AF873756

# TOKEN RING TECHNOLOGY REPORT

THIRD EDITION

SEPTEMBER 1991

ARCHITECTURE
TECHNOLOGY
CORPORATION
SPECIALISTS IN COMPUTER ARCHITECTURE

P.O. BOX 24344 • MINNEAPOLIS, MINNESOTA 55424 • (612) 935-2035

ELSEVIER
ADVANCED
TECHNOLOGY

DISTRIBUTED OUTSIDE THE USA/CANADA BY:
ELSEVIER ADVANCED TECHNOLOGY
MAYFIELD HOUSE
256 BANBURY ROAD
OXFORD OX2 7DH
UNITED KINGDOM

DISCLAIMER

# FOREWORD

This report is an overview of the IBM Token-Ring technology and products built by IBM and compatible vendors. It consists of three sections: (1) a summary of the design tradeoffs for the IBM Token-Ring, (2) a summary of the products of the major compatible vendors, and (3) an appendix describing how the ring operates and the protocol analyzer used to test the ring.

Readers wishing more detail on IBM ring products are referred to IBM Token-Ring Report and Reference and IBM Token Ring Product Guide. Readers wishing to know more about rings and ring products in general are referred to the The Ring-Based Local Networks Report. All of the above reports are published by Architecture Technology Corporation.

# Table of Contents

## Section I

# Section II

# Token-Ring Adapter Products and Accessories

## Wiring Systems



## Testing

## New Chip Technology

# Figure List

## Section I



## Section II

# SECTION I

# Introduction to the Technology

# 1. Introduction

The IBM Token-Ring is a networking technology that was initially developed to provide local area network capabilities for IBM Corporation. This technology and its implications take on the same level of importance as the architecture of the Systems/360, IBM's SNA architecture, and the IBM Personal Computer. This technology has the capability to provide long-term significant enhancements to IBM data networking concepts. Because the impact of such a product set is more significant than just the total announced product devices, this report will discuss in detail some of the technology trade-offs and issues within the Token-Ring environment.

The Token-Ring was originally developed in the early 70's at the IBM labs in Zurich, Switzerland. The transmission system (media and data included) was primarily decided upon based on trade-offs that were made to try and achieve higher reliability in a LAN environment. The fundamental concept of the network is that it follows the OSI structured protocols and provides for a long-term consistent growth path with a protocol that gives fair and equal access to all stations at a given priority level within the ring. The initial prototypes were demonstrated at Telecom '83 in Geneva, Switzerland. They were built using IBM PCs, DisplayWriter, 6670 Laser Printer, and a Series 1 computer. These early rings had all the features of the current rings and a majority of the fail-soft capabilities that are provided under the current structures. The Cabling System was announced in March 1984, and the first Token-Ring network products were announced in October 1985.

# 2. LAN Standards

One of the key issues within IBM is that of international standards for local area networks. There are a number of reasons why standards are important to users. Some of the main reasons include the concepts of: 1) greater compatibility of products; 2) higher product volumes (at a lower cost); 3) ease of attachment to a particular network strategy; 4) allowing many different vendors to build multiple types of connection strategies; 5) the ability for the user to choose equipment that best fits a particular need; and 6) the idea that the standards process allows fair and equal opportunity for all vendors (regardless of their size) to impact the capabilities required in the standards.

The dominant standards group in the LAN area is IEEE 802 (see summary in Figure 1). Although other groups are also working on LAN standards, the IEEE is the leading organization. In fact, the European Computer Manufacturers Association (ECMA), Technical Committee 82 has followed the lead set by IEEE 802. Within IEEE 802, the Computer Society sponsors the 802 project, where standards are drafted and then go to the IEEE standards boards. IEEE submits its standards to the International Standards Organization (ISO), where local area networks are the responsibility of Committee 97, Subcommittee 6, for telecommunications and information exchange between systems. ISO standards are then provided to the user community as published standards which provide functional specifications to which manufacturers can build equipment.

Although a number of standards exist within IEEE 802, two are of primary interest to this report: IEEE 802.2 and IEEE 802.5. 802.2 describes a standardized logical link control (LLC) protocol. This LLC protocol is actually a sublayer of Layer 2 (see Figure 2) of the OSI Reference Model (the Datalink Layer), and defines the formats and protocols for exchanging frames between logical link control layers for two devices attached to a local area network. It provides for two kinds of data transfer services: connection-oriented and connectionless (datagram). A third type acknowledged connectionless is in draft status.

Connection-oriented service ensures that a given device can send an error-free, non-duplicated, properly sequenced frame to another user. The connection-oriented protocol permits peer-to-peer communication over the LAN as if the participating peers had a point-to-point link protocol between them. Actually, multiple stations multiplex several logical data link protocols over a single physical link, the shared

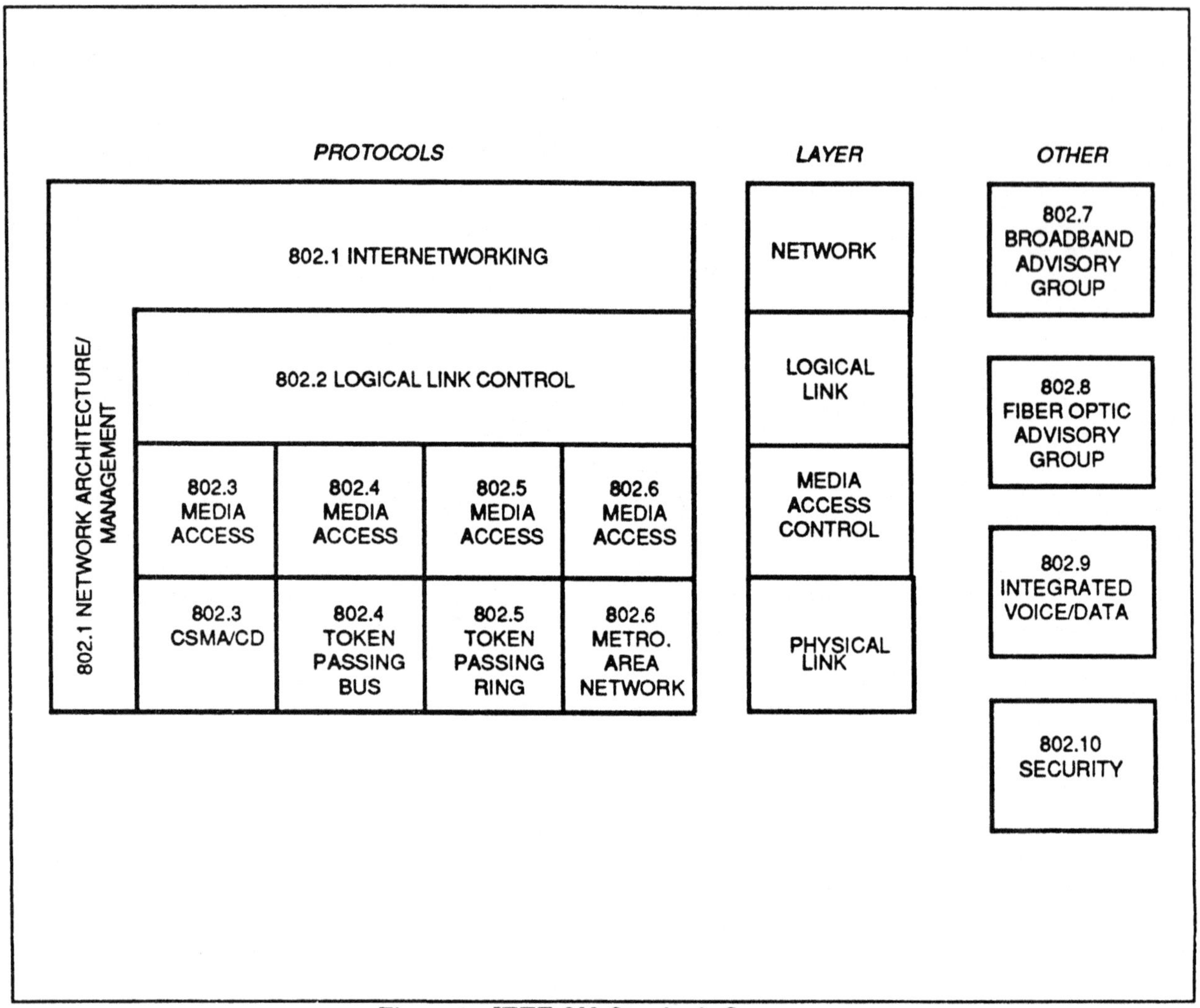


**Figure 1:** IEEE 802 Standards Summary

transmission medium of the Token-Ring. To accommodate multiple data link users at a single station point, service access points (SAP) on the link protocol provide in-point addressing between the data link user and the logical link control layer. In actuality, the logical link protocol of IEEE is independent of the specific Token-Ring medium access control. Generally, IBM tends to favor the connection-oriented services of the logical link protocol. In this environment, a data link connection is established between two service access points prior to any exchange of information and may be reset or terminated at any time by either data link user of the connection.

The connectionless service is a datagram type approach which frames are simply sent and received without any correlation to previous or subsequent frames. Connectionless services are likely to require the use of higher layer error control and sequencing services. All the frames exchanged between stations adhere to a very simple format.

It contains the source and destination addresses, some control fields, and information fields. These address fields identify the service access points of the source and the destination. The control field specifies the type of frame, whether it is supervisory, unnumbered control information transfer, or numbered information transfer. The procedures for connection-oriented service are much more complex than the datagram-level service. There are a series of link protocols which allows the service access point to send sequenced numbers so that end destination users may verify the proper ordering of frames in case of re-transmission. Further, timers are associated with the services to ensure that acknowledgements are received at appropriate times.

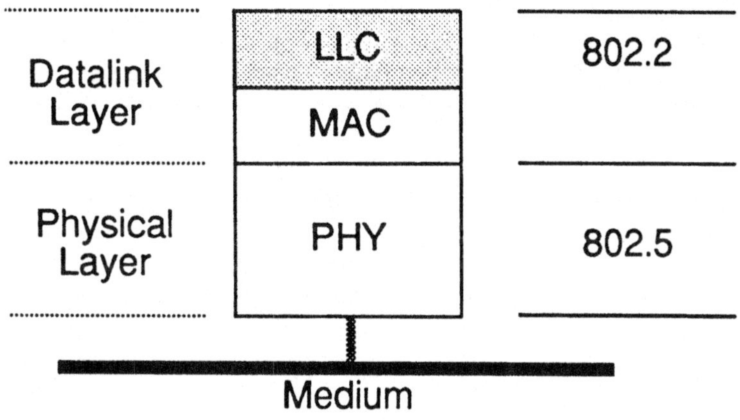


**Figure 2:** 802.2 Relationship To OSI Model

The medium access control (MAC) technique (of which 802.5 is one form) provides a control of media access that is a sublayer of the Datalink protocol and allows that link layer to communicate to an associated physical layer specification. The function of this layer is to ensure that individual stations are properly assigned their opportunity to transmit over the LAN without interference from any other station attempting to transmit at the same time. IEEE 802.5 defines the ring-oriented protocol. Access to the link level is controlled by a token which is sequentially passed around the ring, and by changing the token to a frame, a station gains access to the ring.

This report does not contain an in-depth discussion on token ring standards; IEEE documents contain detailed discussions of these standards. These documents are available from the IEEE Computer Society in Washington, D.C. When we discuss standardized approaches in the remainder of this report, we will be referring to either IEEE 802.2 or IEEE 802.5.

## 3. Overview of Token Rings

The function of a token ring is to provide a means for nodes to be sequentially connected in a circular topology and allow for the transmission of frames to the access control mechanism (token) to a frame and allow for error detection and isolation. Because such networks can be physically limited in size (to areas such as those typically found in offices or campuses), they may run at a very high rate. In data communications, however, the higher the rate of signal transmission, the more prone the signal is to errors. Bearing this in mind, this section will describe general trade-offs of LAN development, as well as IBM's LAN strategy. In the sections that follow, we will look at the protocols and technology of these networks in detail.

The preferred LAN approach of IBM is a technology called a token ring. It is basically a network where devices are sequentially connected together in a circular topology. Each device connects onto the network through an interface called a ring interface adapter. This adapter handles all of the so-called "basic functions." That is, it knows how to recognize frames and addresses; it knows how to buffer data; it knows how to generate and send tokens as they pass by; and it understands a whole series of address translation functions as well as error checking and error control functions.

However, because such a technology is not easily managed in a realistic physical structure, the ring is actually wired to what is called a star ring wiring configuration. That is, the transmission cables for the ring radiate from wiring closets to the work areas. Within the work area, the device uses the network interface to attach itself to the ring. Within the wiring closet, a wiring concentrator called a multistation access unit (MAU) or IBM Part 8228 (a device containing a series of electronic relays), essentially converts the radial star-shaped wiring system into a ring topology. The advantage of this approach is that wiring can be laid out as a series of stars and therefore more easily managed. In addition, wiring lobes--send and receive paths to each device--can be implemented, allowing the device to create a ring topology in conjunction with the wiring concentrator. Connection of the wiring lobes to the concentrators enables the devices to specify serial connections around the ring. One of the functions of the workstation, then, is to direct its network interface as to whether the workstation is active (i.e., involved in the ring), or inactive. If inactive, the wiring concentrator bypasses the lobe of wire from the wiring closet to the workstation location. Thus, by taking a lobe of wire out of the ring, a workstation is removed from the ring and workstations can be moved to any other office which has a lobe of wire installed in it, and reconnected to the ring.

The wiring concentrators tend to segment the ring, providing capabilities to create rings of varying sizes, utilize different forms of transmission media in different parts of the ring, and provide points for users to provide capabilities to facilitate maintenance, reliability, and service functions of the overall network. Furthermore, this ability to form rings of varying sizes means that if the number of workstations, the capacity of a ring, or the physical topology of the environment dictates that multiple rings can easily be built and structured to provide appropriate amounts of capacity, diversity of distance, or topological mapping onto a physical building structure. In addition, the connection of rings would allow a variety of bridges and gateways to be developed so that rings could be connected together or could be connected through some forms of high-speed backbone structures. IBM also believes that different speeds might be useful in different parts of the network and therefore they have provided a wiring structure which can make use of a wide variety of transmission media: unshielded or shielded twisted pair cables, or optical fibers for high speed or long distance requirements. Moreover, the structure of the wiring system is designed so that optical fibers can be mixed in the same network with twisted pair.

Operation of the ring is relatively simple. The following sentences outline this operation (see Figure 3). The sender waits for a token, changes the token to a frame, and appends the data (the data is actually a variable-length field contained within a header, which contains the address information, and an end for physical trailer which contains the frame check sequence), which is then transmitted around the ring. (Note: resident on the ring at any given time is either a token or a frame. The frame is important because it carries the data on the ring.) All the monitoring active stations monitor frames for their appropriate address. When they recognize data addressed to themselves, the data is copied into a buffer. After the sender has completed the transmission of the data and the first part of the frame has come back to sender, the sender places the token back on the ring. This ensures that the ring is not dominated by a single device. It also permits a priority mode to be built in to the token. This allows for multiple levels of access to the ring and ensures equal access to the ring for all nodes. A broadcast option allows any device on the ring to receive or transmit the frame to all devices on the ring. In conjunction with this general capability, each of the ring interface nodes provides monitoring and maintenance functions through the system to ensure that the token or the data frame are not lost and that only one device is transmitting on the ring at any given time. This token protocol, combined with star-shaped wiring, provides several fundamental advantages to the concept of a ring-based system.

## 4. Goals of the IBM Token-Ring

One of the key issues in future data processing systems will be providing for distribution of resources and

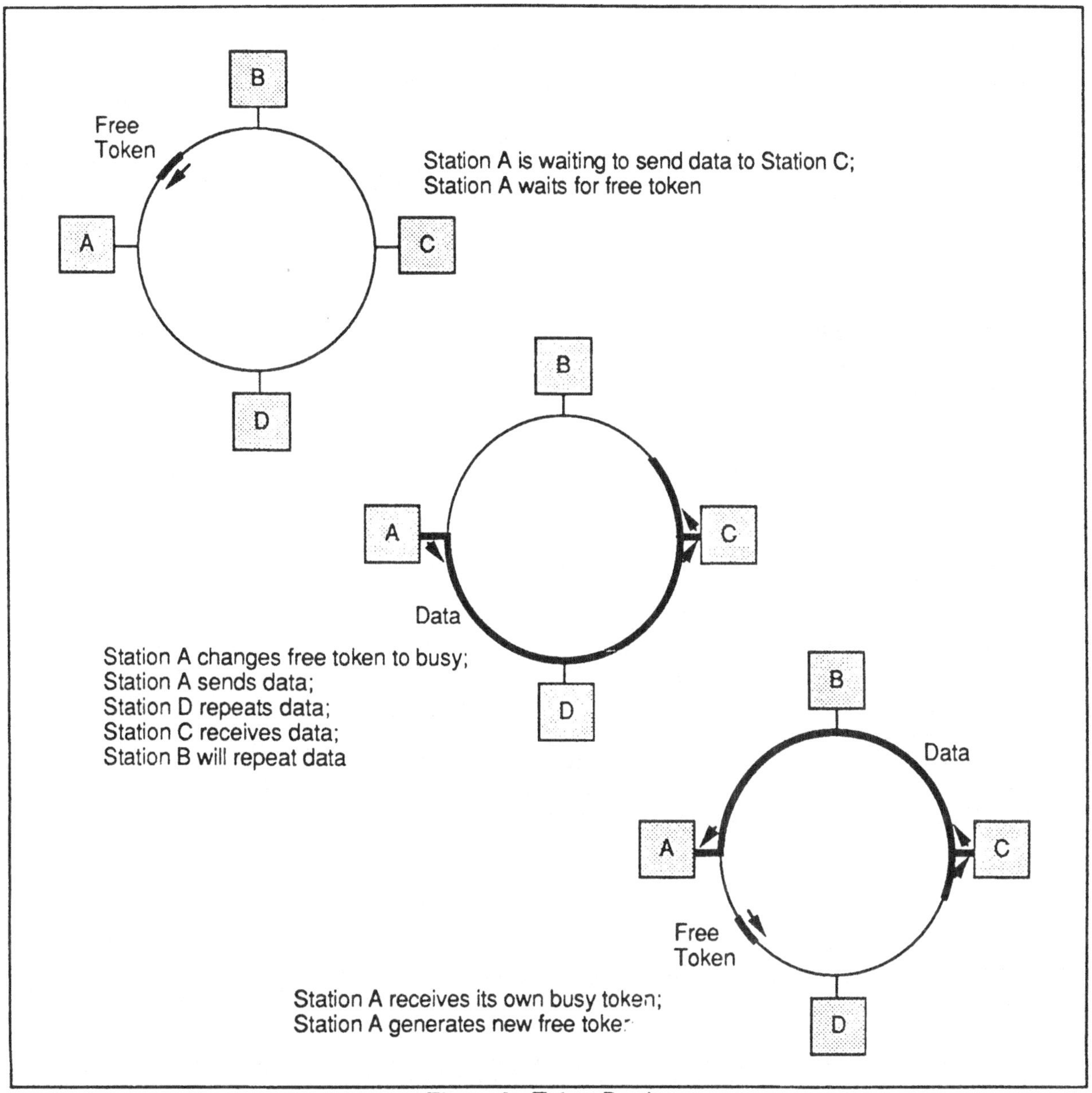


**Figure 3:** Token Passing

information and allowing users to actually execute programs in a distributed data processing environment. However, as resources and information are distributed, there is a greater need for the use of high-speed connections of various kinds of digital devices--from personal computers to large-scale hosts and their associated disk storage units. Furthermore, the computer trend is towards a non-homogenous environment so that even companies as dominant as IBM cannot expect that its system will be the only one with which people want to attach and share information. It is IBM's view that an open token ring protocol, which will permit attachment of multiple vendors equipments, will foster connectivity, thereby increasing sales of IBM-oriented equipment. However, in building a highly diverse distributed data processing system, there is a very difficult systems integration job that must be provided in terms of the underlying infrastructure associated with the rapid transport of information. IBM feels that this problem must be addressed at several levels. The principal trade-offs are summarized below.

IBM believes that for a local area network to be truly effective, it must be open--open in the sense of providing a long-term communications standard to which large numbers of manufacturers can connect their equipment.

Because of the cost and difficulty of installing new equipment, IBM believes that the fundamental technology of transport of information must be on baseband media. The system must have a very simple wiring solution and each new cable type, or cable in the system, must be of a uniform type. (The devices may be required to have adapters to conform to this standardized wiring system.) IBM suggests twisted pair of various forms with various kinds of cable conversion devices. Thus, wiring facilities can be provided and can be pre-wired into a building. The use of baseband, from IBM's viewpoint, provides the lowest cost form of data transmission. With respect to speed, IBM believes that a PC-based LAN must operate in at least 4 megabits per second. For some of its other systems, IBM favors up to 16 megabits per second.

Because not all vendors use the same protocols, and because there are long-haul and international standards, IBM believes that a critical function that must be provided by a LAN is gateway connections. So, within their products, they are endeavoring to provide gateway functions to the popular standard capabilities such as ISDN. And because the Token-Ring is open, other vendors will be able to derive connections to their sets of protocols.

Because many different vendors may wish to have their systems run on the Token-Ring, IBM proposes that a token ring must have multiple external application interfaces (e.g., NETBIOS to support personal computer LANs and a Logical Unit 6.2-oriented interface to connect the environment into SNA environments).

Because of physical device limitations and limitations of the ring as implemented on the cabling system, there is a physical limitation of only 260 devices per ring. In large-scale systems, multiples of these high-speed rings may connect together. Later, as we discuss different characteristics of the IBM system, it becomes evident that network management is the key issue with multiple rings.

The two primary levels of the Token-Ring LAN that we concentrate on in this report are the use of the cabling system and its technology, and the use of the Token-Ring protocol technology.

## 5. Wiring Systems

The Cabling System is IBM's primary view of how a customer should wire a building. It is a hierarchically structured wiring system designed for local networks, PBXs, and to connect existing systems together. It offers cable conversion devices or baluns to convert coax devices to run on twisted pair plan. It is designed to allow you to install both voice and data wiring at the same time in order to save costs. And, because of the way it is installed and the way it can be reconfigured from the wiring closet, it is designed to allow for a highly flexible installation.

With protocols such as the Token-Ring protocol, then, one could then run multiple logical local networks on the same cable plan. The idea is to increase the connectivity by allowing up to 260 devices to share the cabling system. If, for example, one began to run a large personal computer LAN that outgrew its capability, one could then go up to through a variety of products and connect into the IBM mainframe environment.

Therefore, the Token-Ring protocol is designed to provide a resource-sharing capability so the user can share input/output devices and hard disk devices, and then migrate into the SNA environment. From IBM's point of view, the 4-megabit-per-second capability allows the user to have proper distribution of software to provide what it considers to be high-performance data connection.

## 5.1 The Need For A Common Wiring System

IBM maintains that its system permits a building owner to install one common wiring system and use it for both voice and data. Regardless of the terminal families involved, all devices can run on the common wiring system. Then, since all future devices will be attached to the same wiring scheme, it is likely that additional wiring will never have to be installed. Over time, however, one may have to add different kinds of adaptation units to the wiring system to tailor it for a particular form of terminal device. One may choose to run a variety of different protocols or logical connections on top of the installed infrastructure topology, and then to run different devices with cable conversion mechanisms.

To summarize, the general strategy is to: 1) install a common wiring scheme into a building; 2) utilize the wiring closets and specialized equipment at these wiring closets to connect together a variety of cables to build a specific form of topology or connection; and 3) adopt the terminal or other digital device to the wiring system through the use of special conversion devices. This allows one to completely prewire the building and to re-use the wiring in each office without supplementary wiring. This is possible because the wiring closets are used to build the topologies and each device is rebuilt or readapted through the wiring system via appropriate connection technologies. This connection technology is primarily developed using the concept of a balun. (A balun is a balanced/unbalanced cable conversion device that converts the impedance of one type of wiring to the appropriate impedance of another type of wiring.) Because of this design consideration, one can build a concept in the wiring system for the migration of capabilities. That is, one has the ability to migrate technologies but need not completely prewire the building initially. The building can be prewired or rewired in sections, depending on internal needs and growth.

A major problem with designing and installing such a cabling system is keeping track of the cables. IBM asserts that if one develops a cable system designed for the long term, then it must be built and labeled based on the cable database. Such a product--a cable planner--is available from Architecture Technology Corporation. This design aid helps one establish the cost and maintain a cable system database. At one time IBM introduced its own product to keep track of such a process. However, it was inadequate, and IBM removed it and discontinued production.

## 5.2 Detailed Design of Certain Aspects of the Cable Plan

In order to develop a Token-Ring system running at a high-performance capability, a special connector must be utilized. This combined male/female IBM data connector allows concatenation of several connected paths so that the same connectors and cables can be used with the smallest PC LAN system up to the largest mainframe LAN system.

One of the critical issues in this environment is to allow for the development of simple, versatile cables. And, because of the topological aspects of a star-shaped ring, the connector uses a self-shorting contact. Then, when a ring or station is disconnected, it does not interrupt the operation of the ring but can be immediately inserted into the ring by electronic signal, or if it is out of the ring, it is automatically provided with a wrap path so that the wiring system can be tested. The main idea is that the connector allows the contacts to short on themselves and convert the ring-in/ring-out paths into a single contiguous loop when the connector is unplugged. Accordingly, if a station is disconnected, it does not impact the ring operation.

The design of the connector's case essentially shields the cable on all sides from radiated noise from high-speed transmissions. The importance of this is that if the connector does not induce noise onto the transmission lines, the signal-to-noise ratio is effectively enhanced.

By proper design, it is easy to assemble cables into these connectors in the field. First, one inserts a shielded twisted pair into the shell, assembles the contacts, connects the bottom or top cover, and ends up with (with the simple use of very simple tools) an in-field, molded connector design. This way, almost anyone in the field can quickly assemble connectors for token rings.

A key issue in designing the connector and shield of the cabling system (in addition to allowing devices to go on and off the ring systematically) is achieving a properly grounded system. The connectors and the shield of the signal conductors provide a continuous electrical path which help to ground the entire system. The problem is that in addition to grounding the AC power system of the building (and ensuring that noise is not induced by the power system or other operational equipment within the building), components of a LAN distributed throughout the building(s) may cause individual pieces of the equipment to be grounded at different parts of the complex. This can potentially induce a dangerous ground potential difference into the system. Furthermore, if the cable is not properly shielded, the AC power system, radars, signals from radio and television systems, or thunderstorms could exacerbate these undesirable effects. Therefore, because of the distributed nature of a Token-Ring, a multipoint grounding scheme has to be developed.

**5.3 Grounding**

The key to this grounding scheme is the fact that the distribution racks within the wiring closets are grounded to the nearest transformer grounding system. That ground is then built up throughout the complex, and within the system; each distribution rack grounds to the closest power service grounding electrode. The power source grounding electrodes are then connected together to form the ground for the entire building. These grounding electrodes are, in effect, bonded together. The metal conduit is bonded to the grounding conductor to lower the impedance and thereby decrease the ground potential difference. (This is done in accordance with national, state, and local electrical codes.) This grounding should ensure that there is no impedance derived between devices on the Token-Ring. To make this effective, each device attached to the Token-Ring must provide a grounding path through the shield of the signal cable. Each device must be grounded properly to its AC outlet giving the Token-Ring a low impedance path through the shield of the signal cable into the ground system of the building or campus. With the correct type of connector and a shielded conductor, the Token-Ring has the effect of noise immunity, and it is safe for operators to use.

**5.4 Signalling**

The actual transmission of the signal on the cabling system is performed using the technique known as the Manchester Differential Code (see Figure 4). With this technique, information based on the transition of wave forms from a positive to a negative or a negative to a positive state is derived. This occurs via a positive pulse followed by a negative pulse for each databit. By detecting the appropriate 0 crossings, and when they occur, one is able to determine the type of bit sent. This technique has another advantage: the clock for the system can be derived in the data transmission. However, because of the sequential nature of the transmitters and receivers, as the signal propagates around the ring, there is a shifting of the information within a time slot. This shifting is referred to by IBM as jitter.

**5.5 Jitter**

Jitter is important in figuring out the number of devices and length of cable that can be allowed. The jitter phenomena occurs as you send a nice clean pulse, the impedance of the wire causes the pulse to be elongated in time, then skewed, and to be shortened in amplitude due to the loss of energy between devices.

To elaborate on jitter or clock skew, the Token-Ring "assumes" that there is a master clock time standard in the system. This time standard is made available to the system through a clock and the active monitor. From the point of view of the time standard, the Token-Ring looks like a series of regenerated repeaters--one per node, separated by cable. As each signal is transmitted from node A to node B, it is distorted, attenuated, and may pick up noise. In node B the amplifier reshapes the wave form, re-times the wave form, and retransmits it. Because the devices are sequentially placed, there may be an error rate of

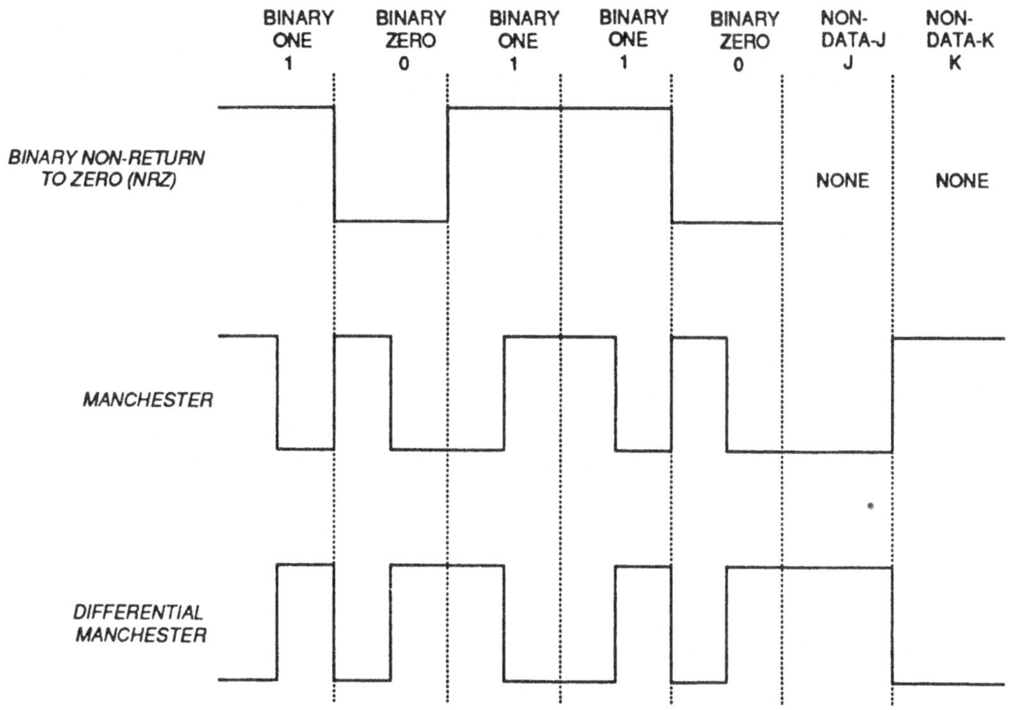


**Figure 4:** Manchester Encoding

transmission between each pair of devices, and the system error rate is then the sum of these individual error rates. However, because of the sequential error problems between any two stations, it is limited to between the two stations because the regenerative repeater reshapes the wave form and re-times the wave form. Thus the only implication of this technology is that the total number of devices is limited, based on the sequential build-up of both clock skew/jitter and error rate.

The solution to jitter is to provide a variable length buffer within the system at the monitor. This buffer is about 12 bit-times long and allows the system clock monitor to anticipate and adjust itself so that the system clock will not be effected by jitter. This is essentially accomplished by using a variable length delay buffer.

For the IBM system, it was initially believed that to achieve safe transmission on shielded twisted pairs, one could not run much faster than 4 megabits per second. However, because AT&T's Premises distribution system (which competes with IBM) was able to run at 4 megabits per second on unshielded, IBM devised its own Type 3 Wiring (or unshielded twisted pair), which also allows 4 megabits per second transmission.

#### 5.6 Type 3 Cable

In many installations there is a need not to have to rewire the building so in addition to the cable technology provided by IBM, IBM provides a specification of what is called a Type 3 wire. This Type 3 wire can basically be equated to common garden variety unshielded telephone twisted pair (Telco). Since much of the wiring inside buildings has been designed for low speed (i.e., hertz-per-second voice transmission, as opposed to high speed, megabits-per-second transmission), there is some question as to the suitability of the wire for high-speed transmission.

Furthermore, because of the competition presented by AT&T, it is even more important that IBM follow this technology. The basic strategy for IBM was to specify the type of wire, in the Type 3 media specification, and then show to the user how to use this wire to develop token ring protocols. Because these twisted pairs are generally unshielded, and you can put out high frequency radiated noise which is beyond the specifications of the FCC limits, a special media filter is provided. This media filter connects with unshielded, twisted pair cable, which terminates in a six-or eight-pen modular jack. This modular jack is then connected into the regular building wiring system using unshielded twisted pairs.

Because the multistation access unit will have a valid data connector on it at some point, these unshielded twisted pairs are carried all the way into the wiring closets where they are terminated and connected to a special cable called a Type 3 media jumper cable. This jumper cable has either a data connector or color-coded twisted pairs at one end which connect to a Type 66 connecting block for a telephone system (also known as a punch down block), and has at the end of this, a jumper cable, and the data connector. IBM claims that one can therefore build small networks using unshielded twisted pairs (see Figures 5 & 6). (However, the company does not recommend the mixing of voice and data grade lobes on the Token Ring.) One can, however, use the Type 1 wiring to connect two wiring closets, for example. As mentioned previously, it is important to note that the wire is unshielded and a media filter has been put in to remove some of the high-frequency components of the signal. Consequently, there is more distortion, there is a factor of about three times larger signal attenuation, and jitter is increased in the system. Accordingly, the total number of devices which can be sequentially connected together is decreased from around 260 to around 72.

As long as one remains within the limits of the recommended performance capabilities of the wiring system, the system should perform as specified, regardless of whether it is running on shielded or unshielded twisted pair. However, one should be wary of any unusual sources of electromagnetic interference in the building, for there may be a higher than normal amount of error conditions on the

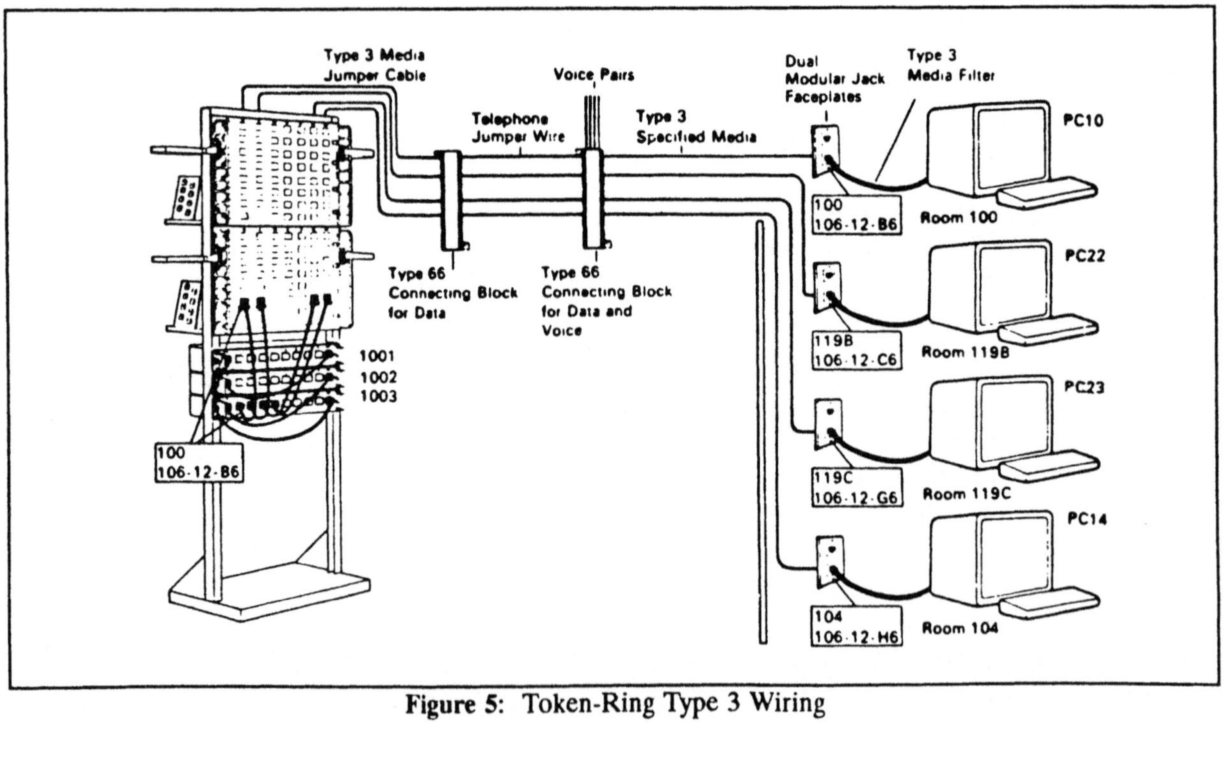


**Figure 5:** Token-Ring Type 3 Wiring

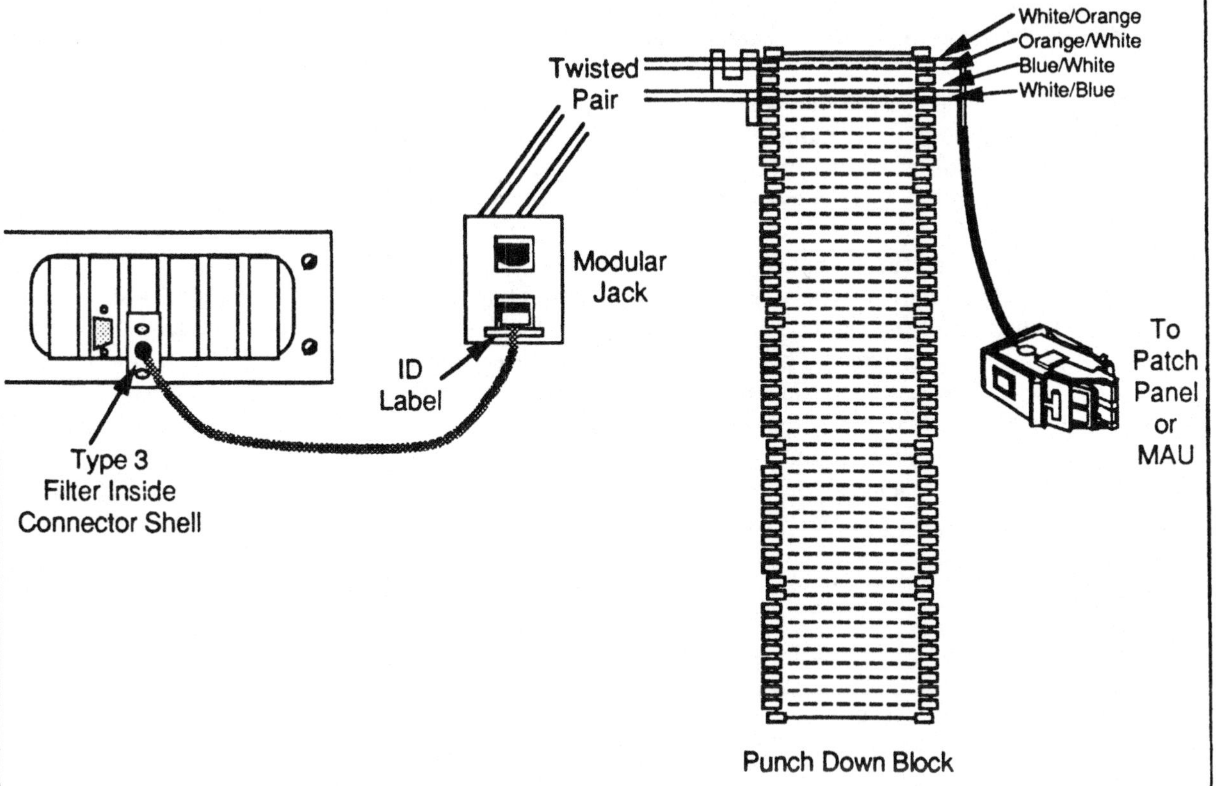


**Figure 6:** Type 3 Wiring Components

Token-Ring. This could trigger automatic re-transmission and recovery procedures. Generally, the rules for Type 3 wiring are that it will work as long as the number of devices is restricted to 72, and the distances that join either the wiring closets or the devices to the closets are reduced by about a factor of 3 from the capabilities associated with Type 1 or Type 2 wiring.

## 6. Use Of The Cabling System In Operational Environments

Once one has understood the theory of a twisted-pair cabling system, one can begin to conceive of using it in actual operational environments. Some of the considerations for such a system will be discussed briefly below.

### 6.1 Baluns

If the cabling system is to be a truly general-purpose system as described by IBM, it must be able to transmit coaxial cable-type signals as well as twisted pair-type signals. However, a twisted pair system is generally known as a differential balanced system and as a coaxial system is an unbalanced system. The critical technology to connect these two different kinds of cabling schemes together is a device known as a transformer balun.

A number of different types of baluns can be made, depending on whether or not one wants DC isolation of the signals. However, the critical design issues associated with a balun are whether or not it increases the capacitance and changes the impedance of the fundamental signal law. Balun transmission lines essentially use multiple signal conductors to transmit part of the signal on one conductor and the other part of the signal is shifted on the other conductor. In the shielded baluns system, the cable shield is held at 0 volts to provide a reference between the two signal voltages.

If the line is properly balanced, induced noise will be cancelled, but if the system is not properly balanced, or the balun is not properly balanced, noise will not completely cancel itself. Thus, it is critical in the design and evaluation of the balun to achieve a coupling which does not increase or decrease the impedance of the balance signal. This is one reason that on very short runs, one could actually run the Token-Ring on unbalanced lines. The ability of the Token-Ring adapter to differentiate between noise and to connect devices together and minimize jitter, is based on a worse case design. On the cabling system, one could use baluns to connect coax-based devices onto the twisted pair wiring scheme and use the twisted pair wiring scheme as the replacement to coax. However, it must be understood that the quality in distance of the signal is related to the quality of the twisted pair wiring scheme and the quality of the balun.

### 6.2 Configuration Rules

The cabling system configuration rules are basically designed around the operating characteristics of the components on the network and the types of twisted pair media that are available for the Token-Ring. Given the network parameters topology and the station insertion statuses, one can calculate the strength and relative positioning with respect to clock skew or jitter of any given signal along the ring. Then, by determining whether the ring has a single or multiple wiring closet configuration, you can build a loss budget and you can figure out what kind of losses are allowable along the ring. This enables one to determine the length of any device from the wiring closet, the number of allowable wiring closets, and the distances between the wiring closets. These signal paths then allow one to compute the type of signal loss between any two devices in the system and determine whether it is an acceptable loss in the system. Depending on the type of cable used, various forms of loss will occur, yet a distance trade-off can be made in the system. By assuming that the longest load is available for every device in the system, a longest-ring-path calculation can be created, and the worse-case signal loss within any given type of network can be identified. A summary set of equations can therefore be built, and one could summarize the configuration rules for allowable token rings. IBM provides tables to guide the process. These equations are actually built into the Token-Ring Cabling Planner.

### 6.3 Data Grade Cable

The data grade twisted pair cable is known as Type 1 or Type 2 cable. For the data connection two twisted pair, 22-gauge wires are utilized. These twisted pairs are enclosed in a polypropylene jacket and surrounded with an aluminum shield which is enclosed in a braided shield and a PVC jacket. The twisted pairs are twisted with different lengths of twist to reduce crosstalk between the pairs, and are then laid parallel to each other producing an oval cable. Since the pairs do not nest into each other, this also reduces crosstalk.

The impedance of this cabling system is around 150 ohms. This is a compromise between cable diameter and attenuation. IBM suggests that for maximum performance, Type 1 or 2 should be used to have the ability to run up to 16 megabits per second. If the user also wants to put in telephone wires, IBM suggests using a type 2 cable: shielded cables surrounded by four telephone - grade twisted pairs. This phone twisted pair cable receives in its frequency range: approximately 4 megabits per second--a low level of induced noise (approximately 1/800 times smaller than the transmitted signal). And, if data pairs are near voice pairs, the induced noise is less than 1/10,000 of the transmit signal. This provides for a very efficient system in which the signal-to-noise ratio is easy to detect.

## 7. The Move To Optical Fiber

For data communications systems, one may begin to consider the use of optical fibers as opposed to copper wire. Optical fiber is desirable in many circumstances, such as running long distances, or running at very high speeds. Typically, copper and fiber complement each other in terms of one's strengths making up for the other's weaknesses.

Copper-wire-based systems are a mature, well-understood technology. A variety of technologies are available within the copper industry, and the wire is easy to cut and install. If one is only going a few hundred feet and the rates are fairly low (i.e., a few megabits per second), the low cost of copper wire supplants the advantages of fiber. However, signal attenuation and noise problems occur on a copper media as distance or speed is increased--especially into an electromagnetically noisy environment or when there is a need for a high degree of shielding of electronic-emitted noise. The solution to such problems is fiber. Fiber provides for electric isolation of component parts. Fiber's one disadvantage in such circumstances is that it is restricted to point-to-point usage because of the kinds of connectors available. In other words, it is very difficult to splice or tap the fiber. The disadvantages of optical fibers will decrease over time as technology increases the capability for manufacturers to produce high-speed, low-cost fiber techniques. As data rates continue to increase, the ultimate solution is that of an optical fiber. With that in mind, IBM has provided for a Type 5 optical cable within the Cabling System.

Generally speaking, fibers have been successful in long distance data communications environments and voice communication environments such as Trans Atlantic Cable or Continental Cable Crossings. One of the major challenges within the fiber industry is tackling the development of a fiber with a low-loss connector, and then placing this fiber in an environment such that it is easily installed by unskilled labor. This cable also should be able to withstand large ranges of temperature, humidity, flexing, impact damage, and other destructive forces. The performance of a fiber system for short distance communication is highly questionable at this time. However, because AT&T is working very hard on fiber optics, it appears that fiber will be feasible for the Token-Ring in the future. Unfortunately, at least four or five different companies claim to provide the standard fiber for local area networks. At IBM - Raleigh in Research Triangle Park, in fact, the IBM Token-Ring runs on a fiber system installed by AT&T which does not meet IBM's own specifications for token ring fiber systems. Generally, it is common to find that IBM and many of the other manufacturers view the fiber as: a way to increase the data rates of the overall system; a mechanism to increase both the data rate and the distance between wiring closets; or a technique to connect devices that need to be electrically isolated or to eliminate radiated signals. Accordingly, it makes sense to use high-speed fiber in some places, and low-cost, well-understood copper in other places. Even though IBM has announced both fiber and fiber repeaters for use within Token-Rings, it is likely the company will choose copper-based technologies for the next few years.

## 8. Multistation Access Unit (MAU)

Once the wiring fundamentals of the Token-Ring are understood, one must then bring together the equipment to develop the ring itself. As we have stated before, the strategy is to develop a star-shaped ring. The critical element in this structure is the multistation access unit (MAU) (see Figures 7 & 8).

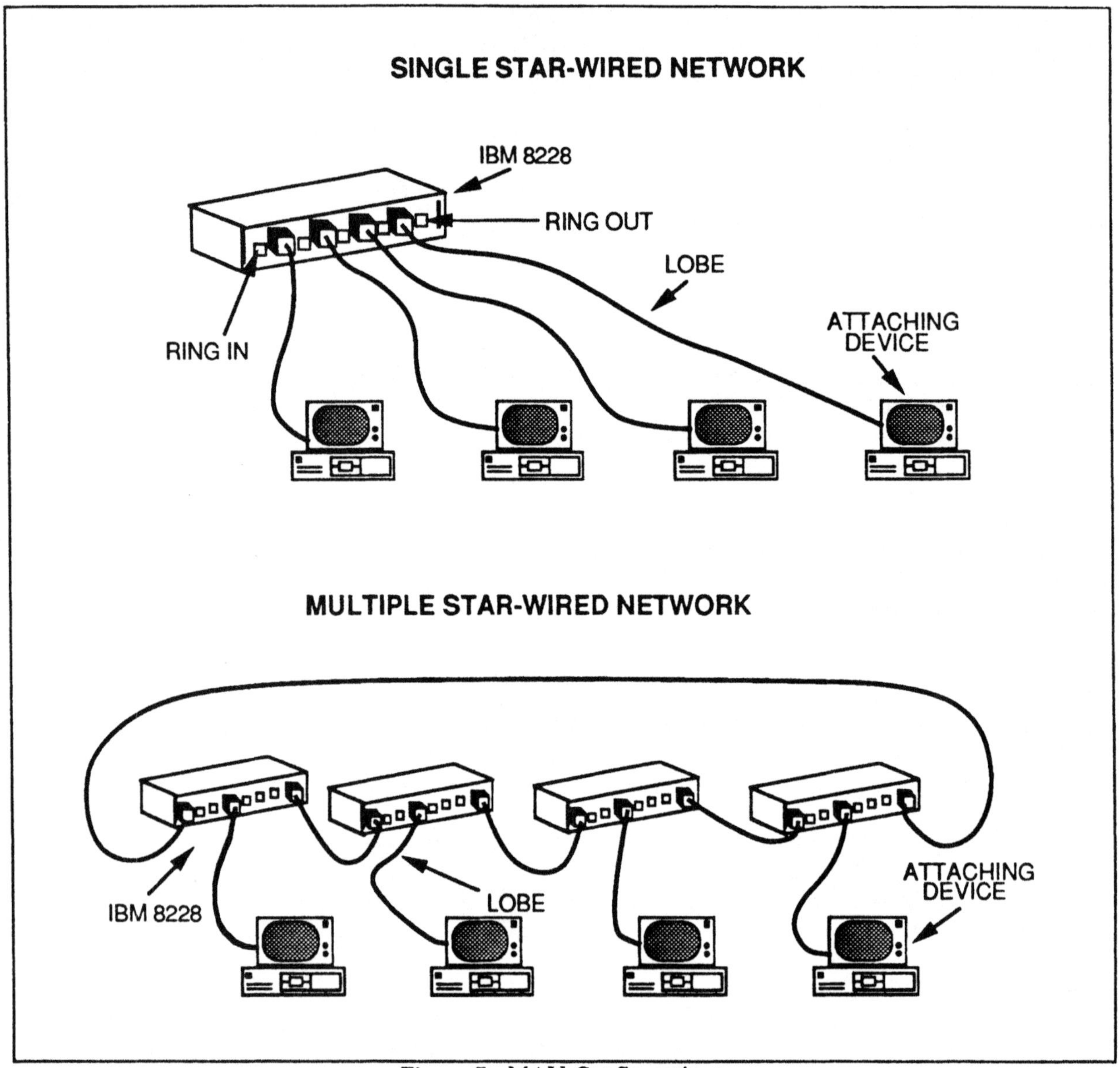


**Figure 7:** MAU Configurations

These are generally located in a wiring closet, but could actually be distributed anywhere around the Token-Ring. The MAU is a device that essentially allows a lobe of wire connecting the device's ring interface unit to be inserted or removed from the ring. If the device is not inserted in the ring, a relay in the MAU allows the ring signal to bypass through the device by bypassing the lobe of wire. Thus, any unit that is on, is not participating in the ring. When a device is inserted in the ring, the overall lobe of wire is then included in the ring path and the device's ring interface unit participates in the ring protocols.

The current MAU sold by IBM can attach up to eight units. Other manufacturers, such as Ungermann-Bass, provide MAU-like devices which can attach into two or eight units. Having an empty MAU port is the same as having a station which is not connected on the ring. Furthermore, when the unit is powered on but is not inserted in the ring, this ring interface unit can be testing the lobe of wire between the device and the MAU. After ascertaining that the lobe of the wire at the ring interface is operating properly, the device can then insert itself to the ring. This insertion is accomplished by sending a signal to the MAU which essentially switches a relay in the MAU. It inserts the ring interface and its associated lobe of wire into the system. This is done by a signal provided by the adapter. Thus, the MAU itself is passive. The power to set the relays is derived from a "phantom" voltage from the ring adapter.

This is done using less than 200 micro amps of current running at less than 4 volts. The circuit that is able to spec this energy is activated; it essentially draws and stores enough current to activate the relay. If the span of current is in any way disrupted, then the device is dropped from the network.

In conjunction with the MAU, there are other kinds of devices available for the Token-Ring. For people who wish to make large rings, high-speed copper and high-speed fiber repeater devices designed to allow the ring to be extended, are available. For people who wish to make very small systems, IBM proposes a fan-out connector.

This fan-out connector (similar to one offered by 3Com) is able to eliminate an MAU. Currently the MAUs can insert up to eight stations in the ring. For a location that requires some small additional connectors, the fan-out connector can be used. This is essentially a version of a passive wiring concentrator which is designed to insert one or two stations onto a Token-Ring. These fan-out connectors could be used in place of a MAU by properly concatenating such devices together. A fan-out connector would be a smaller, less costly way to connect the small number of stations into a ring. By using bridges and gateways, that ring could be connected into a larger network. With a prewired data cabling system where more wall outlets were needed, instead of running additional wires, the devices could be connected together using fan-out connectors. These could be connected in series and then attached to the wall outlet. If a device were to be inserted into the ring, it would have to serially activate the appropriate fan-out connectors and then the wiring concentrator. The signal would then bypass the inactive fan-out connectors, and activate the appropriate fan-out connector as well as the MAU connection. If other devices were to be inserted in the ring at this point, they need only activate their fan-out connectors.

## 9. The Ring Adapter

It is IBM's intent to provide a series of devices called ring adapters on top of the wiring system, to work in conjunction with the MAU. These devices provide the IEEE 802.2 link protocol interface to the Token-Ring in a single package. These adapters allow, for example, a PC to attach directly to a ring lobe and insert or delete the device from the ring. The fact that the adapter (and therefore the Token-Ring) uses IEEE standard protocols, does not mean that the user cannot have other adapters which operate IEEE 802 protocols on the same ring.

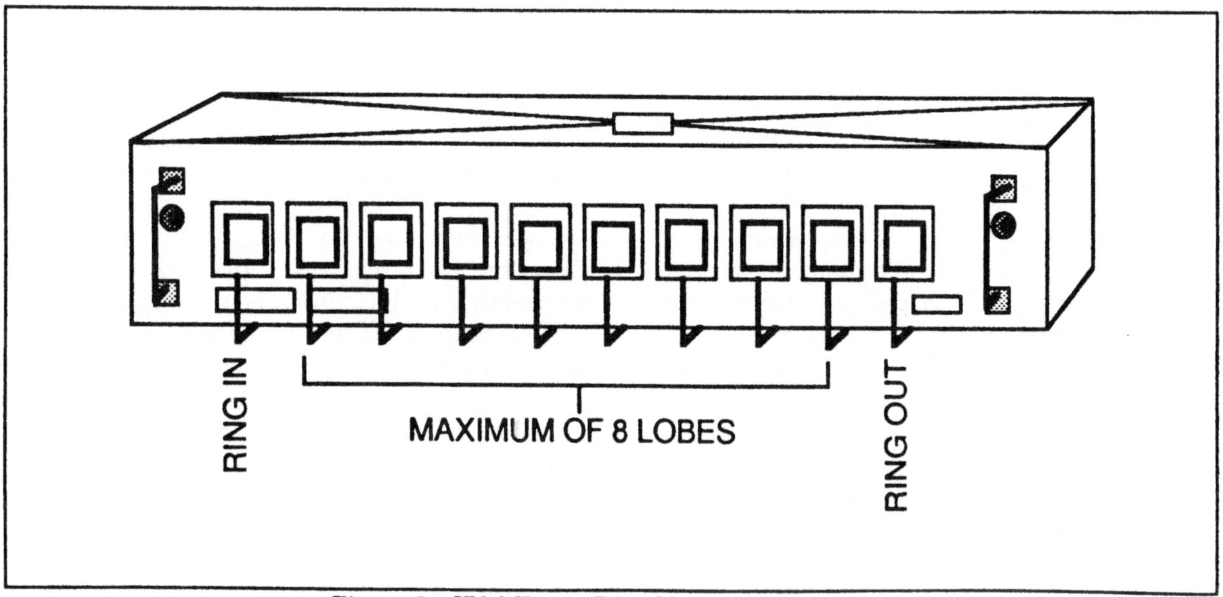


**Figure 8:** IBM Token-Ring Network Multistation Access Unit

The adapter itself is really a small processor or series of processors that perform three major functions. One function is to interface with physical signals on the Token-Ring. This is accomplished by a series of analog, front-end chips, operating in conjunction with various protocol handlers and a message processor. The protocol handler converts the information to digital data and places the information in the main memory of the adapter. It also extracts data from the main memory and prepares it for transmission. The message processor controls the overall processing of the ring protocols and controls the interface to the user.

The ring adapter essentially provides the lowest two layers of the OSI Reference Model: the link and the physical link. It actually provides the complete IEEE datalink control layer (i.e., the logical link control and the MAC frame control), and the physical layer of the IEEE 802.5 and 802.2. The actual interface between a host and the adapter, is by a set of shared memory buffers. Provision is made within the adapter and its associated support software so that one may use NETBIOS, the 802 LLC, or direct interface.

### 9.1 Specialized Adapter Functions

There are a number of specialized functions designed to assist in the operation of the Token-Ring that are built into the adapter itself. Some of these functions are described below.

One of the critical functions in the ring is its synchronization capability. The ring essentially uses a master clock. There is one master clock on a ring. Each device which is not the active monitor uses phase-lock loop technology to synchronize itself with the clock signal. The reason for this is that as the ring is operating and the signal is propagating around the ring, timing jitter or clock skew builds up. Each device attempts to remove or reshape the wave form. It is the function of a device acting in the mode of an active monitor to remove this accumulated time skew of the system. With this concept of a single master unit and simple phase lock loop design, it is possible to attach up to 260 devices onto the system.

### 9.2 Reliability Functions

It is critically important that the Token-Ring be highly reliable. If the ring were to fail, it could possibly bring down the entire system. Because of the sequential nature of the connection of the devices, it is vital that a single failure not be allowed to destroy operation of the total system. Thus, the Token-Ring has a number of major goals that are designed to enhance its reliability, availability, and serviceability. A couple of the key goals are that no signal failure can bring down a ring system, and secondly, that hardware can be used to diagnose or repair a failure.

Some of these features have been built directly into the ring interface card and other features have been built into programs which can be run on processors on the ring. Standard techniques for the development of highly reliable circuits, including burn-in life cycle testing, protocol validation, etc., have been used to make the fundamental ring's adapter reliable. A series of specialized protocol processes and ring recovery protocols are available and running on the Token-Ring constantly to ensure that it operates correctly. For serviceability, the star-shaped ring allows the user to add or delete facilities from the network at will to ensure the maintenance and diagnosis of failed parts. For example, the wiring system is designed so that stations can be switched in and out of the ring quickly. It is easy to disconnect the device form the system and check its lobe of wire. In fact, there is a specific function on the protocol board, allowing a wire fault detection to cause the adapter to be removed from the ring. Also, there are timers on the adapter that sense if the microprocessor has stopped or has begun to loop. Lastly, the connector itself, is a special self-shorting connector. If someone accidentally unplugged the device, the ring will continue operating (with one station removed).

The adapter itself contains a whole series of tests designed to test the adapter, do a functional check out of the adapter, check out the wiring lobe all before the adapter is inserted into the ring. If an adapter is in a ring, it can signal a hard error through the use of a so-called beaconing condition, and cause itself to be removed or remove itself from the ring. Any time that a device has removed itself from the ring, and has satisfied its own self tests, it can attempt to put itself back into the ring. While operating on the ring, but not actively transmitting, adapters also execute a series of background tests to verify the operation of the adapter.

Network diagnostic programs provide information to the ring for reconfiguration and for further test of units on the ring. Failure of a multistation access unit will cause a device to be automatically removed from a ring. Multistation access units also contain a second path which allows a parallel path inside the MAU in case of failure of a connection between MAUs.

Another important issue with respect to the Token-Ring is errors and error detection. When the ring is brought up, an active monitor is established. The active monitor is either the first station to be attached to the ring or is the station that has the largest physical address if an active monitor has had to be re-initialized. It is the function of the active monitor to maintain the proper clocking on the ring, to compensate for ring jitter, to ensure that there is enough buffer space on the ring for a token, to remove invalid frame or tokens, and to generate a new token in case of a lost token. Any station that is on the ring but is not the active monitor runs in the standby monitor mode and monitors the active monitor's operation. If it detects a failure of the active monitor, it chooses a new active monitor, via an election process from the actively operating stations on the ring.

Other important processes are also occurring. One example is ring poll (neighbor notification), which allows each device to obtain the addresses of its upstream neighbor, provide the address of itself to its downstream neighbor, to notify other devices of proper operation. This series of programs operate in a set of sequences. For example, if an adapter is attempting to insert itself, it checks to see that it is operating correctly and has a valid lobe of wire. It inserts then itself in the ring and checks to see if there is an active monitor by waiting for neighbor notification. If there is no monitor, it starts the contention process to become the active monitor. If there is a monitor, it goes into the passive monitor state. It then checks addresses to make sure that its own address is not equal to that of one that has already been inserted, and notifies the network management function (if present) that it is inserted in the ring. A failure to be able to do any of these insertion checks causes the station to remove itself from the ring.

Once a station is actively operating in the ring, it may participate in a series of recovery protocols. These are used to recover from either hard or soft errors. Typical recovery protocols are: ring purge, a technique by which the active monitor tests the ring capability to deliver frames and generate tokens; a monitor contention technology whereby if there is no active monitor detected, the stations can create an active monitor; a technique called beaconing which is used to identify a fault domain; and a variety of soft error detection and recovery facilities.

### 9.3 Management

Management of the Token-Ring is difficult because of its highly distributed nature. Therefore, there are a series of basic techniques designed to monitor and maintain a distributed link protocol operating on top of the Token-Ring.

The IBM Token-Ring offers a series of products essentially designed to provide network management capabilities. Some of the capabilities we have just been discussing are part of the network management function. Certainly, there are capabilities which allow for problem determination and ring recovery, but network management can also include problem isolation and management of multiple Token-Ring systems. These technologies can be implemented at several levels. Some of the implementations at the adapter level have been discussed, but these functions also could be put into bridges and gateways. In the IBM system, this is very complex because the size of any given Token-Ring might vary from one to a series of multiple rings connected together.

IBM's general strategy has been to build a hierarchical network management facility. This way, at any given level of the hierarchy, a collection of information is under the control of a network manager that knows about a specific size universe. Accordingly, the network manager in a multiple ring system manages each ring as if it were a single ring and knows how to gather information from different network managers. The basic requirement for such a function is to be able to isolate and report failures in order to determine when stations are inserted or withdrawn.

Some of these functions are associated with the protocol, and some are associated with address changes when an adapter notifies a server on a ring. Further, some of these functions include collecting errors and reporting statistics (The adapter reports an error to the network manager and includes its address. This way, the source of the problem can be isolated.) The strategy is based on the concept of determining the difference between hard errors which can make the ring inoperative, and soft errors which cause the ring performance to degrade. Because it can be difficult to determine who is causing the hard error, each adapter can withdraw itself from the ring and initiate ring recovery procedures. In the case of soft errors, each adapter performs error-checking procedures and checks for analysis problems. Because some rings might be very small, network management is not the type of function that should be required full-time so you want to be able to run the manager on a PC and insert it in a ring if you choose. With multiple rings along with bridges and gateways, it becomes important to be able to build a hierarchy of network managers so that each network manager knows about its ring and the fact that there are other network managers in the system.

To effectively manage multiple rings, functions must exist which allow the network manager to collect information from each ring and then forward it to a specific network manager for overall analysis. In fact, these procedures need to be defined so that the procedures do not have to be decentralized and that they could actually be stored in multiple locations. Bridges are a good source of such information because bridges exist on multiple rings. Bridge can also report on internetwork traffic and congestion that occurs on any given system. Furthermore, a bridge can provide information on congestion between rings. Another type of function one may choose to have is a configuration report server. This server can track the actual configuration, over time, that exists within any given ring.

Another feature that is desirable in a network manager is the ability for the network manager to command an adapter to withdraw from the ring. Thus, if a network manager found an adapter that was misbehaving over a period of time, the network manager could take that node off the system and cause that node to go into error recovery procedures which would hopefully clear up the problem and allow the other device and its adapter to heal itself before coming back on the network.

The network manager could also be implemented with a feature to control the number of active stations on a ring to ensure a certain level of performance. In fact, IBM is trying to position its NetView product to allow PCs to act as network managers that collect and provide information to a higher-level function on S/370 hosts. (In other words, it is a centralized management node that exists somewhere within a large set of physically connected rings.) The basic management hierarchy envisioned by IBM to implement such technologies is a three-tier hierarchy. It consists of stations, various forms of management servers, and a Token-Ring network manager. This can be extended one more level under NetView so that each Token-Ring network manager constitutes part of a larger scale data communications network facility. In this case, the ring board and the station tend to monitor the MAC in the physical communication layers. The management servers collect and distribute data to and from the stations. They also would check on error reports and configuration changes to the network manager. The network manager would be responsible for the overall management of that particular local area network. There would be a higher level centralized network management node which then knows about the total overall system.

Management servers usually are data collection and distribution points that range in a series of programs available from IBM. There are four types of functions performed by the IBM LAN Manager Program: the ring error monitor, the configuration monitor which collects configuration reports and knows about the status and configuration of the monitor; a ring parameter server, which initializes and maintains operational parameters such as timer threshold values; a process which can request the status of the stations, change the values of parameters, and force configuration of changes on the Token-Ring. This information is collected into logs and can be made available to an operator who runs the network management service of the local area network. In a much larger scale network, such information eventually is collected together and sent up through the hierarchy of Token-Rings to the centralized management node.

# 10. Other Capabilities On The Token-Ring

In this section, we illustrate some uses and specialized features of the Token-Ring, and describe some of the ways that higher-level functions can allocate some of the bandwidth or address space on the Token-Ring to achieve certain levels of capabilities.

One problem with the synchronous token ring is that one would like to support on the token ring asynchronous as well as synchronous multiplexing. This is achieved by quasi-synchronous multiplexing, a technique that tries to allow for efficient asynchronous utilization of bandwidth while guaranteeing certain minimum transmission delays for synchronous stations. In a synchronous system, bandwidth is divided into fixed-length slots which are numbered in reference to a position according to their relative positions to the synchronization pattern. Periodically, a control station places the synchronization pattern onto the channel. Bandwidth is guaranteed because a certain number of slots is assigned in any interval of synchronization. This assignment is maintained for a long period of time. In an asynchronous environment the bandwidth is divided into variable-length packets. Each packet contains an address field located in a fixed position. An assignment of the bandwidth is dynamic.

The Token-Ring Network uses a circulating pattern called the token, and transmission cannot be performed until a token has been received. IBM asserts that this technique allows for efficient integration of synchronous and asynchronous operation. A strategy to quasi-synchronous multiplexing would be to take an asynchronous multiplexer and transmit synchronous data by collecting data over a short period of time and then put them into a single packet. The problem with this technique is that large buffers would be required in the stations because of long end-to-end transmission delay possibilities.

Another technique would be to periodically interrupt the asynchronous traffic and introduce synchronous traffic. If fixed-length packets were used, it would be easy to introduce a synchronous packet periodically. The problem with this is that fixed-length packets are inconsistent with Token-Ring technology. Consequently, synchronous packets are periodically transmitted between asynchronous packets. This is not controlled from a centralized station. This protocol is integrated into the access procedures.

The way the technique works is as follows: Each packet contains a control field. This control field dictates whether the transmission is synchronous or asynchronous, and whether or not the transmission of asynchronous packets is to be suspended. This suspension is controlled by a centralized station called the synchronous bandwidth manager. This packet essentially interrupts the ring. If no synchronous traffic is in progress, the control field is modified to indicate that the token is to be used for transmission of synchronous traffic. If asynchronous transmission is in progress, the synchronous bandwidth manager sets the control field to indicate that a synchronous interrupt has occurred. When a station is about to release a token, it examines the control field of the header of the packet that is purging from the ring. If the interrupt has been set, the station transmits a synchronous token instead of the usual asynchronous token. Therefore, synchronous traffic can be interspersed within asynchronous traffic. The number of channels that can be multiplexed depends on a wide variety of parameters. This technique allows asynchronous traffic to be interrupted periodically for the insertion of synchronous traffic, thus giving the ring both synchronous and asynchronous capabilities.

Another key issue within the communication system of the Token-Ring is allowing equipment to be easily moved and reconfigured. This is done through the use of address classes. The basic idea is that when a user wants to move to a physical location, the equipment will be reattached but the name of the equipment is associated with the equipment and not its physical location. This is accomplished through the use of specialized addressing features. An adapter address then constitutes a node address. There are three different kinds of addresses: specific addresses, group addresses, and functional addresses. Adapters may have different numbers of these addresses.

The most basic address is the specific address. Each adapter has a specific address, or unique address. When it inserts into a ring, it checks to make sure that a specific address is unique. If it is not unique, it removes and reports the condition to the node user. If properly inserted in the ring, it can then copy frames that are addressed to it.

Group addresses are different form specific addresses. Group addresses are there to provide multipoint operation. This is accomplished by having each node in a multipoint link assigned the same group address but a different datalink control identifier.

Functional addresses are a subset of group addresses. They allow a frame to be sent to a specific designated function, such as an error monitor. This can be accomplished regardless of the physical node residency of the service. Functional addresses provide a way to avoid processing long lists of frequently searched addresses. When moving a node, one must be able to connect with these different kinds of addresses and capabilities. This is performed via a routing information exchange sequence which is specified and provides a source control route between any two nodes on any set of interconnected rings. Another important concept in the Token-Ring is that of priority. From the earlier discussion of algorithms, it was learned that every time a transmission is completed, the token is retransmitted. What we failed to mention in detail is a station has the ability (by setting appropriate bits in the token) to implement an algorithm called priority with fairness. It does so by making a priority reservation in the token. The essential mechanism of this algorithm concern the eight priority levels within the Token-Ring. At each given priority level, the algorithm works exactly as we described before, except that, if there is a priority higher than the priority of the incoming token, the incoming token can be blocked and a token can be re-issued at a higher priority. The effect of this algorithm is that at every given priority level fairness is maintained but fairness is given a priority. Thus, at any given priority level, the tokens still make complete circuits of the ring. But, upon seizing a token and going to a higher priority level, one remembers stopping the token, and when the token comes back, lower priority token is re-admitted. This ensures fairness within each priority level, but allows high priority levels to usurp bandwidth of the ring. This still allows fair access to the ring but allows higher priority messages to have faster fair access to the ring.

## 11. Source Routing

Another key design issue concerns routing.

The IEEE 802 standard was designed with the purpose of building a standard for a single LAN. As an after thought, the group is working on "enhancements for multiple ring networks." This functionality is commonly known as source controlled routing (SCR). SCR is implemented in the current IBM products. DEC favors a technique called spanning tree routing. It appears that hybrid solutions will occur with spanning tree implemented at the 802.1 level and SCR at the 802.5 level. This discussion below will cover SCR.

It is very difficult to figure how to route in large networks. Yet, because the Token-Ring consists of a number or series of potentially small networks, bridged together, efficient routing is important. Furthermore, the network may consist of not just simple networks connected together, but a hierarchical structure of networks. The technique that IBM chooses to implement such a concept is called source control routing.

Source control routing is a specialized form of routing wherein the source controls the route to the receiver by inserting that route within the frames it transmits to the destination or receiver. This field will then contain a specific list of bridges that are required to relay the frame on its route from the source to the destination. In this technology, a frame can have one of three routes: broadcast to the segment only, (i.e., this frame is not intended for relay by any of the bridges); limited broadcast (bridges can be configured to relay this frame so it appears once and only once in every part of the network); general broadcast strategy (in which case a frame appears on every segment of the network at least once; frames may potentially flood the network in this particular case); and point-to-point routing (in which a frame travels over a specific designated path between the source and the destination).

In point-to-point routing, the source finds out about the paths or possible paths to the destination station by sending a query frame and receiving special frames which contain the routing information. The major advantage of this procedure is bridges do not actually have to perform routing. They simply pick the frames up and forward them on to the appropriate network. This way, the hardware and software for bridges have lower costs and the bridges perform very well.

The disadvantage of this technique is that while searching for a route between two stations in the network, if the network is complex, it is possible to generate a substantial amount of traffic because of these query packets.

This source routing is currently under consideration for acceptance by the IEEE 802 Standards Committee. There are several ways to implement this technique such as having route loaded by an operator who knows the route, or by building a routing server which knows valid routes for all stations. This dynamic query formation defines the route between the source and the destination, and allows for dynamic reallocation of routes and adaptation of source and destination stations to the actual current state of the network without actually having to have any forms of previous information. This routing technique is very similar to the kinds of techniques that are used within the ARPANET. Because this function is essentially a link-level passthrough, it is viewed as being implemented in a bridge as opposed to being implemented in a gateway, and consequently, IBM makes a very dramatic distinction between a bridge and a gateway. IBM considers a bridge something that connects similar networks. A gateway is something that connects dissimilar networks and provides address and protocol translations. For the Token-Ring, IBM's predominant capabilities provided at this time are based on bridges.

The performance of the local area networks can be hindered because of congestion in bridges. Source control routing makes the network look like one giant logical network (which is made of multiple physical rings). To avoid performance degradations, a technique called the dynamic window which is used by a station that is transmitting through a bridge that has become congested.

The essence of the algorithms for dynamic window flow control are as follows. A device may transmit as many internet packets as it wishes. However, if the receiver detects a lost frame and notifies the transmitter, or if the transmitter detects a lost frame, then the transmitter will not transmit a frame until it receives an acknowledgement of a frame. Thus, when there is no congestion in the network, one can transmit as many frames as desired. But, if the network becomes congested to the point that a frame is lost, it can only be transmitted after the user has been informed that a frame has been received. This way, one throttles back the large window of transmission to a very small window of transmission, decreasing the number of retransmitted or lost frames.

The basic mechanism of the algorithm includes two functions: the detection of the congestion (which is done by determining that a frame is lost) and the modification of the transmission window. If there is no congestion, the largest window can be utilized, because one can transmit as often as desired. When congestion is detected, the smallest window must be used. In other words, one can only transmit after receiving acknowledgement of the frame. The key to this algorithm is in assuming that the loss of frames due to a random bit error is very small.

## 12. 4/16 Mbps

For performance reasons, IBM has provided a second solution for the token ring which runs at 16 Mbps. Thus, the product set of IBM can run at either 4 or 16 Mbps. However, any given ring must have all of the devices that are attached to it running at the same rate. A set of rings that are running at different speeds could be bridged together. In some of the new IBM products, the rate is electronically programmable so that the user can use a single card in either a 4 or 16 Mbps mode based on the users speed selection for the particular card (and thus the overall speed on the ring).

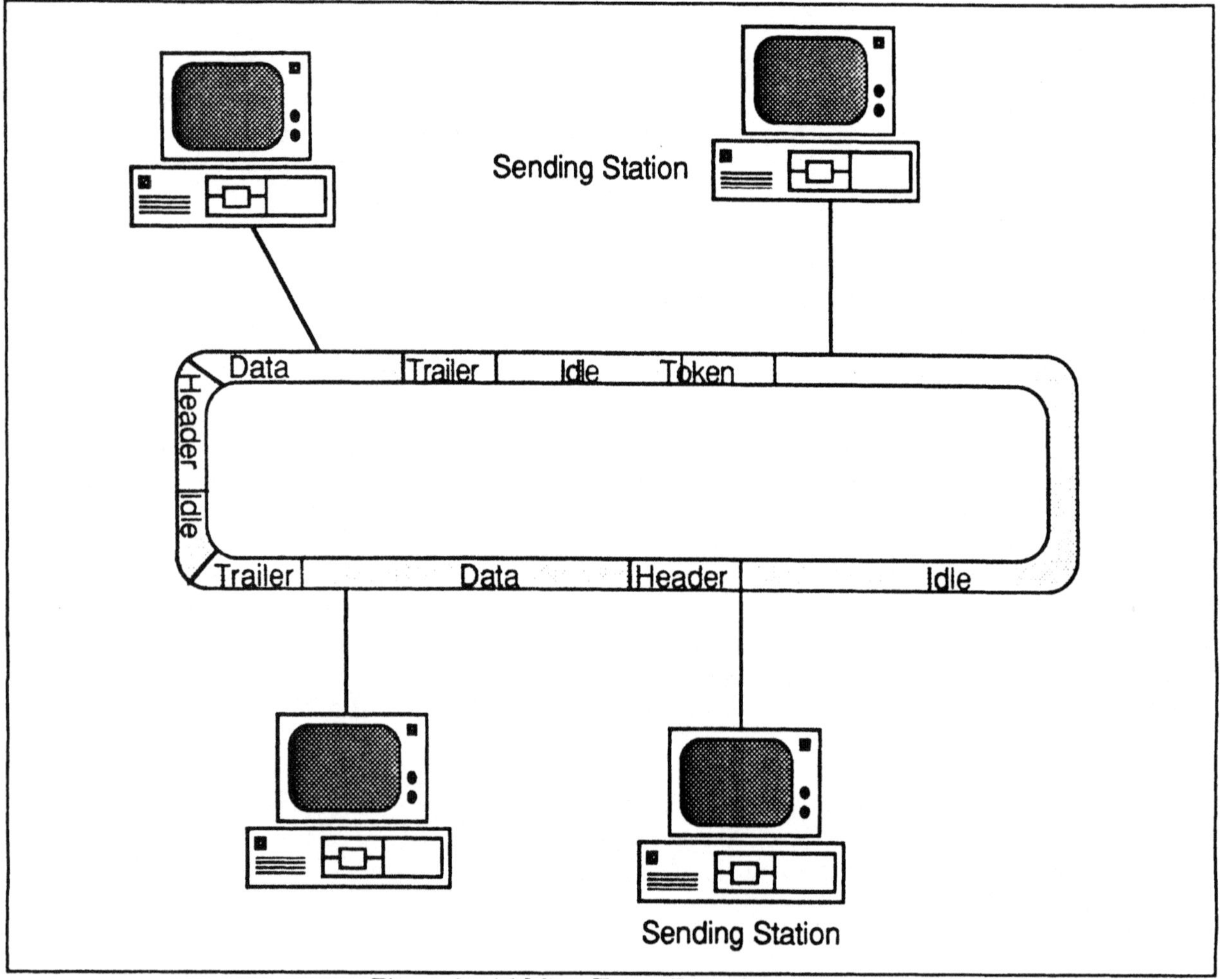


**Figure 9:** 16-Mbps Token-Ring Operation

## 13. Early Token Release

In large rings that are operating at 16 Mbps, the idle time on the ring can become a large factor in the performance of the ring. However, since the token is released onto the ring only after the frame has traversed the ring, time waste is occurring. Thus, IBM has implemented on its 16 Mbps products, a technique that allows the source of a frame to release the token as soon as the frame is transmitted. This leads to a functional capability as illustrated in the figure where there may be multiple frames on the ring but still only one token. This enhancement of the technology is in direct conflict with the priority capabilities of the 802 standard and again is causing great consternation in the standards process. However, IBM has implemented early token release on all of its 16 Mbps products.

# 14. Conclusion

In this section, we reviewed some of the key technology trade-offs made by IBM at the lowest level of the Token-Ring protocols. We discussed wiring details, as well as the ways in which the adapter, low-level network management, and some of the routing controls work. One of the first uses of the Token-Ring is as a replacement of the SDLC protocols in SNA networks. To complement the technology capabilities of the wiring system, the link protocols, and the routing structure, IBM will be supporting more advanced protocols such as peer-to-peer protocols like LU6.2 (APPC) implemented directly on top of the Token-Ring. We can expect other such capabilities in the near future.

From the point of view of this discussion of the Token-Ring architecture, future IBM systems, we have just seen the most significant advancements described in terms of IBMs overall long term direction. We hope this discussion of these trade-offs has been illuminating to you, and that you will find the remaining part of this report discusses vendor's Token-Ring products of interest. There are literally hundreds of products available, so we have enclosed several of the products that we find most interesting. Inclusion or non-inclusion in the next section should not be construed as a judgment on a particular company or its products.

# SECTION II

# A Closer Look at the Key Systems

# Token-Ring Adapter Products and Accessories

## 1. Andrew Network Products

Andrew Network Products wants to known as the 16-Mbps token-ring specialist and has concentrated much of its product development effort on products aimed at 16-Mbps token-ring systems, namely:

- The Bridgeport/7606, a local source-routing token-ring bridge that works cooperatively with IBM source-routing bridges, IBM LAN Manager, and NetView
- The TRA 4/16 family of switchable adapter cards, designed for compatibility with IBM PCs or PS/2s and the 802.5 standard
- The 8229 Fiber Optic MAU, which permits users to take advantage of existing fiber cabling
- 8221 and 8222 Fiber Optic Converters, which increase geographic distances on token-ring LANs

Andrew Network Products is a division of Chicago-based Andrew Corporation, a $365 million worldwide supplier of communications products and systems. Andrew Network Products offers a range of connectivity products for token-ring systems, including media management, source routing, token-ring bridges, copper and fiber-optic repeaters, and adapter cards. Andrew also provides connectivity products for the IBM midrange system and mainframe computers, as well as cable and wire management products.

# 2. IBM Token-Ring

### 2.1 Introduction

On October 15, 1985, IBM put an end to years of speculation and announced major enhancements to its work group connectivity product line. Among the new products announced was a local area network, the long-awaited IBM Token-Ring Network. Also, the IBM Cabling System was extended with a new media, the Type-3 Telephone Twisted Pair Specification, which supports the IBM Token-Ring Network and 3270-to-3274 attachment.

The IBM Token-Ring Network is a 4-Mbps baseband PC network that conforms to IEEE 802.5 and ECMA 89 standards. It can use either the IBM Cabling System or IBM's newly announced Cabling System specification for telephone twisted-pair wiring. If the data-grade medium is used, up to 260 devices can be attached to the Token-Ring; if the telephone medium is used, up to 72 token ring devices can be attached to the network.

A token-ring access protocol is employed for network traffic control. The various devices to be attached to the network are cabled together through a network access unit to form a logical ring. Access to the shared ring is controlled by a token. Each networked device regenerates the signal as information is passed around the ring. The access protocol and baseband signaling are implemented by a network adapter in each attached device.

Hardware components of the Token-Ring Network include an adapter card with logical link control for the attachment of a variety of IBM products to the network, a multistation access unit, and cabling. Software components include a program that provides an IBM PC Network NETBIOS interface to the network, an SNA programming interface for the PC, a program that links the PC Network and the Token-Ring Network, communications servers, and network management software.

The IBM Token-Ring Connectivity is illustrated in the Figure 1.

### 2.2 16 Mbps Token-Ring

The 16-Mbps IBM Token-Ring Network was demonstrated publicly for the first time November 14, at the opening of the 1988 COMDEX computer trade show in Las Vegas, with an appropriate mixture of showmanship and IBM technological thoroughness.

The products announced by IBM at COMDEX included:

- A series of hardware attachments and software products that allow workstations, communication controllers, and computers to connect to the IBM Token-Ring Network operating at 16 or 4 Mbps

- An optical fiber converter operating at 16 or 4 Mbps

- A token-ring bridge program operating at 16 or 4 Mbps and supporting local and remote bridge functions

- An enhanced version of the IBM Token-Ring Network PC Adapter II for 4-Mbps transmission rates

Operating at 16 Mbps, the new IBM Token-Ring Network provides a new capability called "early token

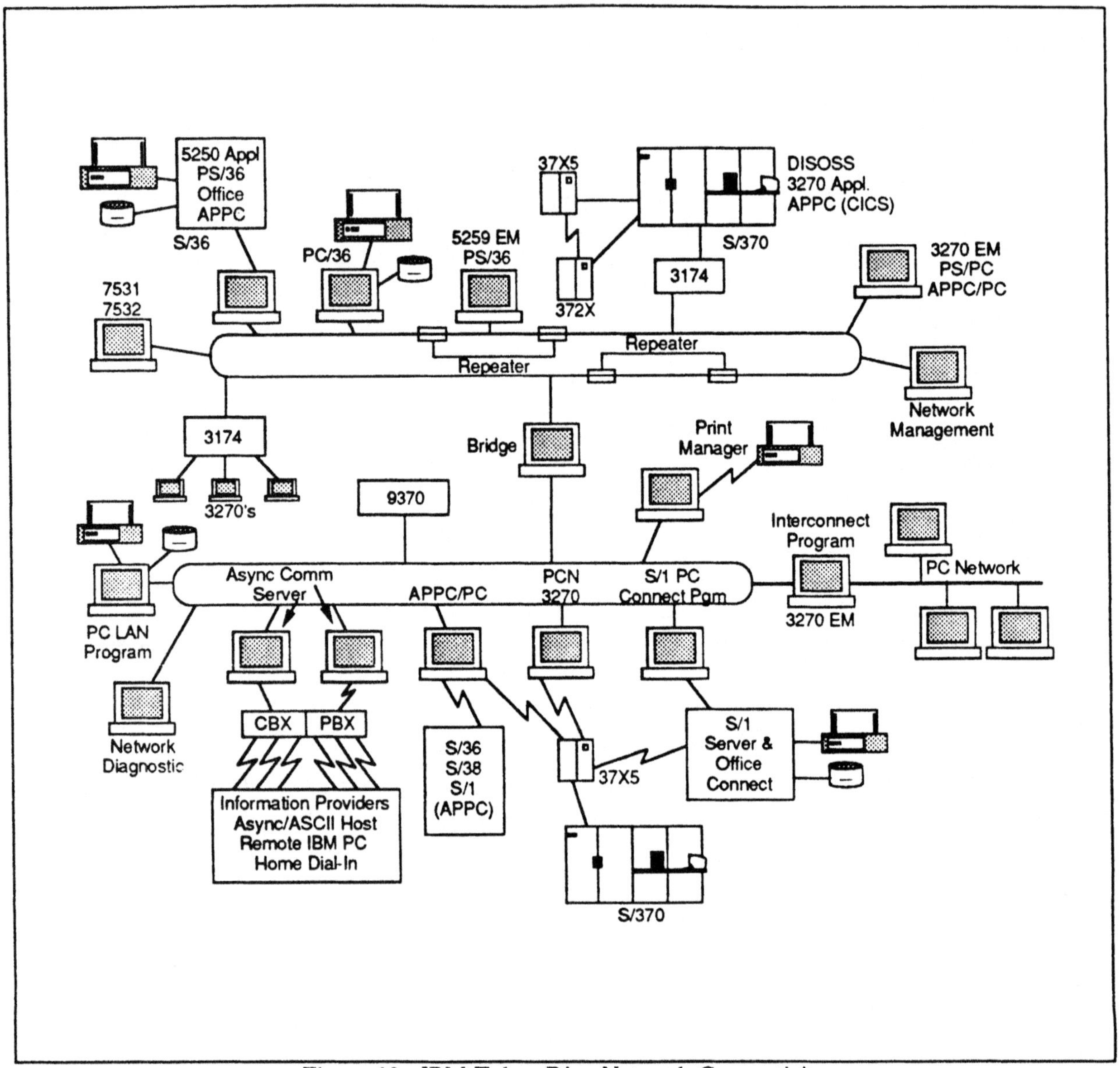


**Figure 10:** IBM Token-Ring Network Connectivity

release." An enhancement to the original token-ring architecture, early token release allows multiple "frames," or units, of data to be on the ring at the same time. Thus, a workstation on the ring now can transmit a token immediately after sending a frame of data, rather than waiting for its frame to return.

This enhancement to the IEEE 802.5 standard permits more efficient use of the 16-Mbps LAN, in that early token release enables ring efficiency to exceed 95% for all frames larger than 128 bytes, regardless of the length of the ring.

In terms of increased frame size, the IBM Token-Ring Network now supports frame sizes up to 18,000 bytes on 16-Mbps rings and up to 4,500 bytes on 4-Mbps rings. The new, larger frame sizes are said to be able to increase data transmission efficiencies by as much as 300% for specialized applications; previously, frame sizes were limited to 2,000 bytes. The large frame sizes also will accommodate high-volume RAM-to-RAM transmissions, such as those required for image applications, and can improve individual work-station performance.

## 2.3 IBM Token-Ring Network Hardware Components

Adapters

4-Mbps token-ring adapters are available from IBM for the following machines.

- 3174*
- 3720
- 3725
- 3745*
- 4702*
- 8100
- 9370*
- AS/400*
- ISA (PC, AT)*
- Micro Channel (PS/2, some 9370's, RISC System/6000)*
- RT/PC
- Series/1*
- System/36 (5363)
- System/88

Those marked with an * are also available in 16-Mbps versions. Here, we will examine the IMB PC and Micro Channel adapters in more detail.

### 2.3.1 The First Token-Ring Adapter

The original Token-Ring adapter card for the IBM Personal Computer is a full-sized (4.2 inches by 13.2 inches) card that works with industry standard architecture (SA) busses (i.e. the PC and PC/AT). Although no longer available, this adapter was the first to use IBM's 4/Mbps token-ring chip set upon which other all currently available IBM 4-Mbps adapters are based.

Five custom analog and VLSI devices handle the protocols and interface to the two twisted-pair. The non-analog devices were developed by IBM Burlington, using high-density, high-speed bi-polar technology. An on-board 16-bit processor aids in initial diagnostics, on-going diagnostics, and communications functions.

The microprocessor executes resident (on-board) microcode (32K 16-bit words arranged as two 32K by 8-bit EPROMS) which provides the host access to the data link functions per IEEE 802.2 LLC or physical link functions per IEEE 802.5.

When an IBM token-ring adapter is turned on for the first time, diagnostics built into the Token-Ring adapter perform a power-on-self-test (POST) procedure. This will check all the internal operations of the adapter, including the on-board timers. The adapter also checks the lobe cabling (up to the MAU and back) with loop-back tests to ensure that the cable is performing properly.

A single chip functions as a front-end. It is essentially an analog device which performs differential Manchester encoding/decoding, data synchronization, and physical insertion/removal from the ring. The chip is transformer-coupled, to electrically isolate the adapter from the cable.

The two-chip (one for transmit, one for receive) protocol handler performs parallel-to-serial conversion, encoding/decoding of data (from the front-end), cyclic redundancy check (CRC) generation and checking (removal), DMA to shared memory, monitor function, and detection of ring errors.

The shared memory is organized as four banks of 4K by 4-bit static RAM. It can be accessed as 8K by 8 from the host, or 4K by 16 from the adapter's microprocessor. The shared memory starting address is programmable by the host, eliminating the need to set switches. Any 8K boundary can be programmed, and certain areas of the shared memory can be protected (set to read-only) from corruption by the host. Figure 17 illustrates how the shared memory can be mapped into the PC memory domain, and how one might protect certain areas.

With the introduction of the PC Token-Ring adapter II, adapter II 8 Kbytes of static RAM was added. In addition, there were changes made to the microcode to support the IBM Attachment/36 and Token-Ring Bridge products.

In addition to the shared memory interface (also referred to as the memory mapped input/output (MMIO) interface), certain functions are controlled by the programmable I/O (PIO) interface via an I/O location in the PC's I/O space. The address of this I/O location is set via a dip switch on the adapter. This I/O port gives access to one of sixteen 8-bit control registers. Functions provided by the control registers include: bi-directional interrupt and status; the PC shared RAM starting address; the PC shared RAM management (i.e., setting protected areas) timer control which provides millisecond (ms) level timing; and the PC timer value register.

Five timers are provided by the adapter to supply interval and dead-man timings. The interval timers ensure proper token operation of the ring, as well as a general-purpose 10 ms timer accessible by the host PC. The dead man timer is a 120 ms timer which checks if the adapter code is executing. If the timer expires, a procedure is initiated to get the bad adapter physically off the ring.

To connect to the network, the adapter card provides a widely available DB-9-type connection to the PC adapter cable. Pins 1 and 6, 5 and 9 are used to connect to the transmit +, transmit -, receive +, and receive -. The adapter cable consists of a flexible 8-foot, Type 6 cable for connecting to data grade (Type 1 or 2) media. An optional Type 3 media filter is available for use with Type 3 telephone-type wire. In addition, the adapter supplies the phantom voltage required to drive the insertion relay in the MAU.

### 2.3.2 PS/2 Adapter

The IBM Token-Ring Adapter/A is used for the Micro Channel found in Personal System/2 Model 50 and higher. It contains the same basic chip set as described above and has 16 Kbytes of static RAM. About the only real enhancement to this adapter is that it is a 16-bit interface to the host and has a provision for remote program load (RPL), a feature for diskless or network boot (where the operating system is downloaded from a file server) operation.

### 2.3.3 16/4 Adapter

The 16/4 Token-Ring Network adapter cards feature the first analog/digital chip built with IBM's one-micron complementary metal oxide semiconductor (CMOS) technology. Taking advantage of the cooler-running CMOS technology, IBM engineers at Research Triangle Park, NC, and at Essex Junction, VT, jointly developed the new 40,000-circuit interface chip, integrating functions that previously required six chips. This increased integration enhances reliability and allows the new 4-Mbps adapter to be packaged in a half-size card.

The 16/4-Mbps adapter cards provide 64 Kbytes of RAM; as previously noted, IBM Token-Ring Network adapters used 8-Kbyte or 16-Kbyte RAMs. The 64-Kbyte RAM on the 16/4 adapters permit the use of larger data frames and allows more concurrent sessions to be established.

The IBM Token-Ring Network 16/4 Adapter and 16/4 Adapter/A, permit attachment of IBM PC's and compatibles (with ISA buss) and IBM PS/2 and compatibles (with Micro Channel buss) to the token-ring with switchable data rates of either 16 or 4-Mbps (the adapters will operate with older 4-Mbps adapters at the 4-Mbps rate). A remote program load is available as an option.

### 2.3.4 Busmaster Server Adapter/A

The IBM Token-Ring Network 16/4 Busmaster Adapter/A is used to attach an IBM with Micro Channel architecture, configured as a server, to an IBM Token-Ring Network operating at either 16 million or 4 million bits per second. The IBM Token-Ring Network 16/4 Busmaster Server Adapter/A provides high throughput capability while requiring less host-processor involvement than previous IBM Token-Ring adapters.

This reduction in host-processor involvement is enabled through the busmaster capability of the IBM Token-Ring Network 16/4 Busmaster Server Adapter/A, which allows adapter-to-system-memory transfer of data independent of the host processor. The server's processor is available for other tasks.

## 2.4 Mainframe Connections

### 2.4.1 3720

The IBM 3720 Communication Controller and IBM 3721 Expansion Unit are a lower-cost, lower capacity entry in the 3725 communication controller family. A link-attached model has been specifically designed for remote operation.

The 3720 provides four host attachments via two channel adapters and two 2- processor switches, up to 60 lines, and a maximum of two IBM Token Interface Controllers (TIC). Specifically, Models 11 and 12 support the Token-Ring. Advanced Communication Function/Network Control Program (ACF/NCP) Version 4 Release 2 or greater is required for the 3720. Alert support for the Token-Ring is via the hardware monitor component of NetView; NCCF/NPDA does not support alerts from the Token-Ring. NetView is discussed in greater detail in Chapter 7.

### 2.4.2 3725

Special hardware features support direct attachment of the 3725 front end processor (FEP) controller to the Token-Ring. The Token-Ring Subsystem permits attachment of appropriately equipped 3725s as well as 3726s to IBM Token-Rings. The subsystem consists of Line Attachment Base (LAB) Type C and Token Interface Controller (TIC).

The Line and Token-Ring Attachment Base provides a Token-Ring multiplexer and a physical base for up to four TICs. In addition, each LAB Type C provides a communication scanner and a physical base for up to 16 line attachments. The TIC provides one attachment to the Token-Ring. It contains a microprocessor operating under control of a resident microcode. Under control of ACF/NCP, the coupler provides logical link control functions conforming with the IEEE 802.2 standard.

One LAB Type C can be installed in a 3725 Model 1 or 2. In a 3725 Model 1 with a 3726, one LAB Type C can be installed in the 3726 if a LAB Type C is installed in the 3725, or two in the 3726 if no LAB Type C is installed in the 3725.

### 2.4.3 3174

The IBM 3174 Subsystem Control Unit (cluster controller) large cluster Models 1L, 1R, 2R, and 3R attach up to 32 3270 Information Display System terminals. The small cluster Models 51R, 52R, and 53R attach up to 16 terminals. These control units provide attachment of 3270 system displays, printers, and workstations to IBM host processors via a local channel, remote link, Token-Ring, and IBM Token-Ring LAN gateway. An optional feature permits attachment of ASCII terminals and attachment to ASCII hosts via telecommunications links.

The 3174 models are functionally equivalent to the IBM 3274 Control Unit Models 41A, 41C, 41D, and 61C but offer improved price/performance, usability, and increased functional capabilities.

It is the 3174 Models 3R and 53R that provide direct host attachment via the Token-Ring. These models communicate with the host via an IBM 3720 or 3725 with the NCP/Token-Ring interconnection facility interconnection of ACF/NCP Version 4 Release 2, or via a 3174 Model 1L with the IBM Token-Ring Network 3270 Gateway Network optional feature.

As an option, IBM Token-Ring Network 3270 Gateway is available for a 3174 Subsystem Control Unit Model 1L using SNA protocol. This option provides the capability for up to 140 Token-Ring attached devices, as PU 2.0 nodes, to communicate with an IBM host. Any combination of the following Token-Ring attached devices are supported by this feature:

- 3174 Model 3R or 53R
- PC using IBM Personal Computer 3270 Emulation Program Version 3.0
- PC using APPC/PC (as a PU 2.0 node)
- System/36 with the LAN Attachment Feature and using 3270 emulation or APPC (as a PU 2.0 node)

The devices and workstations directly attached to the 3174 and those attached via the Token-Ring can coexist and operate concurrently.

Support-S Release 2 adds Token-Ring Gateway support for remote 3174 Models 1R, 2R, 5R, and SNA/SDLC mode. (The gateway is defined by IBM as 3174 Model 1L, in which other remote 3174 control units that are attached to the Token-Ring may communicate to it -- up to 140 PU2.0 connections on the Token-Ring are supported.) The previous release supported the Token-Ring Gateway option feature with only the 3R and 53R models. It appears that the 3R and 53R continue to be the only models that can also attach locally to a 3720 or 3725 front-end processor.

The 3174 Subsystem Control Unit Type 3A Dual Speed Communication Adapter and supporting microcode, provides both gateway and alternate host attachment for IBM Token-Ring Networks operating at either 16 or 4-Mbps. The 16-Mbps ring can attach to an IBM mainframe, whether it is a backbone or application ring. Substantially improved gateway throughput can be achieved at either speed with the use of larger frame sizes.

3174 Configuration Support-B Release 2 contains functional enhancements to the 3174 including Multi-Host Token-Ring Gateway, which provides enhanced connectivity options for devices attached to the Token-Ring.

The Multi-Host Token-Ring Gateway allows a Token-Ring attached device to take greater advantage of the multiple host connectivity options available in the 3174 Establishment Controller, to access hosts through the primary host link and/or the Concurrent Communication Adapter. With the Multi-Host Token-Ring Gateway function, a user can have sessions with up to three different SNA hosts concurrently through the Token-Ring network using the 3174 configured as a gateway. A maximum of 50 downstream physical units may access the SNA host through each Concurrent Communication Adapter.

Token-Ring-attached devices that require access to multiple hosts via the Multi-Host Token-Ring Gateway will define the path through the 3174 gateway to the specific host link via the SNA Service Access Points portion of the gateway address. This requires definition during the customization of both the Token-Ring-attached device and the 3174 gateway.

Alerts and problem determination statistics from the Token-Ring continue to flow through the 3174 gateway to the SNA host over the primary link. Link events, specific to the sessions in progress via the Concurrent Communication Adapter links, flow to the appropriate host via that link.

### 2.4.4 3745

The 3745 Communication Controller is the newest member of the IBM Communication Controller family. The 3745, in conjunction with up to four IBM 3746 Expansion Units, offers modular growth for up to 16 host attachments, 512 line attachments, 8 high speed line attachments to T1 and CEPT channels, 8 IBM Token-Ring attachments and provides interfaces for local and remote consoles and the Remote Support Facility.

The 3745 is a medium to high end communications controller which operates under the control of the Advanced Communication Function/Network Control Program Version 5 (ACF/NCP) licensed program.

The 3745 supports IBM's network management direction by sending error related information to the NetView program running in a host processor. Alerts generated for the 3745 are displayed on the network control terminal by NetView, which also provides support for the IBM Token-Ring Network.

The 3745 controls data communications between modem attached, directly attached (without a modem) or IBM Token-Ring Network attached terminal devices, or between such terminal devices and one or more directly or remotely connected IBM 4341, 4361, 4381, 937X, 3033, 308X or 3090 host processors, or between host processors.

It can attach to a byte multiplexer, block multiplexer or selector channel and supports the Data Streaming mode when attached to a block multiplexer channel of an IBM 937X or 3090 system.

The Token-Ring Adapter and the Token-Ring Adapter Type 2 (16-Mbps) features on the same 3745 may be mixed. The Token-Ring Adapter Type 2 supports two attachment ports, software selectable ring speed of 4 or 16-Mbps per port, the use of large I-frames on the ring, INN/BNN traffic on the same Token-Ring Adapter Type 2 port and the Early Token Release option at 16-Mbps. The Early Token Release option allows improved ring utilization particularly on long rings with short I-frame traffic. At 4-Mbps, the Token-Ring Adapter Type 2 has higher data throughput than the current Token-Ring Adapter. Up to four Token-Ring Adapter Type 2 features can be installed on a 3745 allowing attachment to up to eight rings.

The 3745 can support up to 9,999 Token-Ring attached devices operating on 16 or 4-Mbps IBM Token-Ring Networks.

### 2.4.5 3172

The new IBM 3172 Interconnect Controller is a Micro Channel/80386-based intelligent controller that provides channel attachment of LANs to IBM System/370 host processors. Through multiple LAN attachments, the 3172 provides connection and data transfer services between LANs and IBM System/370 host processors in Transmission Control Protocol/Internet Protocol (TCP/IP) and Manufacturing Automation Protocol (MAP) Version 3.0 networks.

The LANs supported by the 3172 are Token-Ring and IEEE 802.3 (CSMA/CD) which includes Ethernet via TCP/IP protocol and MAP 3.0 (IEEE 802.4 Token Bus) protocol. The data stream is transparent to the 3172. Up to four LAN attachments and two channel attachments can be used with the 3172 Interconnect Controller. The 3172 is available in the IBM 9309 Rack Assembly or may be ordered as a stand-alone unit that can be housed in any compatible EIA 19" rack.

## 2.5 IBM Token-Ring Network Software Components

### 2.5.1 Interfaces

One of the key questions facing software developers is what token-ring interface should be written to. For the IBM PC Token-Ring adapter operating under PC DOS, there are four major interfaces to choose from: NETBIOS (Network Basic Input/Output Systems), APPC/PC, 802.2 DLC, and 802.5 MAC (direct). For OS/2, IBM offers these plus additional interfaces via the Communications Manager found in the OS/2 Extended Edition (see Chapter 6).

#### 2.5.1.1 PC Adapter Interfaces

All interfaces to the IBM PC Token-Ring Adapter require an adapter support interface (handler) once known as TOKREUI (Token-Ring Extended User Interface). TOKREUI was included with the adapter card on a 5-1/4" diskette as TOKREUI.COM. It is now incorporated as part of the IBM Local Area Network Support Program for DOS that was announced at the same time as Personal System/2 and also incorporated into the OS/2 EE Communications Manager.

#### 2.5.1.2 IBM LAN Support Program

The LAN Support Program is designed providing an interface to NETBIOS and IEEE 802.2 LLC and to enforce interface consistency for the various IBM PC LANs: Token-Ring (all PC and PS/2 adapters), PC Network Broadband (Adapter II and II/A only), and PC Network Baseband (a 2-Mbps Starlan-like network). All models of IBM PCs are supported from the XT to AT to PS/2. Both XT and AT versions of the 3270 PC are supported except for model 5271.

The equivalent of TOKREUI (as well as NETBEUI for NETBIOS and TOKR3270 for an IBM 3270-PC version of TOKREUI) is supplied by the PC LAN Support Program. Unlike TOKREUI, which is a "terminate stay resident" program, device drivers used for the appropriate adapter/interface that is loaded by DOS at boot time. DOS 3.3 or higher is required for proper operation of the device drivers.

The purpose of the adapter support interface (handler) is twofold: to supply the Token-Ring interface to canned programs such as NETBIOS and to relieve the programmer of the Token-Ring adapter complexities when designing custom applications. The handler essentially provides a direct (802.5 MAC) and logical link sublayer (802.2 LLC) of the data link layer (DLC) interface for the adapter as indicated in Figure 2.

There are a total of six device drivers supplied by the Support Program. One device driver called the interrupt arbitrator, is always used regardless of the adapter. It has one parameter that defines the language that load-time error messages are displayed in. In the first release of the Support Program, this parameter has no effect and error messages are displayed in English.

The other five drivers are as follows: two for Token-Ring; two for PC Network broadband or baseband; and one for NETBIOS. A program called DXMAID can be used by the user to automatically generate or modify the CONFIG.SYS file with the appropriate drivers and associated parameters for the desired adapter and optional NETBIOS support.

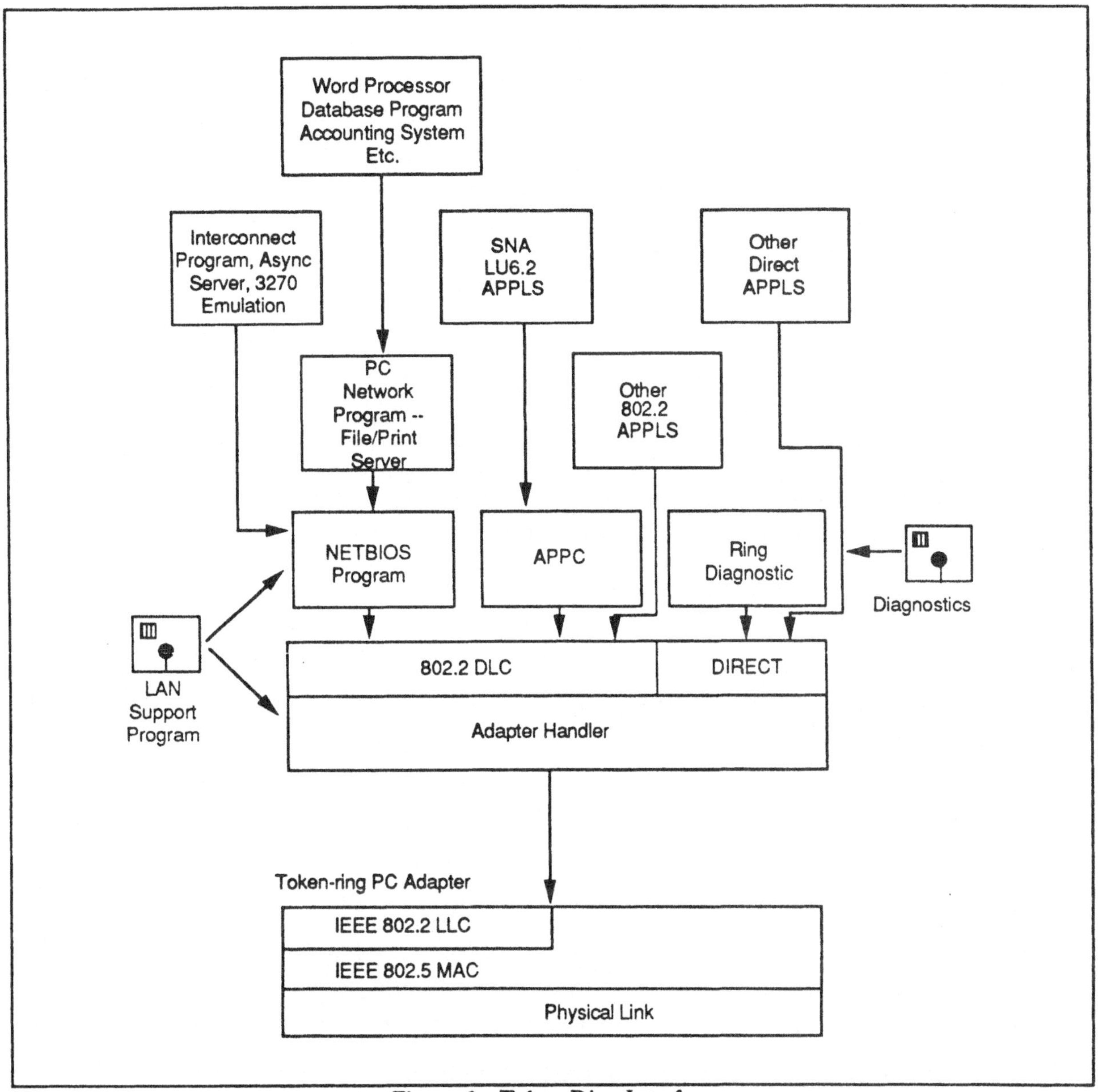


**Figure 2:** Token-Ring Interfaces

2.5.1.3 Token-Ring Driver

The two PC-DOS Token-Ring drivers are called DXMC0MOD.SYS and DXMC1MOD.SYS. The latter is used if operating the 3270 Workstation Program. The standard driver occupies 8Kb of RAM and the 3270 version occupies 14Kb. Both drivers support up to two adapters.

Adapter addresses and shared RAM locations are optional parameters for both drivers. If an adapter address is given, it overrides the universally administered address (the one burned into the adapter -- a 48-bit address that is uniquely assigned by a vendor who has obtained a range of addresses from IEEE) with a locally administered address. Locally administered addresses are handy for supporting applications such as 3270 workstation emulation, where a person may move to a different PC on the Token-Ring and yet retain the same physical address.

2.5.1.4 Direct Interface

The direct interface allows an application to obtain error status and logs, and to generally control the Adapter. The programmer must refer to the Token-Ring Adapter Technical Reference Manual for programming information.

Primitives (commands) are included to configure and manage the Adapter microcode and to support auxiliary commands that control buffer management, the 100 millisecond timer, and operational characteristics of the Adapter handler.

2.5.1.5 DLC Interface

The data link control (DLC) interface provides the IEEE 802.2 Type 1 (connectionless) and Type 2 service interface with link station characteristics. These include: support for node hierarchy with the station component; the SAP (Service Access Point) components and connect components; XID (eXchange IDentification) and TEST commands issued on a 'per SAP' basis; and XID and TEST responses issued by the station component (i.e., transparent to local applications).

A link station (link connection component) is a protocol machine used to manage elements of the procedure required to exchange data with a communicating link station in an adjacent node.

The SAP is an 8 bit architected code point/address through which an application is identified to the data link (DLC) software. SAPs allow multiple applications to share the same adapter (for example APPC/PC and NETBIOS), simultaneously.

2.5.1.6 NETBIOS

Network Basic Input/Output system (NETBIOS) was originally developed for the IBM PC Network by Sytek (now Hughes LAN Systems). The Pc Network version operates with Sytek LocalNet 20 protocols and provides an interface for various levels of protocol to the host. IBM reiterated the importance of NETBIOS by offering a NETBIOS emulator with the Token-Ring. This allows applications originally developed for the PC Network to be run on the Token-Ring. Most services provided are at the session level. Supported session services include peer-to-peer communication and naming.

Since NETBIOS is backed by IBM, many developers of LAN software and hardware have developed NETBIOS interfaces (also called NETBIOS ("emulators").

The IBM PC Local Area Network Program (formerly the IBM PC Network Program) is an example network application that relies on NETBIOS for its operation. It implements the Server Message Block (SMB) protocol. The PC LAN Program provides the user with workstation functions (redirector, receiver, and messenger) and non-dedicated server functions (workstation and server functions).

It should be noted that the NETBIOS interface option available for the Token-Ring is am "emulation" of the NETBIOS contained within the PC Network adapter card. Therefore, the actual protocols used within the various layers differ between the Token-Ring and the PC Network but what the user or programmer will see are identical interfaces and operation (except for response times, which are much faster in the Token-Ring).

The NETBIOS session layer interface provides host access to several protocols. Session management provides support for user sessions between nodes allowing users to establish connection to a named process and is responsible for determining the named process address. Once the destination node is determined, the initiating application can communicate with the destination node to provide session level services. In conjunction with naming, a datagram service is available for sending datagrams between two names (nodes).

NETBIOS name management provides binding of alias names and network addresses within the entire local network providing all name management services, including the translation of remote names to a network address. This mechanism of NETBIOS is one reason why it takes so long to initially become part of a NETBIOS network--the node will broadcast (a number of times to ensure reception by all other stations on the network) its names(s) to other stations--this ensures that the node has a unique name. Broadcasting also occurs to establish a session connection with another name.

Once supplied as the NETBIOS Extended User Interface (NETBEUI), NETBIOS is now configured into the IBM PC LAN Support Program as a device driver. Applications (i.e., the PC Network Program) written to NETBIOS for PC Network will work "as is" with the Token-Ring emulator. The device driver occupies 23Kb of RAM in its default configuration.

### 2.5.1.7 APPC/PC

Advanced Program-to-Program Communication for the IBM Personal Computer (APPC/PC) is a licensed program that supports the SNA application programming interface (logical unit [LU] Type 6.2, physical unit [PU] type 2.1) and allows program-to-program communication over an IBM Token-Ring Network and synchronous data link control (SDLC) communication links. As a common protocol for communication, APPC can provide improved connectivity among distributed transaction programs.

APPC/PC supports both the IBM Token-Ring Network PC Adapter and SDLC adapters. It provides a common program-to-program protocol that allows multiple conversations between applications running in an IBM Personal Computer and a System/370 (CICS/OS/VS Version 1, Release 7), System/36, System/38, AS/400, Series/1 (Realtime Programming System Version 7.1), or another IBM PC, APPC/PC does not provide direct connectivity between sessions on the IBM Token-Ring Network link and sessions on the SDLC link, but it does provide the application programming interface to allow a user-written program to communicate between sessions on the two links. It conforms to SNA LU Type 6.2. The support is based on SNA LU Type 6.2 sessions. APPC/PC supports PU2.1 architecture and provides a peer-to-peer relationship between the IBM PC and other PU2.1 nodes, such as the System/36, System/38, and Series/1. APPC/PC attaches to the System/370 as a PU2.0 node.

APPC/PC can be used by IBM PCs to help satisfy the requirements to attach to other SNA products using the SNA LU6.2 architecture. It provides communication services for applications in much the same way that IBM PC DOS provides disk input/output and file management services.

The program has been designed to have an open API. APPC/PC appears as a set of communication services provided by the operating system. It is loaded into the PC and remains resident, much like NETBIOS. An application accesses APPC services through PC DOS interrupt 68H. THE SAP assigned to APPC is 94H (F0H is assigned for NETBIOS). If NETBIOS is to be run concurrently, the NETBIOS must be loaded first, specifying an additional non- NETBIOS SAP value of 04H. APPC/PC will consume 160Kb of main memory in the PC. An additional 21Kb is required for menus, up to 5.5Kb for each additional LU, and 2.5Kb is needed for each additional concurrent conversation/session.

It supports a program interface through a set of verbs that allows application transaction programs to communicate at a conversational level with no session awareness. Application programs can engage in tow types of conversation: mapped conversation--intended for use in communications between user-written programs; and basic conversation--intended to provide a lower level interface, such as that required by logical unit service programs.

APPC/PC security support is provided to the IBM PC application program at both the session and conversation levels.

Network management data can be created by APPC/PC or by the user application program. The data can be sent to the network problem determination application.

An IBM PC application can use both this program and the LAN Support Program NETBIOS for concurrent access to the Token-Ring Network. Only one Token-Ring Personal Computer adapter is required.

Connectivity supported by the program includes: IBM PC to IBM PC, using an IBM Token-Ring Network communications link; IBM PC to IBM PC, using an SDLC communications link; and IBM PC to System/370, System/36, System/38, or Series/1, using an SDLC communications link.

To IBM, Lu6.2 is the technology, a base, and a strategy for future program-to-program communication interface (independent of operating systems) hardware, programming languages, data formats, communication protocols, and network configurations.

## 2.6 PC-DOS Services

### 2.6.1 PC LAN Program

The IBM PC Local Area Network Program (formerly called the IBM PC Network Program) was originally designed to operate with DOS 3.1 and the IBM PC Network (broadband). NETBIOS support available via the PC LAN Support Program, along with DOS 3.3 or higher, is required to operate the PC LAN Program on the Token-Ring.

The PC LAN Program consists of a single large executable file which can be brought up one of four ways: the user executes a NET START command and then specifies a redirector, receiver, messenger, or server. The first three (redirector, receiver, and messenger) are for workstations, and the last one (server) is a non-dedicated file/print server implementation which runs as a background task in a workstation. Figure 3 shows an example implementation with one PC configured as a file server and another as a print server.

Using the redirector is the most basic way to get onto the local network. It intercepts the workstation's printer and disk I/O to send to a server; users can also send messages to other machines. The receiver messenger and server perform the same as the redirector with the addition of: the receiver receives and logs messages to any device or file; the messenger allows a user to transfer files; and the server allows hard disks and printers to be shared.

PC LAN Program Version 1.3 has added the following features to: password controlled access (login) to a server; central resource definition and control including setting the time/date on a master server to synchronize dates and times in all workstations and servers, printer management, define users and modify privileges, and to manage application selector menus for individual users; administrator access to resources from any workstation; support for remote program and operating system load (i.e., support for diskless workstations); the ability to view logged on users; and finally, remote workstation printer selection, queuing, and status. Version 1.3 has also made small improvements in performance.

### 2.6.2 Asynchronous Communications Server

A service introduced by IBM with the original introduction of the Token-Ring, is the Asynchronous Communication Server. The server (an IBM PC) provides access to/from the network via two (per server) switched lines connected to a modem or IBM/Siemens CBX. An example network configuration is shown in Figure 4. The server requires NETBIOS for its operation and works with all IBM LANs that support NETBIOS.

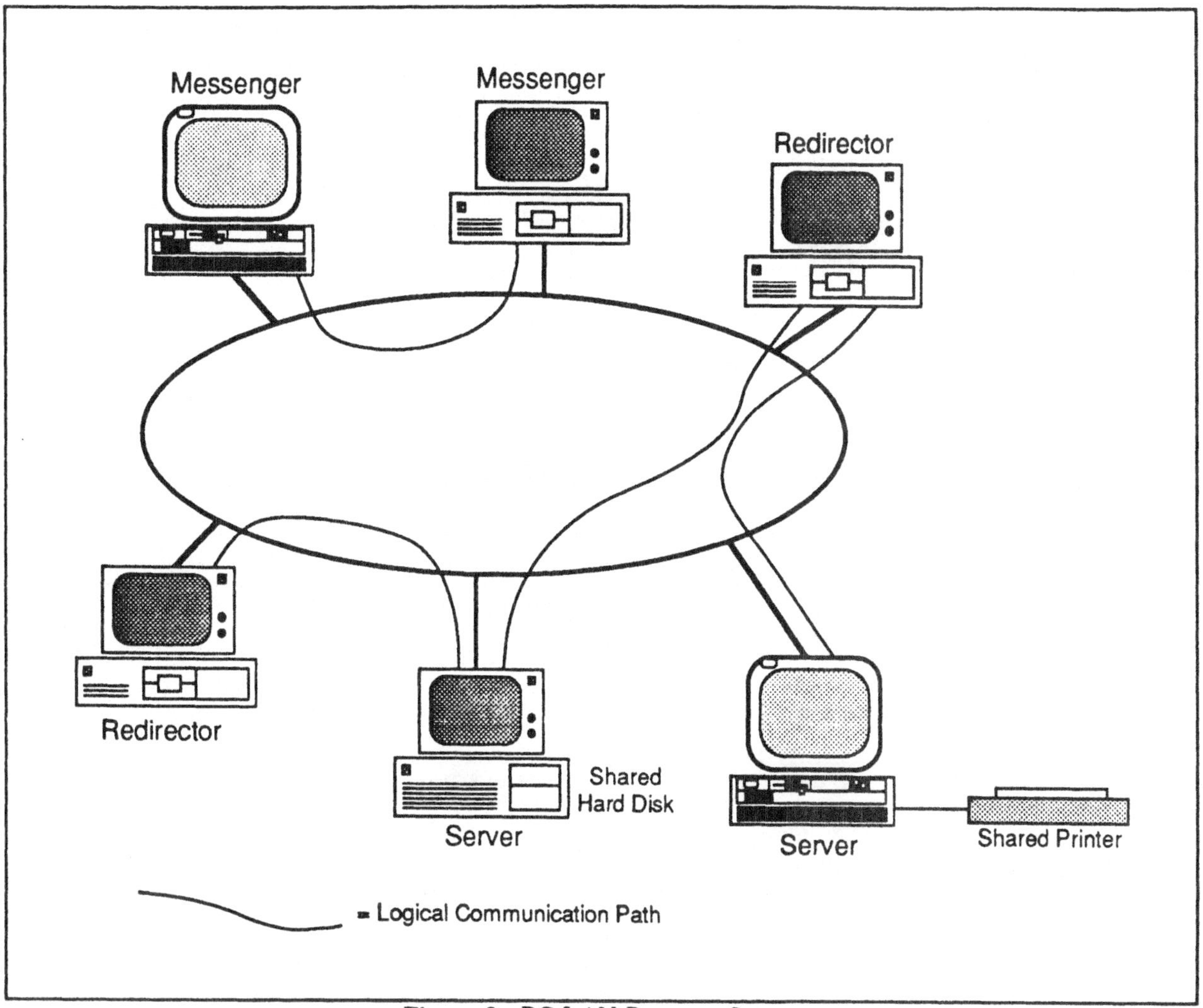


**Figure 3:** PC LAN Program Servers

The server program runs in either a dedicated (executing the server only) or non-dedicated PC (executing the server + other applications). It allows specially programmed applications operating on the network to "dial-out" from the network, or specially programmed applications to "dial-in" to the network. The network must include a complementary application to service the in-coming call. It is important to realize the server is a program and a protocol specification; by itself, it won't do anything. For example, IBM does not provide a network terminal emulation package which runs on a workstation and communicates with the server. The user or third party must supply the necessary applications software. It is possible to set up two applications as "servers" and have them communicate with each other via the LAN. This is useful for debugging new communications server applications.

Third party vendors that have adapted their communications software to work with the server include: Hayes with SmartCom, Crosstalk Communications/DCA with Crosstalk and Software Publishing with PFS:Access.

### 2.6.3 Asynchronous Connection Server

The IBM Local Area Network Asynchronous Connection Server Program functions as an RS-232 communications server for Token-Ring or PC Network (broadband) providing access to asynchronous devices such as modems. The program provides functions similar to devices such as the Ungermann-Bass NIU (network interface unit) that supports serial ports or the 3Com Communications CS (communication

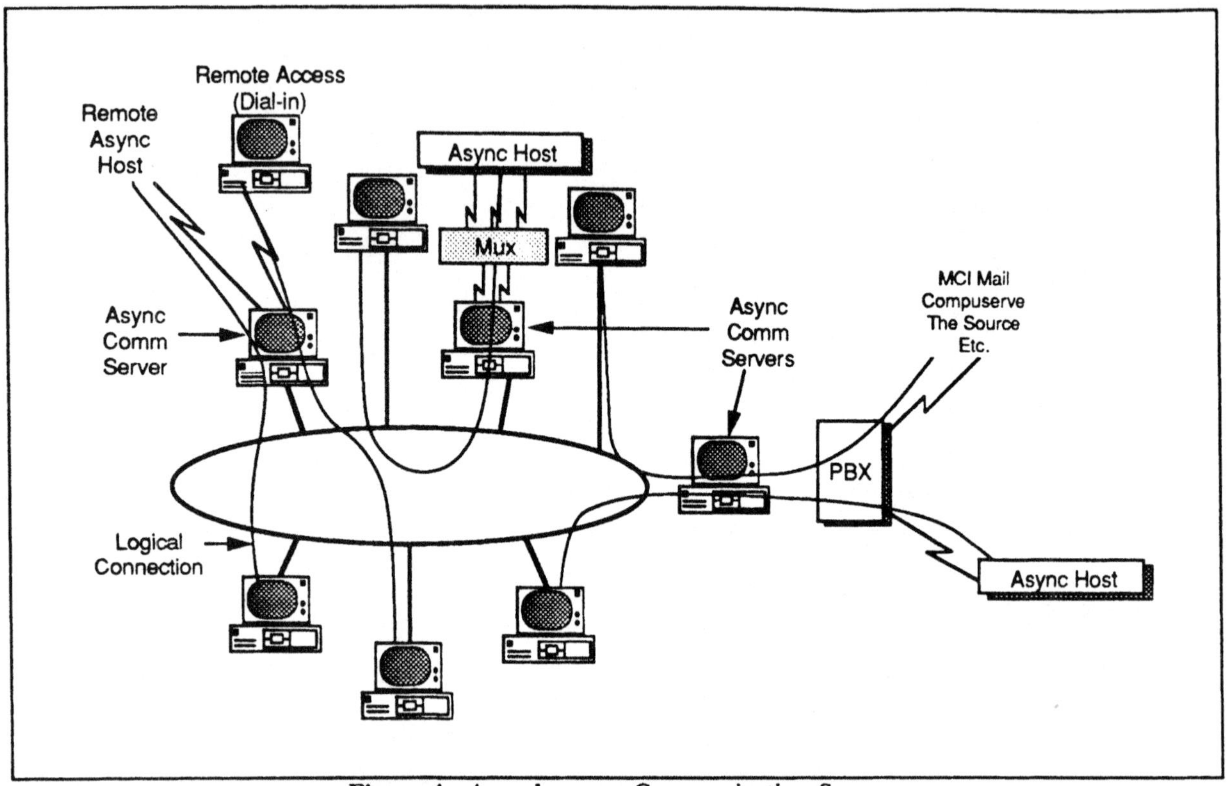


**Figure 4:** Asynchronous Communication Server

server), both of which are available for token-ring operation.

The IBM version is different from U-B or 3Com in that it is based on a PC AT or the Personal System/2 Model 30. PCs communicate via the Token-Ring to the Async Server via an enhanced BIOS interface or via the Asynchronous Communications Server protocol discussed in Chapter 2. In addition to using the COM1: and COM2: serial ports, the server can contain up to four IBM Realtime Interface Co-processor Multiport cards with up to 8 ports per card for a total of 32 ports.

An interesting feature of the Async Server is that devices attached to it, such as an IBM 3101 terminal, can seek a NETBIOS session over the Token-Ring to a second server that has asynchronous devices connected to it. Using this scheme, one can envision building terminal-only token-rings.

The Asynchronous Communications Server protocols are designed to handle data rates up to 64Kbps. The server uses the "AT" command set (used in Hayes Smartmodems and compatible modems). Handling high data rates may require a dedicated PC. One such flow control technique handled by the server is XON/XOFF.

The server relies entirely on NETBIOS and does not use any DOS services. The server runs in the background, relying on the PC's timer ticks (18.2/second) for its operation. The server can only service two lines (COM1 and COM2) but multiple servers can be attached, they then appear to an application as one large server. A server can automatically queue connection requests if all lines of a specified type are busy. Servers can be partitioned by function (i.e., a pool of 1200-baud modems) or group (only authorized groups can access a certain service).

The server protocol consists of a command set of fourteen commands to perform connection establishment, data transfer, and connection termination.

Connection establishment consists of the following commands: connection request (in which you can give the server a telephone number or a name to be looked up in a directory), connection request error (sent back if an error and connection request was to a unique not group name), connection identification and identification response (identify which server responded to the connection request), connection progress (your queue position), request queued (notification of non-immediate line access), and cancel queue (performed by the server -- this will happen if the line is lost, a number dialed is busy, or not answered, etc).

Data transfer consists of the following commands: data (how much data the server is to send to a work station at one time -- e.g., character by character, a text line at a time, x number of characters, time-out between characters received, etc.), transmission status, query parameters, change parameters (specified by the data command), and connection parameters.

Connection termination is one command. With this command, an application can terminate its connection with the communicating device (such as a modem).

NETBIOS commands used for establishing sessions, hanging up sessions, and handling special network situations with the server include: call, listen, add name, add group name, cancel, and delete name.

NETBIOS commands used in conjunction with the server protocol commands are: send or chain send, send datagram, receive, and receive datagram. All are used to send protocol commands to the server.

### 2.6.4 Token-Ring/PC Network Interconnect Program

The Interconnect Program allows a dedicated PC to act as a gateway between the Token-Ring and PC Network. A dedicated IBM PC running only the interconnect program is physically attached to the two networks with one token adapter card and one PC Network adapter card. Applications written to NETBIOS can communicate with devices on either network.

As an example, an IBM PC LAN Program user can access programs or data on a server from one network to another. This requires the Interconnect Program to be "pre-configured" to identify the devices (names) on each network which will be known to the other network. The names can not be dynamically changed during operation and only 16 names on each side are supported. During operation, the gateway receives messages from one network and forwards the messages to the other. Also, during operation, an operator can check device status and monitor the gateway activities.

### 2.6.5 3270 Emulation Program

The 3270 Emulation Program provides users on the Token-Ring access to IBM hosts from their workstations, without having dedicated coaxial wiring and SDLC cards on each workstation desiring host communication.

The 3270 Emulation program can be operated in one of three modes: 1) as a gateway on the network; 2) as a workstation on the network; or 3) as a stand-alone remote user station. The program was originally written for the PC Network; thus it relies on NETBIOS for operation.

As a gateway on the network, the PC requires the IBM SDLC card (for "remote 3274 operation") or IBM 3278/3279 coaxial adapter board (for "Distribution Function Terminal (DFT) operation") to communicate with the host. The gateway then serves users on the network who are running the program as a workstation. Up to 32 concurrent sessions are supported with SDLC; up to five sessions are supported with the coaxial attachment. Multiple gateways can be attached, providing more session access to single host or access to other hosts. The gateway does not have to be dedicated, but dedication is recommended. IBM recommends the use of the PC AT as the gateway.

As a network workstation, the program uses the resources of the PC to emulate a subset or the IBM 3278-2 or 3279-S2A display station with an optional IBM Graphics Printer, Color Printer, Wheelprinter, or Quietwriter attached. The user can then establish a session with a host via the gateway. File transfer (with appropriate host software) to/from local disks or a file server's disk, screen save, and file append are supported. The user can also "hot-key" back and forth between the emulator and network operation.

Another workstation feature is the ability to have host or operator initiated printing to the workstation-attached printer (which mimics the operation of a 3287). The keyboard can be mapped allowing the user to redefine most keys on the PC keyboard to closely mimic the operation of the 3278 keyboard (such as PF keys mapped to the PCs function keys).

The workstation can communicate with a host via a PC configured as a gateway as described above, or via a Token-Ring-attached 3725 front-end processor (FEP) or 3174 cluster controller. An example setup on the Token-Ring is shown in Figure 5.

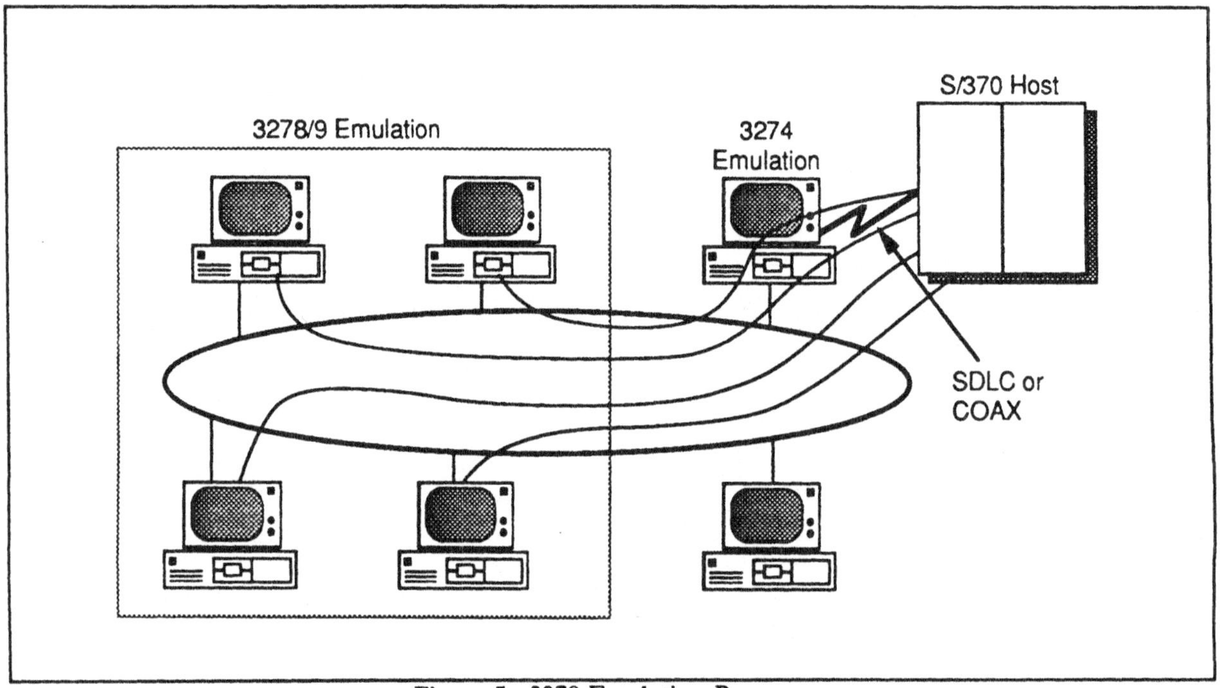


**Figure 5:** 3270 Emulation Program

The 3270 Emulation Program supports most features of a 3274 controller and 3278/3279 display station, but not all. Many functions such as structured field and attribute processing (SFAP) (EBCDIC only); Programmed Symbols (PS) on attached terminals; extended color on terminals; extended highlighting on attached terminals; magnetic strip reader; selector pen; and security keylock are not supported.

#### 2.6.6 3270 Workstation Program

The IBM 3270 Workstation Program version 1.1 allows direct communication to a Token-attached 3174 or 3725. The PC 3270 Emulation Program Entry Level Version 1.2 (for PCs and PS/2 Model 30) and Version 1.2 (for PS/2 Model 50 and higher -- yes, there are two versions of Version 1.2(!)) adds Enhanced Connectivity Facilities (ECF) to Version 1.1 by supporting the Server-Requester Programming Interface (SRPI). Although not a "turn-key" Token-Ring 3270 program, it offers the SRPI interface that can be used across the Token-Ring.

### 2.6.7 IBM Personal Communications/3270

IBM Personal Communications/3270, a DOS program, includes multiple 3270 display or print sessions, Emulator High level Language Application Program Interface (EHLLAPI), and the capability for concurrent connection to one or more IBM System/370* host systems as a 3270 terminal or workstation printer.

This program provides improved file-transfer performance and expands 3270 functions for workstations attached via a Token-Ring Network.

Expanded gateway services provide System/370 host connections to users of OS/2 Extended Edition, PC 3270 Emulation Program Version 3, 3270 Workstation Program Version 1.1, and Personal Communications/3270 via an IBM Token-Ring Network.

### 2.6.8 Series/1 PC Connect Program

Another application written for NETBIOS, the Series/1 PC Connect Program, provides a path between the Token-Ring (as well as PC Networks) and the Series/1, enabling workstations on the network to utilize Series/1 resources and communicate with large IBM hosts. The program requires an IBM PC attached to the network, the NETBIOS emulator, the IBM PC Network Program (configured as a server) and the Series/1 to PC Channel Attachment Feature. The channel attachment consists of a single "cycle stealing" card, a twelve foot intersystem channel cable, and a PC channel interface card. Programming support for the Series/1 is in the RPS operating system.

Figure 6 illustrates the use of the Series/1 PC Connect Program on the Token-Ring.

The PCs in the network can use the Series/1 disks and printers as though they were disks attached to the server. They can also use the Series/1 as a "pass-through" communications controller to communicate with large hosts, using a variety of Series/1 BISYNC or SDLC communications options. The host communication option requires the PC 3270 Emulation Program to operate in a separate PC (the file server and the emulation program cannot operate in the same PC).

### 2.6.9 System/36 Support

A System/36 Model 5360 or 5362 can be attached to the Token-Ring with the IBM System/36 Local Area Network (LAN) Attachment feature with the IBM System/36 PC 5360/5362 LAN Communications PC 5360/5362 Licensed Program and the Model 5364 with the IBM System/36 PC 5364 Local Area Network (LAN) Licensed Program. All models can connect to a maximum of two rings.

The 5360/5362 attachment feature consists of a direct-attach System/36-to-AT adapter that is installed in a dedicated AT that in turn is connected to the Token-Ring via Adapter II. For the 5364 (also known as the System/36 PC), the AT is directly attached. For either configuration, the communications program is downloaded into the AT from the System/36.

With the introduction of the low-end System/36 Model 5363, IBM is offering a direct channel attached Token-Ring adapter. This adapter will eventually be available for larger processors in the System/36 family.

The PC can make use of System/36 resources through PC Support/36 or Personal Services/PC. PC Support 36 allows the user to transfer PC-DOS or System/36 files back and forth, with or without translation, to access the System/36 in terminal emulation mode, or to access disks and printers on the System/36 as virtual disks and printers known to PC-DOS.

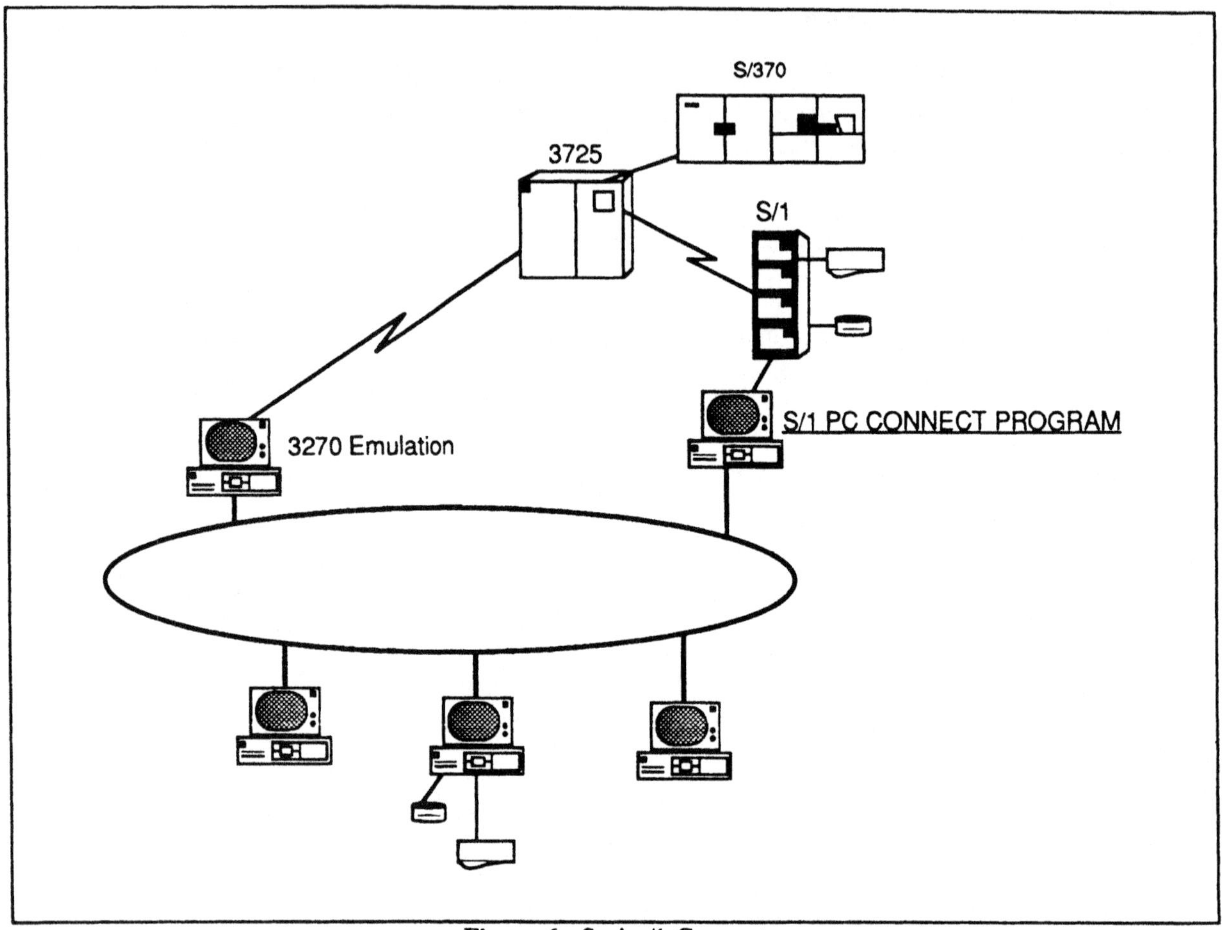


**Figure 6**: Series/1 Connect

Personal Services/PC is more of an office automation package that allows users to exchange files and electronic mail via System/36 and DISOSS (which operates on System/370 hosts). Versions of Personal Services are also available for System/36 and System/370 users.

### 2.6.10 Token-Ring Network Bridge Program

The IBM Token-Ring Network Bridge Program operates in a PC AT or PS/2 Micro Channel between two Token-Rings using a technique known as source routing. Up to seven levels of bridges are supported and they may operate in parallel for increased performance or to provide alternate routes for fault tolerant operation. A frame traverses the bridge in approximately 12 to 17 milliseconds.

The Bridge Program requires two Token-Ring Adapter IIs for the PC AT or two Token-Ring Adapter/As for the PS/2 Micro Channel. All workstation software that uses the 802.2 LLC interface and source routing, can operate transparently across the bridges. All IBM Token-Ring software including NETBIOS and APPC/PC meet these requirements. For non-IBM products, one needs to consult with the vendor of that product. As an example, it took Novell three years to make NetWare work across source-route bridges.

The IBM bridge program monitors error conditions and can give the location and time of occurrence for the two attaching rings. Beginning with the Bridge Program Version 1.1, various error and statistic information can be sent to the IBM LAN Manager Program. The Ring Parameter Server (RPS) provides the ring number to stations as they insert into the ring, and notifies the LAN Manager of the insertion. The Ring Error Monitor (REM) compiles error statistics. The Configuration Report Server (RES) forwards configuration change notifications to the LAN Manager and allows the LAN Manger to query adapters as required and set station parameters for optimal ring operation. Another interesting feature is the ability to trace a specially marked frame through the network for connectivity analysis.

IBM Token-Ring Network Bridge Program Version 2.0 connects both 4-Mbps and 16-Mbps Token-Ring Networks in any combination. IBM Token-Ring Network Bridge Program Version 2.1 bridges remote Token-Ring Networks via leased lines. This program enables the creation of a single logical network composed of many 4-Mbps and 16-Mbps Token-Rings, whether local or remote. As with Version 1.1, Version 2.0 and 2.1 provide network management support to the IBM LAN Manager 2.0 by forwarding ring and bridge error information.

Version 2.0 can be configured locally or by IBM LAN Manager Version 2.0 to communicate with other active bridges in the network to automatically configure the network single-route broadcast path. If this capability is desired, all bridges in the network must be configured to participate in the protocols. Because the existing versions of the bridge program do not support automatic configuration, they must be upgraded to Version 2.0 to utilize this new function.

Version 2.1 can be used to connect either local or remote rings. The local bridge configuration provides all of the functions and capabilities of IBM Token-Ring Network Bridge Program Version 2.0. The remote bridge configuration uses one PC or PS/2 with bridge software at each end of a point-to-point, leased, SDLC line. When the program is configured as a remote bridge, frames are transferred between two rings via a leased teleprocessing line operating in full duplex at speeds from 9.6 Kbps to 1.344-Mbps. The remote bridge can attach to the telecommunication network on one of the following ways:

- Via synchronous modems capable of providing the following interfaces at the indicated speeds:
  - EIA RS-232-C/CCITT V.24 at 9.6 Kbps to 19.2 Kbps
  - CCITT V.35 at 9.6 Kbps to 1.344-Mbps
  - X.21 bis/V.24 at 9.6 Kbps to 19.2 Kbps
  - X.21 bis/V.35 at 9.6 Kbps to 1.344-Mbps
  - X.21 (leased only) at 9.6 Kbps to 64 Kbps.
- Via a multiplexer, such as the Integrated Digital Network Exchange (IDNX).
- Via the T1D3 feature of the ROLM CBX (Models 8000, 9000, and 9751) using the CCITT V.35 interface and a CCITT V.35 to EIA RS-449/RS-422A Interface Converter.

The remote bridge configuration of IBM Token-Ring Network Bridge Program Version 2.1 provides the capability of filtering frames forwarded by the bridge. A programming interface will be specified that will allow a user program to determine whether frames are allowed to pass through the bridge. A sample filtering program will is provided.

Because the performance of the remote bridge is gated by the TP line, network traffic flow should be considered when selecting the line speed. For example, the broadcast traffic generated by a large network could cause severe performance problems at the 9.6 Kbps TP line speed. Because the effective throughput at the slower line speeds is low, the network traffic flow is a determining factor in the number of concurrent links that can be supported by the remote bridge.

To compensate for timing delays created by the TP line, parameters such as frame size and protocol timer values may need to be adjusted in the application. Applications not allowing such adjustments may not be able to communicate across the remote bridge at the slower line speeds.

## 2.7 Operating System/2

Operating System/2 is the "new" operating system developed with Microsoft that was announced in April of 1987 with IBM's family of Personal System/2 computers. This was IBM's opportunity to offer its first Systems Application Architecture (SAA) operating system.

IBM offers their own extended version of OS/2 called Operating System/2 Extended Edition. One of IBM's unpublicized goals of OS/2 EE is its intent to forge strong links with System/370 environments.

OS/2 is the primary operating system for IBM Personal System/2 with the Micro Channel architecture and 80286 or 80386 processors. This includes the Models 50 through 80, and existing PC ATs and the XT/286. OS/2 will support any future IBM Personal Systems based on 80286, 80386 or 80486. OS/2 runs in the protected mode of the 80286 and functions likewise in the 80386 or 80486. Thus, it does not take advantage of additional features available in the 80386/80486 such as virtual DOS machines or large memory segments for programming.

It does however, give users and programmers capabilities not previously available under PC DOS and 8088/8086 processors (such as running programs larger than 640 Kbytes and supporting concurrent multiple applications). OS/2 does support PC-DOS in a "compatibility box" for many (but not all!) existing programs.

OS/2 also takes advantage of the VGA display, which new with the PS/2 (VGA is now the defacto IBM graphics standard for its PCs). The standard VGA and PS/2 standard keyboard are important hardware contributors to the consistency requirement for SAA.

OS/2 standard edition (or the base operating system) does not contain the communication and database managers: users may install the standard edition and later migrate to the extended edition if communications and database support is desired.

### 2.7.1 Communications Manager

The Communications Manager provides communication services for applications written for the IBM Operating System/2 environment, between IBM PC and IBM Personal System/2 and host networks. These services provide communication to personal computers and systems over a wide range of local and remote connectivities -- including SDLC, Distributed Function Terminals (DFT) mode to an IBM 3174 or 3274, IBM Token-Ring Network and IBM PC Network, and asynchronous links -- by utilizing LU6.2, 3270 data stream (LU2), and asynchronous communications protocols. Emulation support for multiple terminal types concurrently is provided, and file transfer and a keyboard remap facility is supported. Several programming interfaces are provided to allow programs to take advantage of the power of the IBM PC and IBM Personal System/2 and to facilitate programmer productivity in applications development. The Communications Manager provides alerts for network management functions for problems determination, and controls for SNA communication services.

Data Link and Data Stream Support - An IBM PC or IBM Personal System/2 may be attached to an IBM PC, an IBM Personal System/2, a host, or departmental system, locally via the IBM Token-Ring Network or IBM PC Network and DFT (to an IBM 3X74 controller), and remotely via SDLC and asynchronous links.

Programming Interfaces (PIs) - The Programming Interfaces (PIs) supported by the Communications Manager include:

Advanced Program-to-Program Communications (APPC) PI: The LU6.2 architecture describes the functions that may be used by conforming pairs of programs for Advanced Program-to-Program Communications over the supported data links. The interface provides programming access to these functions (or verbs). Support is for both Mapped (data stream independent) and Basic (data stream dependent) verbs. APPC applications may be written to IBM hosts with MVS-CICS and VSE-CICS, and IBM System/36, IBM System/38, AS/400, IBM Personal System/2, IBM Personal Computer, IBM RT PC, IBM System/88, and IBM Series/1 systems.

Server-Requester Programming Interface (SRPI): This is the PI for the Enhanced Connectivity Facilities. It enables the writing of simple, communications-independent, requester programs which can call to host server programs, with synchronous returns. It is supported over links using LU2 protocols. Host server support is available under MVS/TSO and VM/CMS.

Asynchronous Communications Device Interface (ACDI): This interface allows the writing of applications (such as other asynchronous emulators or file transfer programs) to exchange data over asynchronous links. The interface provides a high degree of independence of the asynchronous hardware used. Device-specific programming modules are required for each supported device type and are included in the product. They are transparent to user applications. Supported functions include the ability to manipulate the line characteristics and connection control (connect and disconnect) without having to deal with physical device-specific characteristics.

IBM Local Area Network PIs: The IBM NETBIOS and IEEE 802.2 Data Link Control PIs are provided for communicating across IBM LANs.

Programs written for the Communications Manager may invoke the supported communications functions by calls from IBM Pascal/2, IBM Macro Assembler/2, and IBM C/2.

Terminal Emulation - The Communications Manager allows concurrent emulation of synchronous and asynchronous terminals. Emulation includes IBM 3270, IBM 3101, and DEC VT100 terminals.

IBM 3270 Terminal Emulation: The following terminals can be emulated: IBM 3178 Model 2; IBM 3278 Models 2, 3, 4, and 5; IBM 3279 Models S2A and S2B. The following are supported: all base data stream functions; multiple interactive screen; extended attributes; extended data stream (including seven colors, and extended highlights); file transfer; emulator keyboard remapping; LU Type 2, node Type 2.0, to a maximum of five 3270 display sessions per workstation over SDLC, IBM Token-Ring Network, and DFT links.

IBM 3101 and DEC VT100 Terminal Emulation: An IBM PC or an IBM Personal System/2 connected to a host supporting an asynchronous link can emulate the IBM 3101 (Model 20) or the DEC VT100 terminals. Lines can be switched, non-switched, or direct-connected and must be compatible with 1984 CCITT V24/V28 (RS-232-C) as implemented by IBM.

File Transfer - The Communications Manager supports the following file transfer types between supported hosts and IBM Personal Computers and IBM Personal System/2: IBM host file transfer programs are supported under 3270 and asynchronous emulation, (Under asynchronous emulation, file transfer with the 3270-PC File Transfer Program included four-byte CRC error detection); support for XModem is under asynchronous emulation with 128-byte block transfer and one-byte checksum error detection; and Pacing under asynchronous emulation with line delay interval pacing or host prompt character pacing is supported in sending an ASCII text file.

Communications and Systems Management - Communications and Systems Management (C&SM) support (for IBM System/370 host network) includes: C&SM alerts for SDLC, ASYNC (requires a SDLC or IBM Token-Ring Network link to communicate alerts to the host), IBM Token-Ring, and IBM PC Network data links, and problem determination data.

Problem Determination - The Communications Manager provides functions for gathering and processing problem determination data. These functions include tracing of programming interfaces, data units, and/or system events; displaying and printing of all or selected error logs from file; system dumping; and displaying of all or selected messages.

Subsystem Management - The Communications Manager allows a user's system administrator to control and obtain status information on the SNA communication resources maintained by the Communications Manager. As a management tool, it displays information on which programs are in use, sessions in use by the programs, detailed information about the sessions, and resources which are active. It allows the activation or deactivation of sessions, data link controls, and specific links. It also can be used to start and stop an attach manager which allows remote applications to be started.

Figure 7 summarizes the various interfaces available under the communications manager for the token-ring.

OS/2 Standard and Extended Editions Version 1.2 have significant new functions, including many features that better conform to SAA. 1.2 includes enhanced communications functions that allow better connectivity to IBM mainframe computers, multi-user support for remote data services, and support for additional programming languages.

An integral part of OS/2 Standard Edition Version 1.2 is a Desktop Manager/File Manager -- an enhanced user interface to operating system functions such as adding and starting applications, associating files to applications, and switching between applications. The interface also can make use of icons.

OS/2 Standard Edition Version 1.2 also contains the new High Performance File System (HPFS) that may be used to replace the PC-DOS and earlier OS/2 File Allocation Table (FAT) file system. The HPFS can handle partitions and files up to two Gbytes in size and delivers improved performance over the FAT file system. Compatibility between files created by both file systems is maintained for OS/2 programs, as well as for DOS programs running in OS/2's DOS compatibility mode.

OS/2 Extended Edition 1.2 (which serves as the development platform for IBM's new OfficeVision/2 LAN series), has enhanced its Database Manager with Remote Data Services (RDS), an SAA function that provides multi-user database support in an OS/2 LAN environment. RDS gives workstations, attached on a LAN, access to databases on other workstations on the same LAN, without requiring the user to know, or identify, on which workstation the information resides.

Other Database Manager enhancements include: referential data integrity, which helps ensure consistency of data within a database; cursor stability; Cobol, Pascal, and Fortran precompilers; and grant/revoke authorization capability.

A new feature of the OS/2 Extended Edition Communications Manager is an SNA Gateway. This LAN-based Gateway allows customers to support up to 254 workstations on a single LAN. Previously, a maximum of 32 workstations could be supported on a single LAN with IBM's PC 3270 Emulation Program.

Also, the Communications Manager utilizes the Network Driver Interface Specification (NDIS) for two additional LAN protocols: Ethernet DIX Version 2.0 and IEEE 802.3. This support provides the ability for NETBIOS, LU2, and LU6.2 functions to be used across an Ethernet LAN connection.

Other new communications features include a 5250 Work Station Feature; host-directed print; support for the X.25 protocol; and host-graphics view. In order to use the host graphics, GDDM-OS/2 Link is required.

The Database Manager's Query Manager and the Communications Manager's 3270 and ASCII terminal emulators are now Presentation Manager-based.

OS/2 Extended Edition's new SAA Procedures Language is a general-purpose, interpretive language suitable for use as a command processor, a macro language, and a programming language for the casual

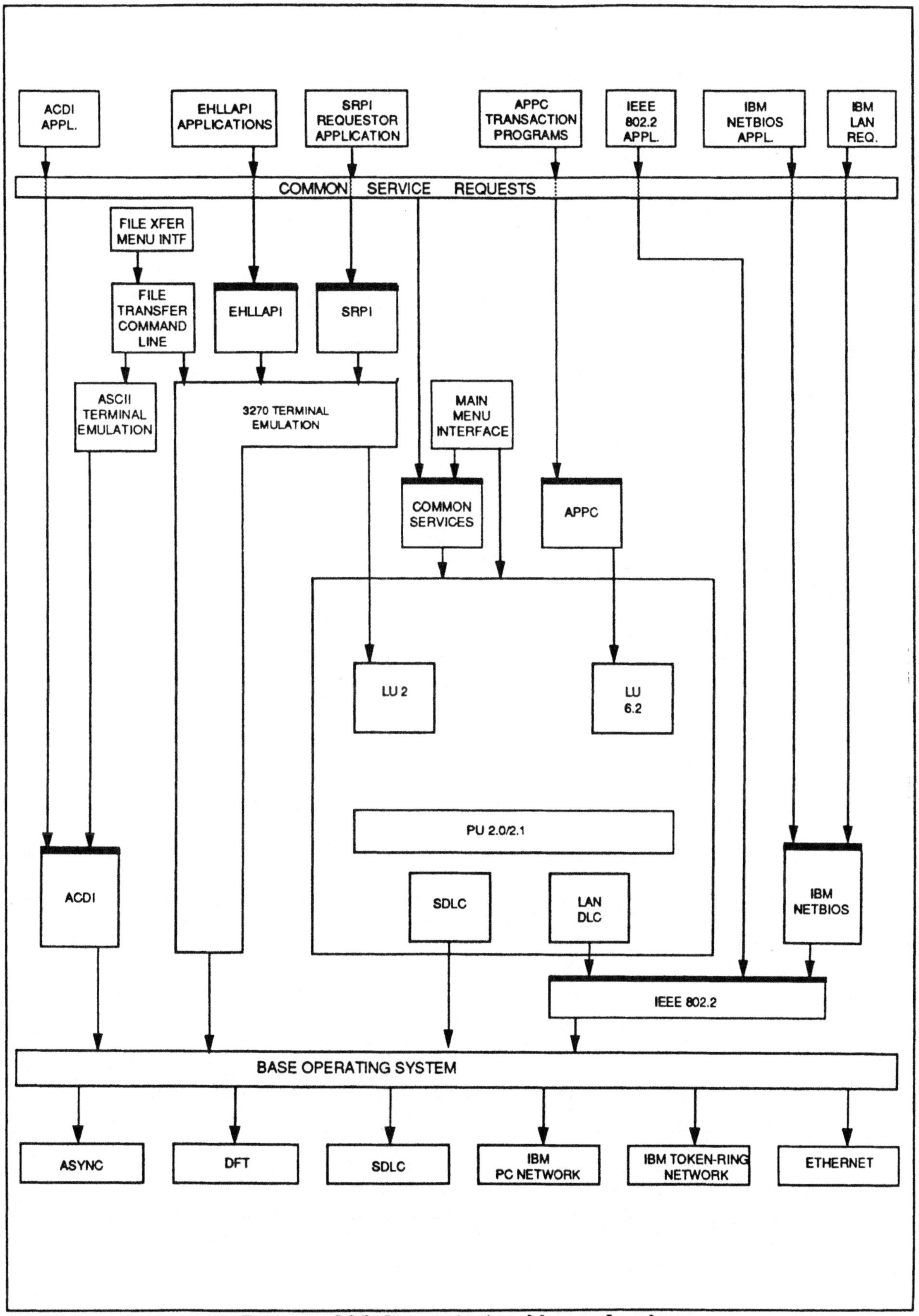


**Figure 7:** OS/2 Communications Manager Interfaces

programmer. It combines the structured logic, general variables, and subroutine calls of a traditional programming language with the ability to execute character strings as system commands.

IBM's OS/2 LAN Application Programming Interface (API) support has been extended to include new APIs, such as Files, Messages, and Sessions. This allows customers and software developers to create distributed requester/server applications that will operate in an OS/2 LAN server environment.

### 2.7.2 LAN to LAN Wide Area Network Program

The IBM LAN to LAN Wide Area Network Program is a licensed program that interconnects remote LANs across a wide area network. Applications written to the IEEE 802.2 interface and using the IBM NETBIOS frame protocol will be able to communicate with remote LANs using the wide area network as a transport medium. The program provides the interface between the LAN and the WAN. Sessions will be established between IBM LAN to LAN Wide Area Network Programs to provide the communication path. This communication will be via the LU 6.2 facilities provided by OS/2 EE Communications Manager 1.2.

- OS/2 EE 1.2 based product with 802.2 and LU 6.2 support that does not require a dedicated processor

  Allows IBM Token-Ring Network, IBM PC Network, and Ethernet LANs to communicate with each other over a wide area network,,using NETBIOS-NETBIOS flows. The connection through the wide area network could be one of the following:

  - LU 6.2 advanced program-to-program communications (APPC) session over Systems Network Architecture (SNA) network
  - LU 6.2 APPC session over X.25 network
  - LU 6.2 APPC session over synchronous data link control (SDLC)
  - LU 6.2 APPC session over LAN

- Interprets IBM NETBIOS session activation and datagram frames and will act upon the name in these frames to determine the target local area network of the request. If another IBM NETBIOS application is to run in the same processor as the IBM LAN to LAN Wide Area Network Program, another LAN adapter will be required for the other NETBIOS application.

- Limits the amount of broadcast traffic on the LAN that passes through the wide area network.

- Uses 802.2. interface for LAN communication.

  Link-Level Control timers (T1, T2, Ti) will be applicable only to the LAN. They apply between the end station and the IBM LAN to LAN Wide Area Network Program but not between the IBM LAN to LAN Wide Area Network Programs.

  However, the NETBIOS and application timers will be between end stations, since the NETBIOS session runs from end station to end station and not from end station to the IBM LAN to LAN Wide Area Network Program. It may be necessary to increase the end station NETBIOS and application timers to accommodate the wide area network delays.

- Allows control of which source and target stations may communicate with each other through supplied or user-written filters.

- Provides full visibility (at the IBM LAN to LAN Wide Area Network Program processor) of the current state of all wide area network sessions and connected IBM LAN to LAN Wide Area Network Programs, as well as detailed logs of errors, events, and statistics; LAN circuit bring-up, takedown, and statistics; and wide area network session bring-up, takedown, and statistics.

- Provides some network management, such as later notification to a host of IBM LAN to LAN Wide Area Network Program error conditions (session lost, resources depleted, processor failure). These alerts will be sent using the Alert Transport Facility of the LAN Manager. If a LAN Manager is not present, alerts cannot be sent to the host.

- Allows a single IBM LAN to LAN Wide Area Network Program to establish wide area connections (up to a Maximum of 48) with multiple other IBM LAN to LAN Wide Area Network Programs on different local area networks simultaneously.

### 2.7.3 IBM LAN Server

The IBM OS/2 LAN Server provides, to both DOS (via the PC LAN Program) and OS/2 applications, resource sharing for disks, printers, and serially attached devices, plus facilities for defining, controlling, and managing access to LAN resources, as well as security and print management (for up to eight printers). These security and administration features are similar to those provided by PC LAN Program Version 1.3 except that file security is down to the file level. The LAN Server requires OS/2 Extended Edition and utilizes the OS/2 multi-session and caching functions. LAN Server also provides facilities for remote execution of programs.

Portions of the LAN Server have been licensed from Microsoft, most notably the redirector. IBM has not implemented many of the Microsoft Application Program Interfaces (API) in LAN Manager, most notably interprocess communication facilities that are inconsistent with Systems Application Architecture (such as Named Pipes -- a facility found in Microsoft's LAN Manager and later added to IBM's LAN Server). IBM and Microsoft are said to be working toward a common server in future releases.

IBM expects one to use the APPC/PC included with OS/2 Extended Edition to develop distributed applications -- especially in mixed computer Token-Rings. For strictly PC LANs, the issue is not as critical -- one is probably safe writing to NETBIOS or Named Pipes. Major third-party LAN vendors such as 3Com, Banyan, and Novell, are offering at least some level of compatibility (such as APPC) with OS/2 Extended Edition and OS/2 LAN Server and will increase this level of compatibility over time.

The newest OS/2 LAN Server (Version 1.2) includes support for more networks including Token-Ring and Ethernet.

Highlights of Version 1.2 include:

- DOS LAN Requester and LAN Support Program -- Requesters allow individual workstations to access the server on a local-area network. The OS/2 LAN Requester continues to be included in the OS/2 Extended Edition operating system. For the first time, the OS/2 LAN Server includes the function previously provided by two products required for the DOS Requester. Moreover, in many PS/2s with extended or expanded memory, the DOS LAN Requester will allow 10-35 Kbytes more space for applications.

- OS/2 LAN Server Version 1.2 Performance Advantages -- By using the High Performance File System (HPFS) capabilities of OS/2 Extended Edition 1.2, file server performance and the number of files available for concurrent access by users on the LAN are increased.

- User Profile Management -- This capability permits workstation users to access both the LAN Server and the OS/2 Extended Edition Version 1.2 with a single user ID and password.

- File Replication Service -- This function allows critical files to be replicated from one OS/2 server to another OS/2 server or OS/2 requester on a time-interval basis for file protection and data integrity.

- New Application Programming Interfaces -- IBM's OS/2 LAN Server 1.2 application programming interface (API) support has been extended to include new APIs. These APIs allow programmers to create applications for network management, network messaging, shared resource management, LAN interprocess communications, and security.

Version 1.3 adds the following:

- Improved performance by using OS/EE 1.3
- Windows 3.0 support
- DOS Requester Ethernet support

**2.8 The IBM Cabling System**

The IBM cabling system has been designed to provide a structured wiring scheme that will work with all IBM communicating devices including Token-Ring networks. It is the intent of the cabling system to replace the ad-hoc wiring of systems which has occurred in the past with a new, moderate-cost, flexible wiring scheme. The system's components consist of: bulk cable, connectors, wall faceplates, wiring closet distribution panels, and cable assemblies (patch cables). The physical topology created by wiring for the Token-Ring resembles interconnected stars, in which all devices share the same dual twisted-pair bus that, if followed from device to device, forms a ring that eventually wraps back upon itself.

A device is connected to the cabling system as follows: A cable runs between the office (or work area) and a central wiring closet. The cable end in the office has a data connector attached to it that is mounted into a faceplate (either wall mount or surface mount). The cable in the wiring closet also has a data connector attached and is mounted on a distribution panel. The distribution panel, in turn, is mounted in a distribution rack above the MAUs. Patch cables link the data connectors on the distribution panel to the MAUs, creating the physical link between the cables. In the case of a small office network--fewer than eight stations--the wires can be connected directly to a single MAU which may be wall mounted in an optional housing.

The Cabling System supports existing non-token products through use of baluns (balanced-unbalanced cable impedance matching devices). The Cabling System can support existing point-to-point 3270 coaxial-based devices, AS/400, System/36 and Series/1 twinaxial-based devices, 5080 graphics systems, and loop systems, such as the finance communication system, programmable store system, and 8100 communication loop (based on a different token protocol) applications. These connections have nothing to do with the actual token-ring and still function as independent devices. The idea is to migrate devices such as the 3278-type terminals to a token-attached cluster controller such as the 3174.

**2.8.1 Cable Types**

For Token-Ring products, baluns are not needed. Devices attach directly to one of six copper cable Types -- Type 1, 2, 3, 6, 8, or 9. Type 5 cable, fiber-optic, can only be used with the fiber-optic repeater.

Type 1 is an overall, shielded data-grade cable with two solid twisted pair 22 AWG wires. Type 1 is available as an indoor version with a braided shield or as an outdoor version with a corrugated metallic shield that is suitable for aerial installation or underground conduit. Type 1 indoor is also available in non-plenum or plenum versions.

Type 2 is basically a Type 1 indoor cable with four solid twisted pairs of telephone grade (26 AWG) wire added around the outside of the shield. Type 2 is not available in an outdoor version. Type 1 cable is used exclusively for outdoor use.

Type 3 is basically (unshielded) telephone twisted pair. wire can be used where existing, un-used phone wire is already in place. A special jumper cable, consisting of Type 6 wire, a filter, and a data connector, must be used to connect Type 3 wire to a MAU. Type 66 connection block (also called a "punch-down block") is used to connect the Type 3 wire to the jumper. The jumper filter removes high-frequency components in order to meet FCC requirements. Figure 8 illustrates the various components in Type 3 wiring systems.

Because Type 3 is comprised of a small diameter, unshielded copper wire, it is subjected to many restrictions when used with the 4-Mbps Token-Ring network. The distance and number of devices it can serve is about a third of the limits for data grade (all other cabling system cable) wire. Type 1 and 2 cable

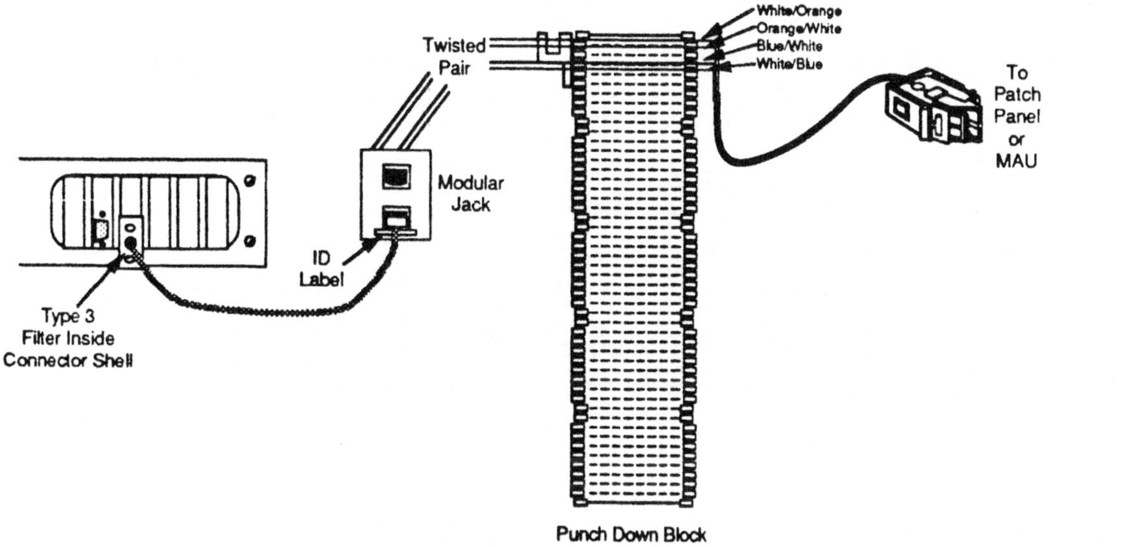


**Figure 8**: Type 3 Wiring Components

is also guaranteed by IBM to support bit rates up to 16-Mbps -- Type 3 is not. Type 3 cable cannot be mixed with data grade wire (except when connecting two wiring closets in which Type 1 wire is used). When using Type 3 wire, care must be taken avoid intercoms, fluorescent lighting, power cables, arc welding equipment, heating equipment, electric motors, or any high voltage equipment.

For more details regarding the use of Type 3, refer to the IEEE draft, entitled "802.5B Recommended Practice for Use of Unshielded Twisted Pair Cable (UTP) for Token-ring Data at 4 Mbits/sec".

Up to 260 devices can be attached to a cabling system configured for the Token-Ring using "data grade" (excluding Type 3 cable) cabling. If Type 3 cable is used, then the limit is 72 devices. Limitations are not dependent on the token protocol or capacity (loading) of the system, instead they result from an electrical phenomenon known as "jitter." The amount of jitter depends on the number of devices passed through by the data signal in the ring, as well as the length and quality of the wire.

IBM's support of Type 3 may not have been intended solely as an effort to counter the lower-cost AT&T PDS as mentioned in Chapter 1. Apparently, many IBM customers already had miles of unused Type 3 wire in place. The Token-Ring Type 3 support is designed to be ad hoc and temporary, with a migration path to the data grade wire that will be required by future 16-Mbps Token-Ring. If Type 3 is not already installed, IBM is discouraging its installation in favor of Types 1, 2, 5, 9, and so on. In fact, two categories of token-rings will be available -- Type 3 rings or Cabling System rings -- because Type 3 cannot be mixed with other cabling types except when connecting wiring closets together.

Type 5 is a 100/140 (100 micron core, 140 micro diameter) fiber cable that can be used with a pair of 8219 fiber optic repeaters. The repeaters essentially bridge together data grade twisted pair to fiber.

Type 6 is a data grade wire of stranded 26 AWG used for short runs in "patch" cables. Type 6 is often used to connect a device to a face plate which in turn connects to a Type 1 or 2 cable. In a small system, Type 6 can also be used to directly attach a device to a multistation access unit (discussed in Section 2.2).

Patch cables are made with Type 6 cable, and are available in lengths of 8, 30, 75, or 150 feet. The eight-foot version is used to connect a device adapter to a faceplate.

Type 8 wire is a 26 AWG twisted-pair data grade wire with a plastic "ramp" used to make under-carpet installation as unobtrusive as possible. Though Type 8 can be used similarly to Type 1, it can only service half the maximum Type 1 distance.

Type 9 wire is a 26 AWG shielded twisted-pair in a plenum jacket. It is designed to be used in environments where stringent fire codes are to be met, such as in plenums. Type 9 is essentially a lower cost version of Type 1 Plenum with a rating of two-thirds the distance capability of Type 1.

Figure 9 illustrates the different cable types.

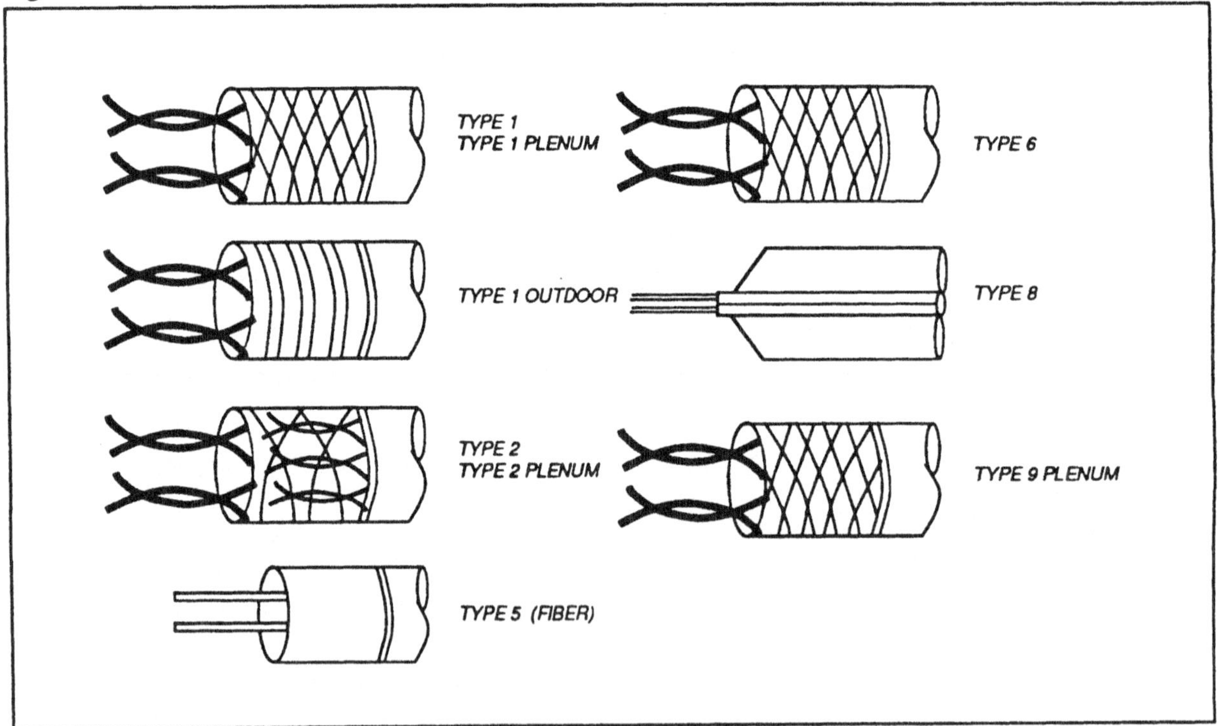


**Figure 9:** Cable Types

The table in Figure 10 summarizes the capability variations among the data grade Types 1 and 2 and the voice-grade Type 3 wire. The drive distances are relative to Type 1. The maximum drive distance (recommended by IBM) for Type 1 is 300 meters from a wiring closet to a work area and 200 meters between wiring closets. These are absolute maximum distances that become shorter as the physical ring wiring becomes larger (as more and more wiring closets, MAUs, lobe wiring, and devices are added). The IBM Token-Ring Network Introduction and Planning Guide provides tables and formulas that can be used to calculate the maximum distances.

| | Cable Type | | | | | | |
|---|---|---|---|---|---|---|---|
| | 1 | 2 | 3 | 5 | 6 | 8 | 9 |
| *Drive Distance ** | 1.0 | 1.0 | .45 | 3.0 | .75 | .50 | .66 |
| *Max. Data Rate (Mbps)* | 16 | 16 | 4 | 250 | 16 | 16 | 16 |
| *Devices Per Ring* | 260 | 260 | 72 | 260 | 260 | 260 | 260 |
| *Closets Per Ring* | 12 | 12 | 2 | 12 | 12 | 12 | 12 |
| *Voice Support* | No | Yes | Yes | No | No | No | No |

* Relative to Type 1

**Figure 10:** Performance Capabilities of Cable Types

### 2.8.2 Data Connector

The data connector is the plug which terminates all twisted-pair wire. Two data connectors can mate together by a 180-degree rotation of one connector -- thus, the same connector can be used throughout a non-Type 3 cabling system. When two connectors are used, one of the connections is contained in a faceplate. For Type 3 systems, faceplates containing RJ-11 jacks are available.

### 2.8.3 Copper Repeater

The IBM 8218 copper repeater extends the allowable distance between MAUs up to 750 meters (2,500 feet). Operating in pairs, 8218s redrive electrical signals on both the main ring path and backup path. Two crossover patch cables are required for each pair of repeaters. An individual 8218 amplifies and reclocks data transmission signals along the Token-Ring.

Typically these units are installed in a standard 19" rack (not supplied by IBM) or attached to flat surfaces such as walls or shelves. Rack installations require a rack mounting assembly accessory which accommodates up to seven individual IBM 8218s. The 8218s may be installed in or removed from a rack mounting assembly without powering down other 8218s in the same assembly. Individual 8218s snap into and out of the bracket.

The 8218s can operate in a Token-Ring environment which has Type 3 media installed. The 8218s are not supported for use on lobe wiring (the wiring from the MAU) the Token-Ring-attached device. In this environment, two data grade media-to-type 3 filters are required where 8218s are used between 8228s, and Type 3 specified media is installed from the office to the wiring closet.

### 2.8.4 Fiber Repeater

The IBM 8219 Optical Repeater extends the allowable distance between MAUs up to 2,000 meters (6,600 feet). 8219 Optical Fiber Repeaters operate in pairs to convert data signals from electrical to optical and back.

The optical fiber repeaters are used in pairs. By operating in pairs, one 8219 converts electrical data transmission signals to optical signals in the main ring path of the network and the second converts the optical signals back to electrical signals. Individual 8219s can convert and redrive data transmission signals on the main ring path or the backup path. Like the copper repeaters, the 8219s are for use on lobe wiring.

Like the copper repeater, the 8219s can operate in an environment which has Type 3 specified media installed. A data grade media-to-type 3 filter is required for each repeater installed in this configuration.

The 8219s can also operate in IBM Token-Ring Network environments that have fiber cable other than IBM Cabling System Type 5 cable installed between 8228s. Fiber sizes that may be used (with restrictions) include 62.5/125 (AT&T), 50/125, and 85/125 micron. These restrictions are called out in the publication entitled IBM Token-Ring Network Optical Fiber Cable Options.

A pair of IBM 8219s requires:

- Crossover patch cable (one per fiber link)
- Two optical fiber BNC-to-biconic patch cables
- Two optical fiber dual socket clips
- Rack mounting assembly or surface mounting brackets
- Optical fiber biconic-to-biconic patch cable (2.5 m or 9.5 m) (optional)
- Data grade media-to-type 3 filter (Type 3 specified media environment at office wall)

### 2.8.5 Fiber Converter

The IBM 8220 Optical Fiber Converter, an electrical-to-optical and optical-to-electrical converter, operates at either 16 or 4-Mbps. It is an "intelligent" repeater, participating in polling and beaconing like other LAN stations on the ring. Two 8220s, connected by a fiber link up to 1.24 miles long, form a subsystem. The 8220 monitors the main token-ring and automatically wraps to the backup ring (a feature missing in the fiber repeater) if it diagnoses a fault, allowing the ring to remain operational for as many users as possible. If the 8220 is defined as a critical resource, the IBM LAN Manager (Version 2 or Entry) can monitor the 8220, detect any errors, and begin the problem determination process.

### 2.8.6 Multistation Access Unit

The IBM 8228 Multistation Access Unit (MAU) is a passive wiring concentrator that connects up to eight stations to 4- or 16-Mbps rings via drop cables (also called lobes). The design and operation of the MAU is what gives the network's physical topology its "star-wired ring" name. A ring in jack on the left-hand side of the device and a ring out jack on the right-hand side of the device provide for a daisy chain connection to other MAUs. The MAU provides for insertion/bypass of lobe segments and associated attaching devices. In addition, it also facilitates write fault detection by an attached device, such as the IBM PC Token-Ring Adapter.

The MAU can be used in many different physical configurations of the ring. Figure 11 shows a network with a single MAU and one with multiple MAUs. A device attaches to the MAU using a Type 6 cable. If the MAU is in a wiring closet as illustrated in Figure 12, then a patch panel is needed to jumper from Type 1 or 2 cable to Type 6. If Type 3 wire is used, a special filter jumper is required.

The attached device (i.e., token-ring adapter), is responsible for activating a relay within the MAU to switch itself into the ring. This is done by maintaining a "phantom" voltage component on the lobe wire. This voltage charges a capacitor on the relay which then inserts the lobe into the network. When the device fails or is turned-off, the relay will de-energize and latch out the device. A look at the operation inside the MAU is shown in Figure 13. Note the automatic wrapping feature of unconnected jacks.

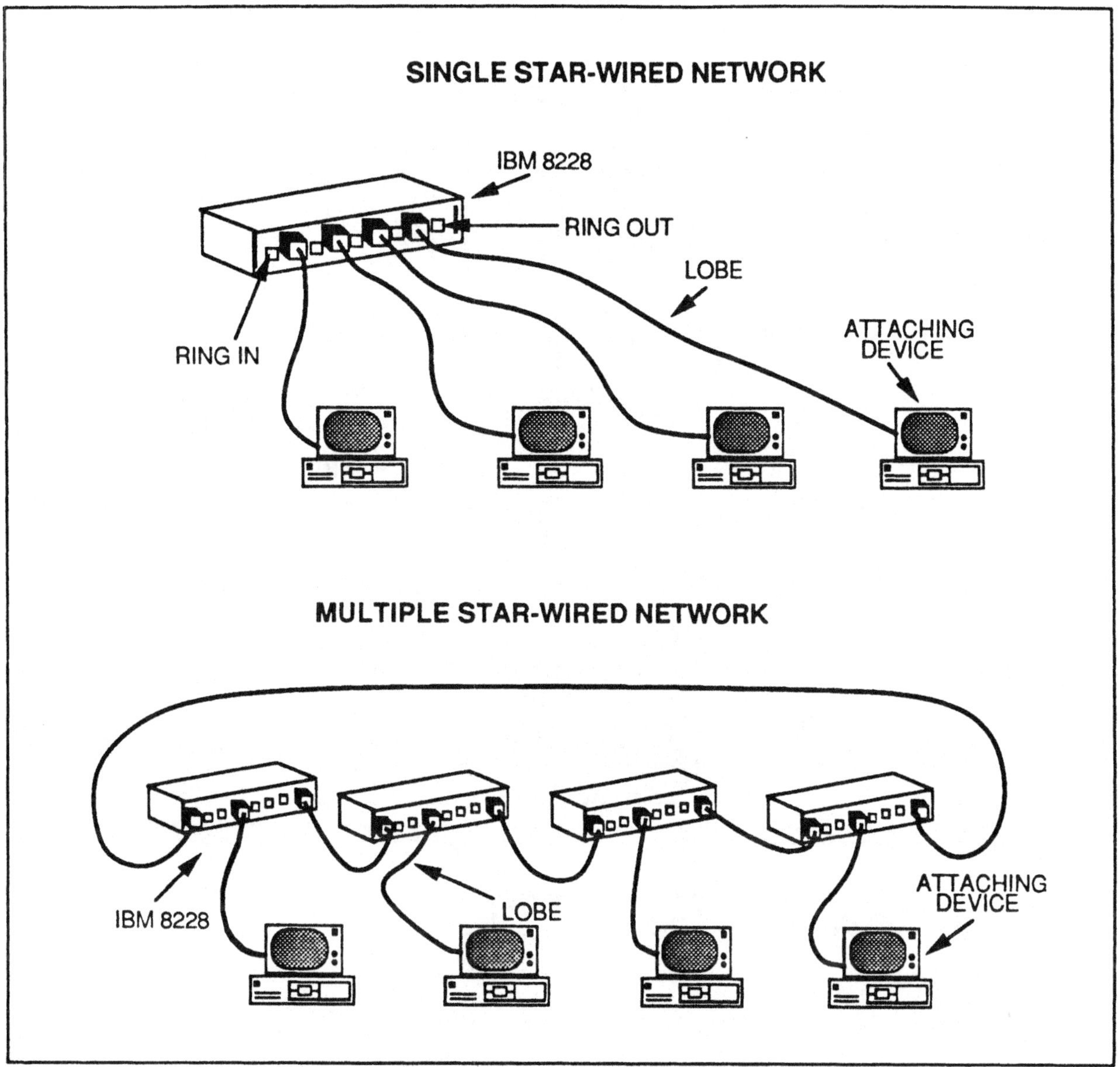


Figure 11: MAU Configurations

The MAU can be rack or wall mounted, as illustrated in Figure 14. The wall mount feature requires an optional wall mount housing, available from IBM. For very small networks (eight or less nodes) a single wall mount MAU can be used with a maximum of 150 meters of Type 6 cable going directly to the device or wall plate.

Though the relays automatically latch when devices are inserted/removed, it is possible during shipment of the MAU, for a sudden movement (such as dropping it) to cause a relay to be latched in the wrong state. IBM provides a testing tool with the MAU. Insertion of the tool into the connected ring tests whether all relays contained are wrapping. If an anomaly is detected, the tool can be inserted into each lobe connection to test the associated relay's status.

There are numerous third-party alternatives to IBM's 8-port MAU. An interesting variation is a "daisy-chaining" MAU such as the 3Com Ring Tap product. The Ring Tap is essentially a single-port MAU, such that one could configure the physical topology as a ring as opposed to a star-shaped ring. Although wiring is simplified, it becomes hard to manage (no centralized isolation points) and adding new Taps can be disruptive.

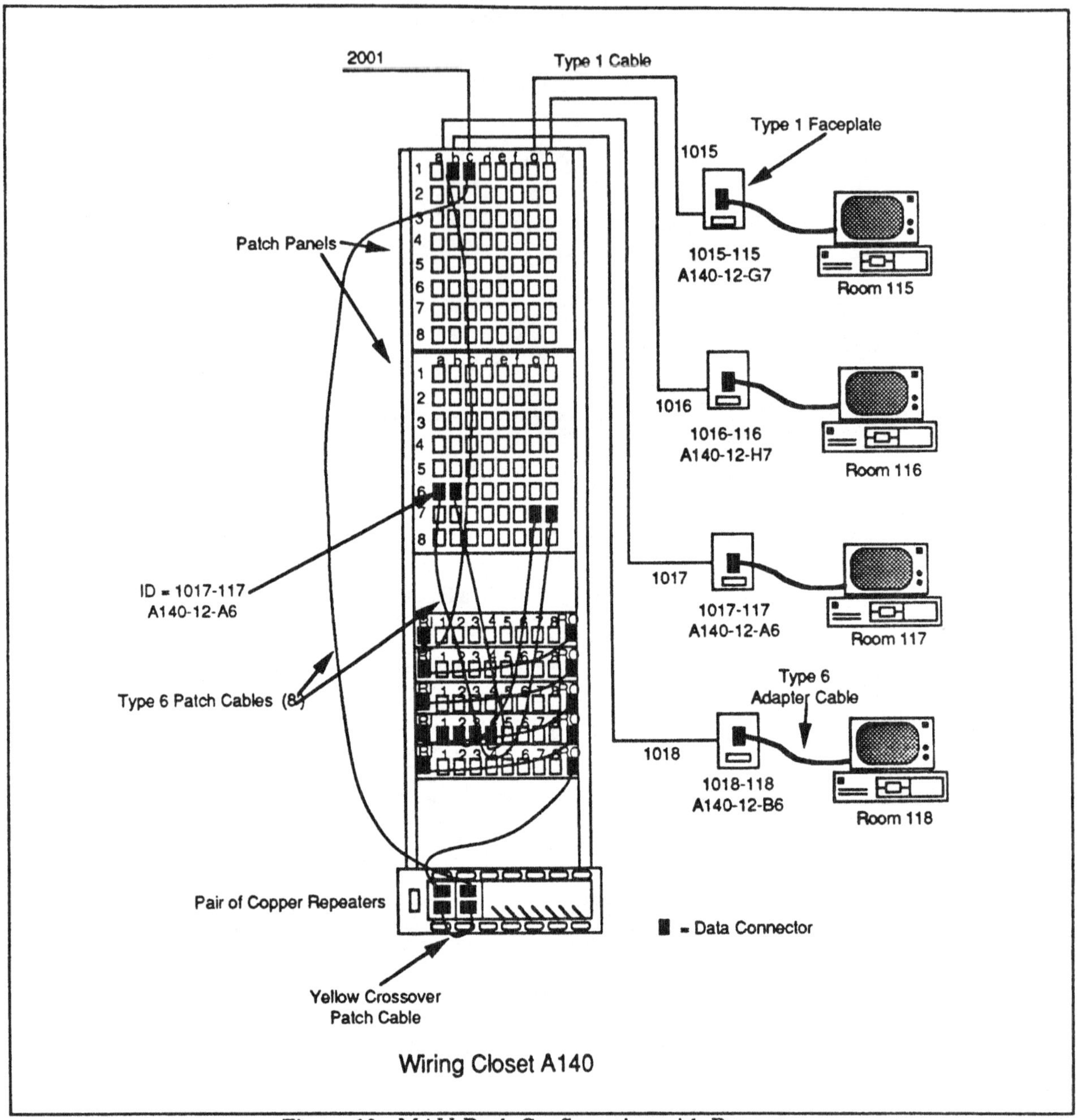


**Figure 12:** MAU Rack Configuration with Repeater

At the other extreme, there are "intelligent" MAU's such as the Ungermann-Bass offers an intelligent MAU called the Distributed Wiring Concentrator (DWC). The DWC offers ten ports (excluding ring in and ring out) and can operate in an active or passive mode (IBM MAU compatible). In the active state (power applied), it allows the U-B Network Management Console (NMC) to perform problem determination, fault isolation and when appropriate, remove stations from the ring.

A summary of the evolution in the IBM Cabling System is illustrated in Figure 15.

### 2.8.7 16-Mbps Over Unshielded Twisted-Pair

There are several vendors offering MAU support for 16-Mbps over unshielded twisted pair, IBM not being one of them!

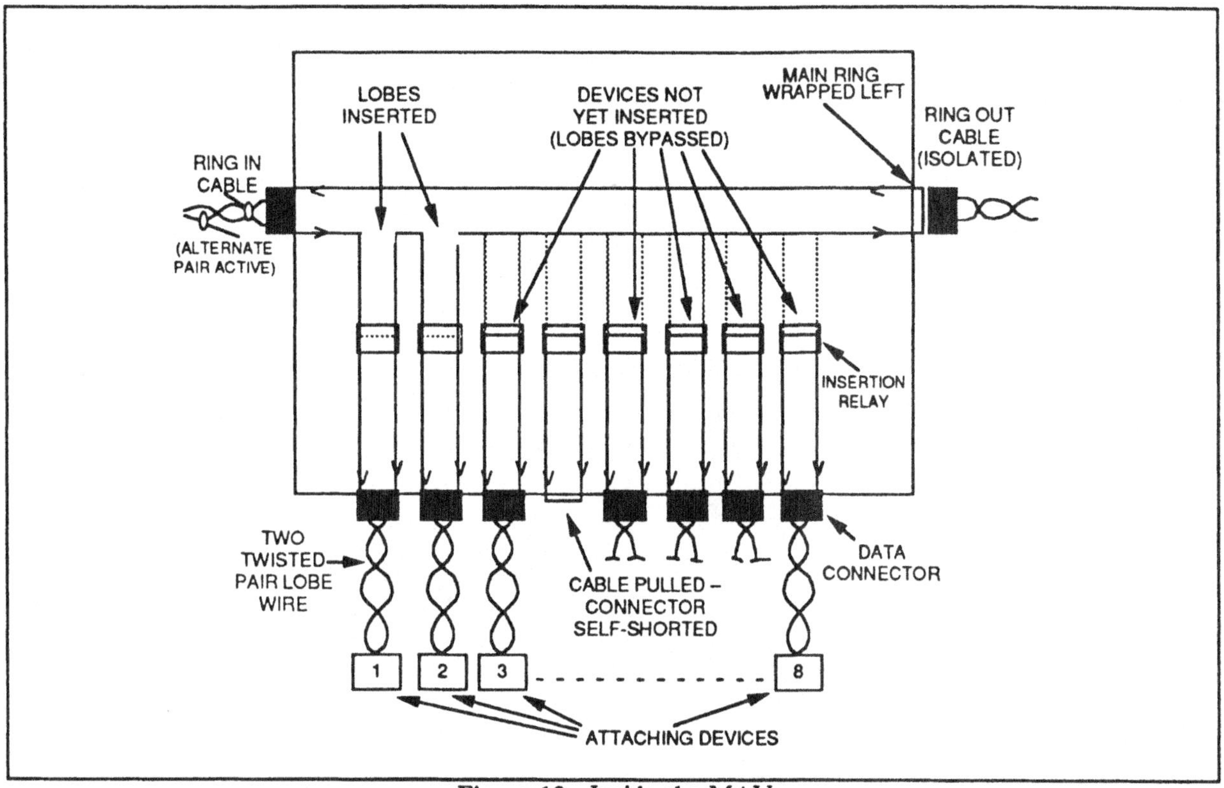


**Figure 13:** Inside the MAU

One such vendor is Proteon who is offering intelligent wire centers that support unshielded twisted-pair (UTP) cabling over 16-Mbps (and 4-Mbps) token-ring networks. Proteon's products feature unified media support and network management capabilities.

The key to Proteon's UTP support is a multi-access unit (MAU) called the Series 70 Intelligent Wire Center. This modular hub presently supports 4-, 10- (for the proNET 10 token-ring), and 16-Mbps networks on UTP and shielded twisted-pair (STP) cables, as well as fiber optics.

The Series 70 is compatible with the AT&T Premises Distribution System (PDS) and the IBM Cabling system. Proteon claims that PDS is often considered to be the best way to run networking cable when the wiring system is in place for telephone communications.

Proteon recommends passive filtering as a simple and pragmatic way to address the technical challenge of 16-Mbps running over UTP: passive filtering at both ends of the UTP cable eliminates electro-magnetic interference (EMI) and facilitates reliable signal transmission, says Proteon. Proteon's filtering approach also limits radio frequency interference (RFI) within the acceptable frequency range.

Proteon's 16-Mbps UTP networks will support distances of at least 85 meters (about 279 feet) between the wiring closet and the workstation. According to AT&T surveys, this distance covers 99% of practical distances between network wire closets and workstations. Proteon supports at least 72 devices on 16-Mbps UTP networks.

The Series 70 uses an independent, out-of-band communications channel for management command and control. This channel enhances the network management capabilities already built into the IEEE 802.5 standard. Network managers using the Series 70 with Proteon's TokenVIEW-4 Network Management software can reconfigure the network to partition large portions of the LAN or individual PCs through the out-of-band channel. Faulty network components and broken cables can be diagnosed and isolated from the rest of the network in five minutes or less, even when the network is down.

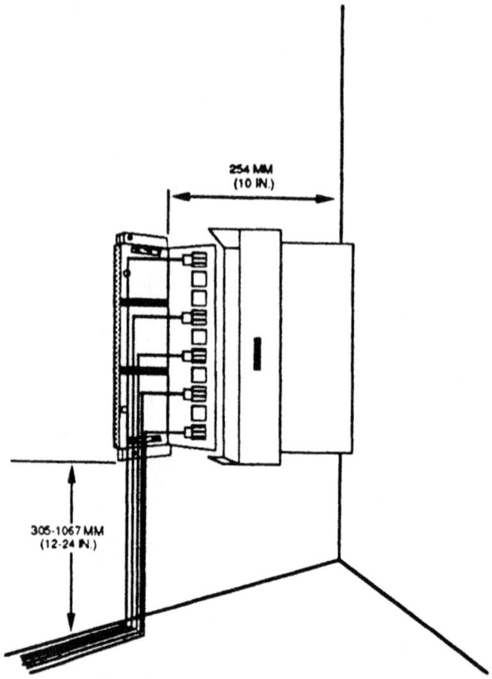


**Figure 23**: MAU Wall Mounting

Proteon is one of several vendors are working together to try to iron out a workable standard for 802.5. Together with AT&T, Proteon has proposed to the IEEE 802.5 standards committee that they define the technical specifications for incorporating 16-Mbps UTP into the 802.5 standard.

### 2.8.8 Network Controlled Access Unit

Citing reliability as a major concern, IBM had been shunning anything but passive MAUs (multi-station access units) for its Token-Ring--until late 1990: the IBM 8230 Token-Ring Network Controlled Access Unit, announced in the blitz of System/390 Enterprise System announcements, is an intelligent access concentrator that allows connection of from 0 to 80 workstations, via pluggable lobe attachment modules (LAMs), to a Token-Ring Network.

The LAMs come in two versions; one accepts IBM Cabling System (ICS) connectors and the other accepts RJ-45 connectors. The 8230 is switchable between 16 and 4 Mbps and has a media access control (MAC) appearance on both the main and backup rings. It is shipped with copper main ring modules and can be upgraded to fiber by plugging in the Optical Fiber Converter Module feature. The 8230 functions as a repeater in both directions. IBM claims that it will be purchased by customers desiring higher ring availability, via automatic reconfiguration, and better access control and "asset management." The 8230, in most cases, will also allow for longer lobe lengths than the 8228. The following lobe lengths will be possible:

- 4-Mbps Data Grade Media (DGM): 375 meters
- 16-Mbps DGM: 145 meters
- 4-Mbps Unshielded Telephone Twisted Pair (UTP): 100 meters (UTP that meets or exceeds IBM Cabling System Type 3 Media Specification)

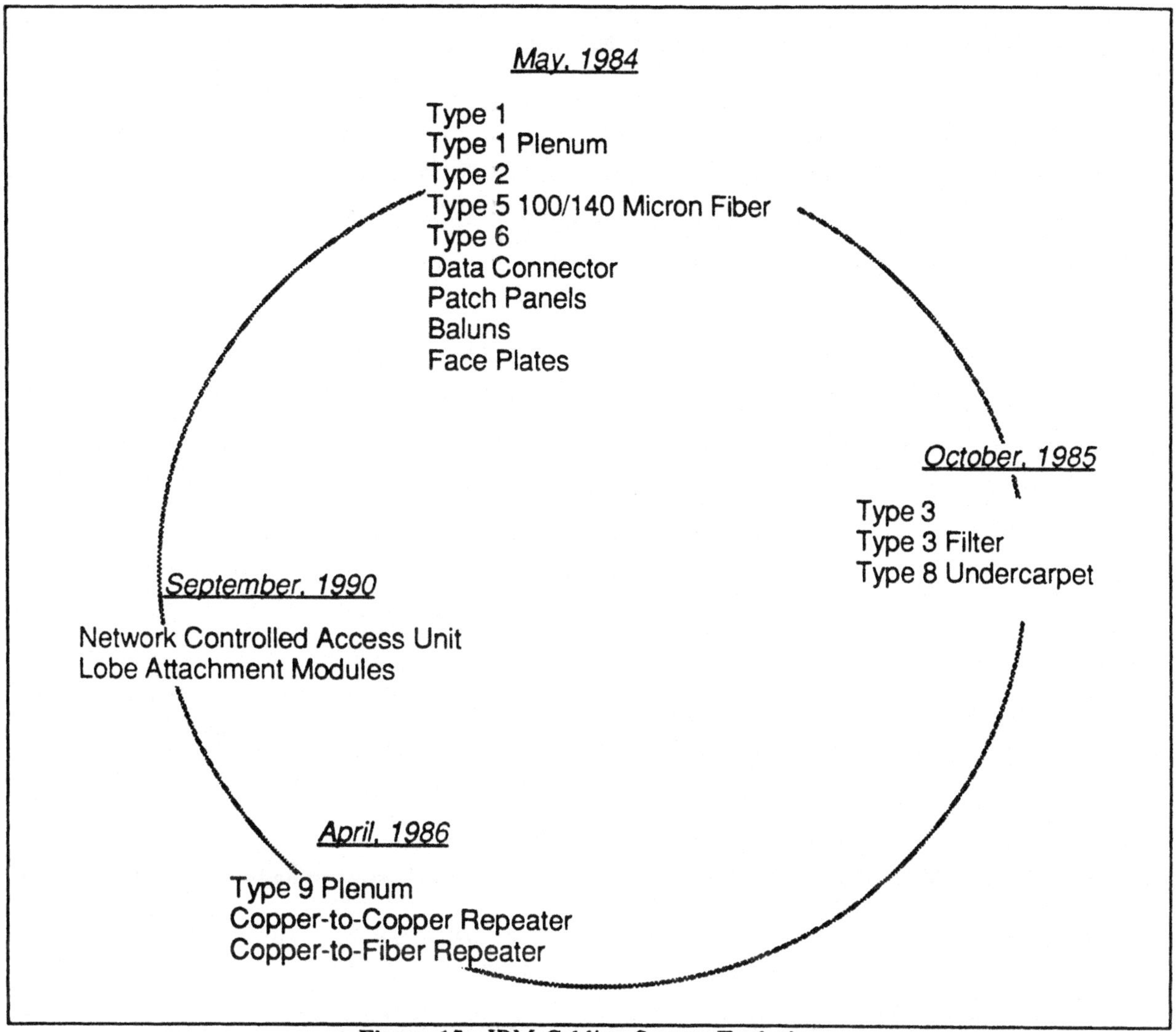


**Figure 15**: IBM Cabling System Evolution

- 4-Mbps Unshielded Telephone Twisted Pair (UTP): 100 meters (UTP that meets or exceeds IBM Cabling System Type 3 Media Specification)

The 8230 has the ability to wrap out a failure automatically, or upon direction from LAN Network Manager (also a new product),in the physical wire or optical fiber cable, a failing lobe, a failing LAM, or the entire 8230.

The 8230"s support of the LAN Network Manager's configuration table provides the adapter address, 8230 number, LAM number, and the lobe number to the LAN administrator, so that a particular workstation can be quickly located for asset control, or if there is a problem that requires maintenance or other attention.

The 8230's support of the LAN Network Manager's access control allows an 8230 port to be disabled via direction from the LAN Network Manager.

The 8230 is modular in design. For example, it can be configured without any lobe attachment modules and be used as a repeater only. From one to four lobe attachments modules, each providing connection for from 0 to 20 workstations, can be added, allowing connection of up to 80 workstations.

The 8230 has interchangeable copper and/or fiber ring-in and ring-out interface modules. If the main ring changes from copper to fiber, the converter modules can be changed from copper to fiber, or one side can be copper and the other fiber without replacing the base unit or lobe attachment modules.

The 8230 lobe attachment modules come in two version, an IBM Cabling System connection and RJ45 connection. This allows the lobe media to be changed without replacing the base unit. The media filter is required when using UTP or the RJ45 LAM.

The 8230 is switchable between 4 Mbps and 16 Mbps, allowing a nondisruptive transition from a 4-Mbps to a 16-Mbps ring. The 8230 supports 4 Mbps and 16 Mbps on shielded cable and 4 Mbps on unshielded telephone twisted-pair.

The IBM 8230 implements a subnet of the LAN station Manager functions and is dependent on the LAN Network Manager for full function. The station manager functions allow the LAN Network Manager to determine the physical location of workstations. The 8230 may reside on a ring that also has 8228s, 8218s, 8219s, and 8220s. The 8218s, 8219s, and 8220s must be operating as repeater pair with these products. The maximum number of workstations capable of being attached to an 8230 is 80.

The configuration-reporting functions of the IBM 8230 are not compatible with any of the following devices, when such devices are attached to any lobes of the IBM 8230 Lobe Attachment Modules: the devices will cause these IBM 8230 functions to provide invalid or incorrect data to the IBM LAN Network Manager. The devices are: adapters that do not participate in normal Token-Ring protocols, such as the neighbor notification process, and fanout devices that attach more than one adapter to a single lobe.

## 2.9 Conclusion

On May 8, 1984, IBM released a statement of direction in which it announced its intention to implement a star-wired, token-ring LAN using the IBM Cabling System within two to three years. On October 15, 1985, the company solidified the statement of direction by introducing a token-ring PC LAN. Not all came off according to plans--IBM was forced to make a concession to other PC local network vendors whose products run on inexpensive telephone wires by introducing an alternative medium to the Type 1 and 2 cables of the IBM Cabling System. Furthermore, products to connect 327x devices to the Token--Ring were conspicuous in their absence.

Six months plus one day from the original IBM Token-Ring Network introduction October 15, 1985, IBM announced major additions and enhancements to its strategic network. On April 16, 1986, IBM significantly enhanced its LANs with new LAN host, departmental systems, and Personal Computer attachments, and with products and programs that support IBM's Token-Ring Network and broadband PC Network. IBM continued to announce additional product releases throughout 1986.

On April 2, 1987, IBM Corporation, with great fanfare, announced "The next generation in personal computing." Introduced was the Personal Systems/2 product line based on advanced technology, new operating systems, enhanced graphics capability, and interesting and important communications options.

IBM's Personal System/2 is a product line in which communications is a key part. Although the PC Network was a part of the Product Announcement, the Token-Ring is still the LAN to use. IBM expects its major accounts to make large purchases of this new personal computer line along with large purchases of Token-Ring products to tie them together.

The November 1988 introduction of the 16 Mbps Token-Ring increases the versatility of the product line and should provide a broader base of market support for the product. At 16 Mbps, the Token-Ring technology appears more attractive against other LAN technologies such as 10 Mbps Ethernet or 2.5 Mbps ARCNET.

IBM's latest release in September 1990 of the Controlled Access Unit and 8209 LAN Bridge upgrades, reaffirms their commitment to moving the Token-Ring forward.

# 3. IBM 8209 LAN Bridge

### 3.1 Introduction

On September 5, 1989, IBM surprised the LAN marketplace by announcing a bridge for connecting an IBM Token-Ring LAN to Ethernet. In addition, IBM announced that the product will be available as early as October 20, 1989.

The new bridge accommodates Ethernets without IEEE 802.2 LLC protocols (the majority of Ethernets), as well as Ethernets that do implement LLC (such as those from Ungermann-Bass). The product will initially be able to recognize TCP/IP frames and pass them through while blocking non-TCP/IP frames. Source routing continues to be supported on the Token-Ring side, while the 802.1 spanning tree algorithm is implemented on the Ethernet side.

This appears to be the first product that will ship which supports both routing protocols (CrossCom has announced such a product but is not yet shipping). Obviously, IBM feels that the "source route" vs. "spanning tree" debate is not an issue and will continue to pursue source routing as a standard for 802.5. As it turns out, some of the spanning tree algorithm is already used in IBM's token-ring bridge product for single-route (limited broadcast) functions.

### 3.2 Description

The IBM 8209 LAN Bridge interconnects an IBM Token-Ring Network with an Ethernet Version 2 or IEEE 802.3 LAN. The 8209 handles the conversion necessary to route information between the dissimilar LANs. IBM and OEM systems and workstations using this connection require compatible protocols such as TCP/IP, OSI, SNA, NETBIOS, or IEEE 802.2 in order to communicate. The 8209 bridges the LAN physical layer differences by providing two LAN ports, one Token-Ring Network and the other Ethernet/IEEE 802.3. The Token-Ring port operates at either 4 or 16 Mbps. When the 4-Mbps rate is selected, the Early Token Release function will be disabled; when the 16-Mbps rate is selected, Early Token Release will be enabled, unless specifically disabled by the customer using the 8209 Utility program.

The Ethernet/IEEE 802.3 port attaches to either an Ethernet Version 2 or IEEE 802.3 LAN. The 8209 accommodates these two CSMA/CD LANs through two modes of operation; the mode of operation is determined by configuration switches. With the switches set for Automatic Mode Detection, the 8209 will examine the data stream and dynamically adapt to the correct operational mode. This allows both modes to be used simultaneously. However, if the destination address of the Ethernet/IEEE 802.3 attached station is not in the 8209 database, the correct format cannot be dynamically determined. In this case the 8209 will perform format conversion based on the setting of the "Mode 1/Mode 2 Priority Operation" hardware configuration switch.

#### 3.2.1 Operational Mode

Mode 1 is used to bridge Token-Ring to Ethernet Version 2 LANs. Above the physical layer, Token-Ring and Ethernet Version 2 differ in Media Access Control (MAC) and user Datagram services. The Token-Ring MAC layer complies with IEEE 802.5, while Ethernet uses Carrier Sense Multiple Access/Collision Detect (CSMA/CD) and does not specify an 802.2 Logical Link Control (LLC) Interface. Additionally, Token-Ring offers both Type 1 (connectionless) and Type 2 (connection-oriented) LLC services; there is no Ethernet Version 2 LLC equivalent function. The 8209 LAN Bridge handles this difference in Mode 1.

LLC information frames, originating on Token-Ring and destined for stations on Ethernet, are stripped of the LLC protocol, converted to Ethernet Version 2 frames, and transmitted on the Ethernet port. A slightly more complicated process is used to convert and forward Ethernet frames onto the Token-Ring. The 8209 retrieves Token-Ring routing information from its data base and inserts it in the frame along with a Sub-Network Access Protocol (SNAP) header.

TCP/IP exchanges between stations on the different LANs would use operational Mode 1.

### 3.2.2 Operational Mode 2

Mode 2 interconnects Token-Ring and IEEE 802.3 LANs. This mode provides IEEE 802.5 (Token-Ring)/IEEE 802.3 MAC-level frame conversion. Protocol layers above the MAC are transparent to the 8209 LAN Bridge and are passed through without modification.

SNA, NETBIOS, OSI, or IEEE 802.2 sessions between stations on the different LANs would use the bridge in Mode 2.

The 8209 LAN Bridge transparently handles conversions for routing information between the two LANs, regardless of the operational mode (Mode 1 or 2). To stations on the Token-Ring Network, the 8209 appears as a bridge to another Token-Ring. A station on Token-Ring uses source routing to communicate with any station on Ethernet/IEEE 802.3. The 8209 is functionally transparent to stations on Ethernet/I-EEE 802.3, appearing as one or more native Ethernet/IEEE 802.3 stations. Ethernet/IEEE 802.3 attached stations can communicate with Token-Ring attached stations as if they were on the same LAN.

The 8209 LAN Bridge maintains two data bases: one contains station addresses for Ethernet/IEEE 802.3 stations; the other contains Token-Ring station addresses and routing information. The Ethernet/IEEE 802.3 data base consists of static and dynamic entries: the Token-Ring data base, however, contains only dynamic entries. Static entries differ from dynamic entries in that they are configured, loaded, and retained in a non-volatile RAM. Dynamic entries are created as part of the 8209's "learning process" and are lost when power is removed.

After power-on initialization, the Ethernet/IEEE 802.3 data base is initialized with static entries. The 8209 enters the learning state, listens to all frames on the Ethernet/IEEE 802.3, and saves each unique source address in the data base. While in this state, the 8209 will not forward any frames. After a few seconds the bridge leaves the learning state and begins normal operations. During normal operations, the 8209 updates the data base when a new source address is detected on an Ethernet/IEEE 802.3 frame.

The Token-Ring data base is dynamically built during normal operations. Entries will be added to the Token-Ring data base only for stations with frames that are forwarded on the Ethernet/IEEE 802.3 port.

The 8209 provides for a combined total of 2048 data base entries. The Token-Ring data base portion of this total may be from 1 to 1024; the number of entries in the Ethernet/IEEE 802.3 data base, however, may range from 1 to 2047. An Aging Timer will determine how long inactive Dynamic Entries will remain in the data base. Static data base entries are not subject to removal by the Aging Timer.

Configurable filters are employed to reduce forwarding of unnecessary traffic. For example, filters may be set up so that only TCP/IP traffic is forwarded to either port. This means even though general broadcast frames are received from either port, they will be discarded if not identified as TCP/IP. Filtering improves performance for the 8209 and ensures no degradation of the attached LANs occurs due to unnecessary traffic.

The 8209 ensures that no traffic is held in the bridge longer than the maximum transit time. If, due to network congestion, the 8209 is unable to forward traffic and the traffic is held longer than permitted, it will be discarded. This function is useful for those high-level protocols that generally retransmit a message unless an acknowledgement is received within a certain time.

Each 8209 has a unique MAC address assigned for each port. The IEEE universal address administration process will be used to assign the MAC addresses.

### 3.3 Configuration Control and LAN Management

The 8209 LAN Bridge is physically packaged in a table-top configuration suitable for stacking or shelf mounting in industry-standard racks. It is designed, manufactured, and packaged to be easily set up and configured by the customer. The 8209 is functionally packaged. The base unit contains Token-Ring functions. Feature #6035 provides the Ethernet/IEEE 802.3 functions, packaged in a module which also contains the configuration switches. Feature #6035 is mandatory and must be specified when ordering the 8209 LAN Bridge.

In most environments, LAN Management functions and configuration customization are not required to install the 8209. The 8209 shipped configuration adapts itself to the installed environment.

The 8209 is shipped with configuration variables set as follows:

- Operational Mode: Automatic Mode Selection Enabled with Mode 1 Priority Operation
- Token-Ring Speed: 4 Mbps with Early Token Release Disabled
- Token-Ring LAN Number: Zero
- Ethernet/IEEE 802.3 LAN Number: 4080
- Initial Bridge Number: Zero

To accommodate additional and more complex environments, three provisions are available: they are hardware configuration switches, Token-Ring Network LAN Bridge Server functions, and an 8209 configuration utility program.

The following options can be selected by hardware switches:

- Enable/Disable Automatic Mode Selection
- Mode 1/Mode 2 Priority Operation
- 4- or 16-Mbps Token-Ring
- Initial Bridge Number (0, 1, 2 or 3)
- Ethernet/IEEE 802.3 LAN number

The Automatic Mode Selection function allows the 8209 to support both Ethernet Version 2 and IEEE 802.3 (Mode 1 and Mode 2) at the same time. The determination for mode of operation is done dynamically.

The 8209 provides Token-Ring Network LAN Reporting Mechanism, Ring Parameter Server, and LAN Bridge Server functions (as defined in the *IBM Token-Ring Network Architecture Reference*, SC30-3374). The 8209, acting as a logical LAN management agent on the Token-Ring Network, will:

- Keep and report statistical frame traffic information
- Accept and respond to requests for Bridge and Route status
- Accept and respond to commands which change Bridge configuration parameters

The controlling LAN Manager can set/reset these configuration parameters:

- Notification interval for performance statistics
- Bridge internal status

- Route active status
- Hop count
- Ring number
- Bridge number
- Enabled functional addresses
- Reporting functional addresses

The LAN Manager will be installed on a Token-Ring station and will establish a link to the 8209 LAN Bridge in order to communicate these management functions. The 8209 can provide management information to the LAN Manager only for the Ethernet/IEEE 802.3 segment to which it is attached.

A utility program is shipped with the 8209. This utility runs under either PC DOS or OS/2 in an IBM PC or PS/2. The utility allows the customer to set up filters, static data base entries, ring numbers, bridge number, and timers which control operation of the 8209 LAN Bridge. The IBM PC or PS/2 communicates the configuration parameters to the 8209 over the Token-Ring. The 8209 Utility program allows the customer to examine and modify the following parameters:

- Spanning Tree Parameters
- Operational Mode
- Enable/Disable Early Token Release
- Filter Definitions
- Ethernet/IEEE 802.3 Static Database Entries
- Ethernet/IEEE 802.3 Port Statistics
- Bridge Number
- Token-Ring LAN Number
- Ethernet/IEEE 802.3 LAN number

In addition to configuration, the 8209 Utility program provides a means to collect Ethernet/IEEE 802.3 port statistics which are gathered by the 8209.

### 3.4 IBM 8209 Token-Ring Attachment Module Upgraded

In September of 1990, IBM announced the IBM 8209 Token-Ring Attachment Module, which connects two local IBM Token-Ring Networks into one logical ring. The connected rings can be any combination of 4-Mbps or 16-Mbps token-ring networks. The 8209 Token-Ring Attachment Module utilizes the IBM 8209 Local Area Network Bridge Base Unit, thus providing this function in a plug-and-play unit with no keyboard or display.

The 8209 Token-Ring Attachment Module provides the same network management and similar filtering capabilities as the local portion of the IBM Token-Ring Network Bridge Program Version 2.2. In addition, the IBM 8209 Token-Ring Attachment Module allows customers to filter on both source and destination addresses, as well as to write their own filters. This enables the customer to control information transmitted over the bridge, and to tailor network management information for the network.

The IBM 8209 Token-Ring Attachment Module provides the IBM Token-Ring Network LAN Reporting Mechanism, Ring Error Monitor, Configuration Report Server, Ring Parameter Server, and LAN Bridge Server functions (as defined in the IBM Token-Ring Network Architecture Reference, SC30-3374). Acting as a logical LAN management agent, it interfaces and is compatible with the IBM LAN Manager and IBM LAN Network Manager.

The IBM LAN Manager/IBM LAN Network Manager program allows the customer to change 8209 LAN Bridge token-ring default configuration parameters (except for the filters) and to collect statistical frame traffic information stored in the 8209.

The 8209 Token-Ring Attachment Module interface to IBM LAN Manager or IBM LAN Network Manager complies with IBM Token-Ring Network Architecture Reference (SC30-3374). It is compatible with IBM LAN Manager/IBM LAN Network Manager and the IBM Token-Ring Network Bridge program.

The Attachment Module is priced at $1,495.

**3.5 Technical Information**

The interconnected LANs and LAN Stations must be compliant with the following applicable specifications in order to correctly operate with the 8209:

- IBM Token-Ring Network
  - Operational Mode 1--IEEE 802.5 and 802.2
  - Operational Mode 2--IEEE 802.5 and 802.2
- Ethernet
  - Operational Mode 1--*The Ethernet: A Local Area Network Data Link Layer and Physical Layer Specification Version 2* dated September 1983, and issued by Digital Equipment, Intel and Xerox Corporations
  - Operational Mode 2--IEEE 802.3 and 802.2

The LAN Manager program allows the customer to change the 8209 Token-Ring default configuration parameters and to collect statistical frame traffic information stored in the 8209.

The customer must supply cables for attachment to the Ethernet/IEEE 802.3 and IBM Token-Ring Network. The 8209 provides LAN interface connectors as follows:

- Ethernet--15-pin female "D" connector; the pin assignments will follow the Ethernet Version 2 convention wherein pins 4, 8, 11, and 14 are not connected; the connector shell will be connected to chassis ground
- Token-Ring Network--9-pin female "D" connector; the mechanical connection complies with the IEEE 802.5 recommendation

The customer should be referred to his/her Ethernet/IEEE 802.3 supplier to procure the Attachment Unit Interface (AUI) cable. This cable connects the 8209 to the Ethernet/IEEE 802.3 transceiver and is often called a transceiver cable.

A 2.44-meter Token-Ring Adapter cable can be obtained by ordering P/N 6339098 as an IBM accessory, or by ordering IBM Personal Computer or PS/2 Feature #3390. This cable will connect the 8209 to the IBM Cabling System or directly to the Multistation Access Unit (MAU). This cable may be extended by using IBM Cabling System patch cables. If telephone twisted-pair (IBM Cabling System Type 3) is used for the Token-Ring, a Type 3 Media Filter cable will be required instead of the Token-Ring Adapter cable. This component is not available from IBM. The Type 3 Media Filter cable is available from ONAN Power/Electronics (P/N 3-50174). Consult your IBM representative or local branch office for a list of suppliers of this part or its equivalent.

*The IBM 8209 LAN Bridge Customer Information*, (SA21-9994) contains a Problem Determination Procedure (PDP)) that allows the customer to isolate a problem to the 8209 or the LAN connections. Once the 8209 is isolated as the failing unit, the PDP specifies that a hardware service representative be called. If the problem is isolated to the Token-Ring, the customer should refer to the *IBM Token-Ring Network Problem Determination Guide* (SX27-3710). If a problem is isolated to the Ethernet/IEEE 802.3 LAN, the customer is advised to make arrangements for further diagnosis and repair.

### 3.6 Enhanced IBM LAN Management and Networking Capabilities

On September 5, 1990, IBM Corporation announced its new IBM System/390 (S/390). The System /390 announcement included:

- Enterprise System/9000 family of processors--a single line of air-and-water-cooled processors, 18 models in all

- Enterprise System Architecture.390--specifically designed for the S/390 environment, including:

  - Enterprise Systems Connection Architecture (ESCON) with fiber-optic channels and a range of new products that enhance systems planning and implementation flexibility and provide for less disruptive dynamic configuration change

  - IBM Common Cryptographic Architecture--featuring new levels of system, network, and workstation security

  - A new architecture--providing data spaces for the VM environment

  - MVS/ESA, VM/ESA, VSE/ESA--Enterprise Systems Architecture throughout a family of new operating systems

- 3172 Interconnect Controller and VTAM enhancements--for improved local-area network (LAN) integration and management, including links to remote systems

- IBM SystemView--enhancing the management of systems and setting a blueprint for systems management products

- Functions, features, and applications for the S/390 environment

### 3.7 Conclusion

The 8209 is priced at $6,265 for the base unit, which includes the Token-Ring 4/16-Mbps interface. To that, the user must purchase and add the Ethernet Attachment Module, for another $935.

IBM was clever in making the 8209 look like its existing Token-Ring bridges, complete with the network management functions. Another interesting observation is that one can now construct scenarios with Ethernet operating as a backbone for Token-Ring networks!

IBM customers will probably like this product. However, marketing into non-IBM accounts could be a problem. Confidence in the 8209 for these customers won't be there until IBM can prove interoperability with existing spanning tree products and Ethernets operating the TCP/IP protocol.

# 4. Proteon ProNET-4

### 4.1 Introduction

Proteon, Inc., is a privately held corporation that markets a line of token-arbitrated, star-shaped ring local area networks. Founded in 1972, Proteon primarily developed advanced communication and computer systems for government and private clients during its early organization. In June 1981 the first ProNET-10 system, a 10 Mbps LAN, was installed.

In February 1984, Proteon received $2.35 million in financing from major high-technology venture capital firms; in May 1985, it received $6.5 million in its second round of financing; and in September 1986, the company received renewed backing from all its existing investors via an additional $6.5 million in mezzanine-round financing. These funds are being used to expand marketing activities, and for research and development of Proteon's ProNET-10, its 80 Mbps ProNET-80 LAN, its new IEEE 802.5- and IBM Token Ring-compatible ProNET-4 LAN, and its multi-network, multi-protocol internetwork router.

ProNET-4 operates over a variety of media including the complete IBM Cabling System and fiber optics, with microwave and infrared in the future. A combination of media may be employed within and between networks.

### 4.2 Host Interfaces

ProNET-4 provides an environment of multi-computer/multi-vendor connectivity through its multiple host interfaces. Current offerings support the IBM PC and AT and compatibles, as well as all systems which use the industry-standard Multibus and VMEbus.

Proteon offers three interfaces for PCs on ProNET-4, all of which are completely interoperable with IBM PC Adapter Cards. The IBM PC Interface (p1340) is for use with PC, XT, XT/286, and compatibles and has a 2.8-Mbps transfer rate. For IBM PC ATs and compatibles, Proteon offers the high-performance IBM PC AT Interface Card (p1344), designed for use in Network Servers. It provides full DMA transfers between the host and ring with transfer rates of 3.5 Mbps. Proteon's p1840 Micro Channel Interface for the IBM Personal System/2 and ProNET-4 network users is a bus master that offers high-performance networking and enhances throughput by using the 16-bit Micro Channel data path on PS/2 models 50 and above. The p1840 supports IBM's Programmable Option Select (POS) software interface, most widely used software environments (PC/TCP, NetWare, VINES), multiple transmission media options, and internetwork connectivity via Proteon's p4200 multi-protocol router.

Proteon offers both intelligent and non-intelligent interfaces for Multibus systems, and a non-intelligent VMEbus interface optimized for use in Sun-2 and Sun-3 systems. The intelligent interfaces have 512 Kbytes of memory and an on-board 68020 microprocessor which offloads protocol processing from the host computer; they are directed towards OEMs and end-users who want the added performance of on-board processing. The non-intelligent interfaces are for those customers who already have networking protocols implemented in the host operating systems, such as UNIX 4.2 BSD. A variety of protocol implementations will be available for the intelligent interfaces in the future. An example ProNET-4 configuration is shown in Figure 16.

### 4.3 Software

IEEE 802.2 Software Support - Proteon's ProNET-4 network is completely software-interoperable with the IBM Token-Ring Network. Proteon provides the IEEE 802.2 standard Data Link Control (DLC) protocol

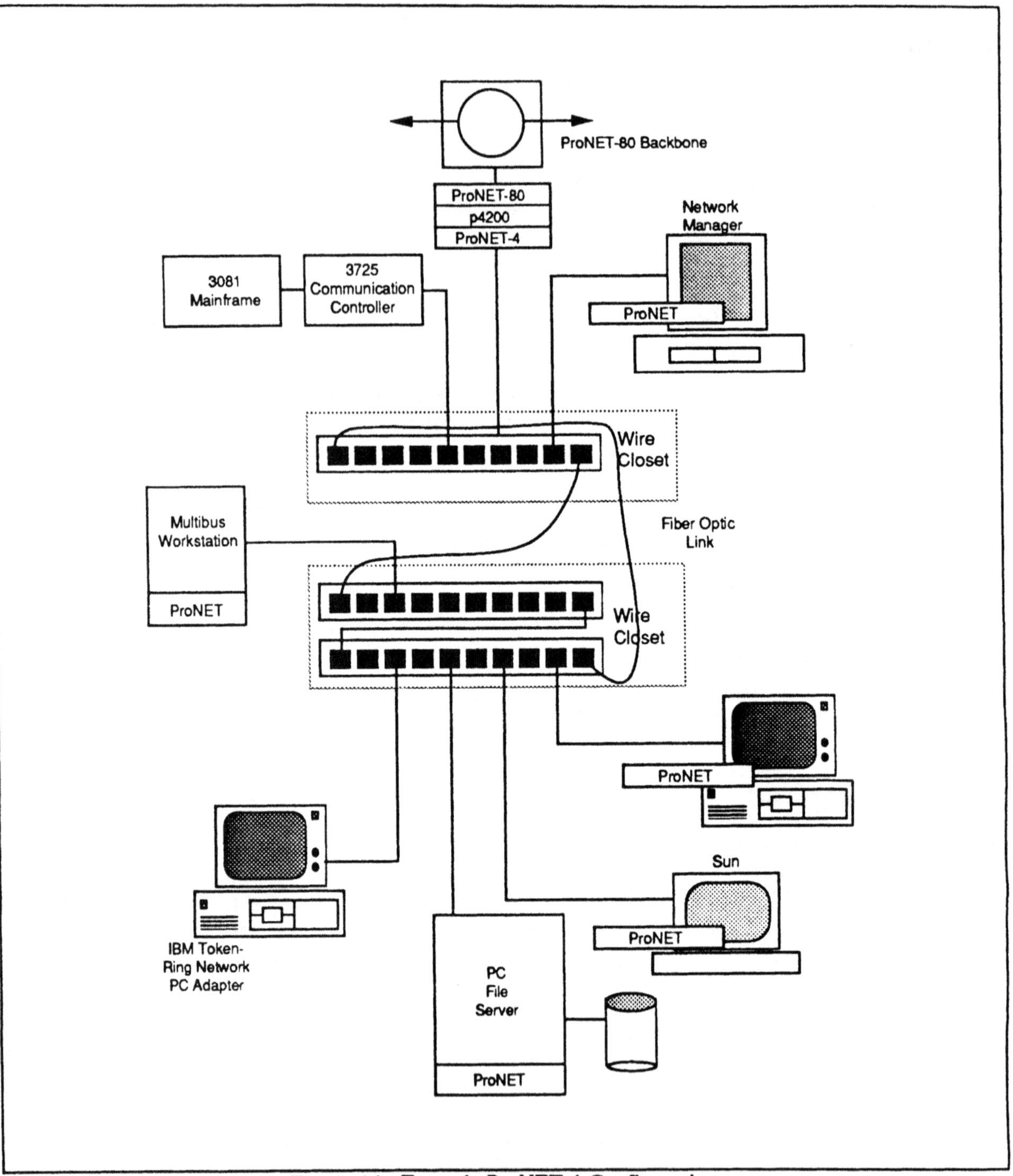


**Figure 16:** Example ProNET-4 Configuration

and IBM Adapter Support Interface (ASI) on its p1340 interface for the IBM PC and XT, and the p1344 interface for the IBM PC AT. The IEEE 802.2 DLC and IBM ASI protocols provide the services used in all IBM Token-Ring Network software programs. With ASI support, users on ProNET-4 can run any program that can run on the IBM Token-Ring Network: this includes programs written for the Advanced Program-to-Program Communications for IBM Personal Computers (APPC/PC), the IBM Token-Ring NETBIOS Program, and the IBM PC LAN Program. The APPC/PC program supports IBM's Systems Network Architecture (SNA) interface LU 6.2, allowing PCs to connect to IBM mainframes over the Token Ring.

Support of the Adapter Support Interface also allows programs using different protocols such as NETBIOS, NetWare, 3270 SNA, and TCP/IP to share the ProNET-4 interface. For example, a user with an IBM Token Ring-compatible version of TCP/IP could transfer a file from a NetWare networked disk to a VAX running TCP/IP.

TCP/IP - Proteon offers industry-standard TCP/IP software for PCs on ProNET-4. The TCP/IP software provides full file transfer, electronic mail, DOMAIN Nameserver Protocol and Name Tables, implementation of Berkeley extensions, and remote logon functions for several host operating systems. As part of the TCP/IP protocols, TELNET software allows a terminal user to "logon" to another machine, eliminating the need for complex and expensive RS-232 port-switching devices.

Network Operating Systems - a variety of network operating systems are supported on ProNET-4. These network operating systems allow IBM PCs, XTs, ATs, and compatibles users to share printers as well as one or more file servers, provide electronic mail services, and run common MS-DOS applications. The users can chose from Banyan's VINES, Novell Advanced/NetWare, or the IBM PC LAN Program.

With these network operating systems, a user positioned at a workstation is provided a simple, consistent method of accessing network resources (file server, print servers, etc.), regardless of the physical location or the workstation or resource. Underlying network topologies and interconnections are transparent to the user. A workstation may simultaneously use files from multiple file servers, allowing data integration across logical and/or physical boundaries. In addition, PCs can access ASCII and IBM hosts through the Network Server. Servers can be located over multiple local area networks. With Banyan's VINES, those servers can also be linked via leased or X.25 lines.

Proteon offers an Advanced Diagnostics package (p5006) for its PC and AT Interface boards (p1340 and p1344): this package offers advanced network diagnostics in a full-screen, windowing environment. The p5006 provides node-to-node communications testing and allows throughput to be assessed for various programming approaches for the TMS380 chipset.

### 4.4 Multistation Wire Centers

The ProNET-4 family of eight-node Multistation Wire Centers is functionally compatible with IBM's Multistation Access Unit for IEEE 802.5 token-ring networks and can be interchanged with IBM units on an IBM Token-Ring network. Four models are available, including intelligent and remote units. The intelligent units also operate with the IEEE 802.5 TokenVIEW-4 Network Management software package to provide advanced configuration management and network maintenance capabilities for IEEE 802.5-based token-ring networks. The family includes:

- p2700 - Non-Intelligent Wire Center
- p2710 - Intelligent Wire Center
- p2711 - Intelligent Wire Center w/Integrated Reclocking Repeater
- p2712 - Intelligent Wire Center w/Integrated Fiber
- p2713 - Intelligent Remote Wire Center
- p2320 - TokenVIEW-4

The ProNET-4 Wire Centers offer enhancements over IBM's Multi-station Access Units (MAUs). Proteon has added LEDs to visibly indicate whether or not a node is in the ring, as well as switches to force connected nodes out of the ring. The multi-station wire centers are easy to install and, unlike the IBM MAUs, require no set-up tool. Another added feature of the ProNET-4 Wire Center is the battery backup capability for enhanced reliability: in case of power failure, the backup unit will support the wire center for up to four hours.

Intelligent Wire Centers - The Intelligent Wire Centers make use of an on-board single chip-computer to: provide advanced ring configuration management; monitor and control signal quality; detect wire faults; and provide information on local node status. For example, when using the TokenVIEW-4 in conjunction with an Intelligent Wire Center, a failed node which is bringing the system down can be removed from the ring without disturbing the rest of the network.

Proteon's Intelligent Wire Centers' integrated media options provide highly reliable connections at a significant cost savings. By integrating the media in a single box, both hardware and cabling requirements can be reduced (see Figure 17). In addition, since the media is an integral part of the wire center, it can be managed through the TokenVIEW-4.

The p2711 Intelligent Reclocking Repeater unit reshapes and regenerates transmission signals to maintain signal quality and to allow the network to expand beyond the limits specified in the IEEE 802.5 specifications. With the p2711, networks limits can be increased up to 200%.

The p2712 Intelligent Fiber Wire Center provides an integrated fiber connection on one end of the wire center. It will support distances up to 2 kilometers and provide continued operation in the event of a failure in the fiber-optic system. All models of ProNET-4 Multistation Wire Centers can be intermixed within a network.

The p2713 Intelligent Remote Wire Center allows economical expansion of a network into areas not

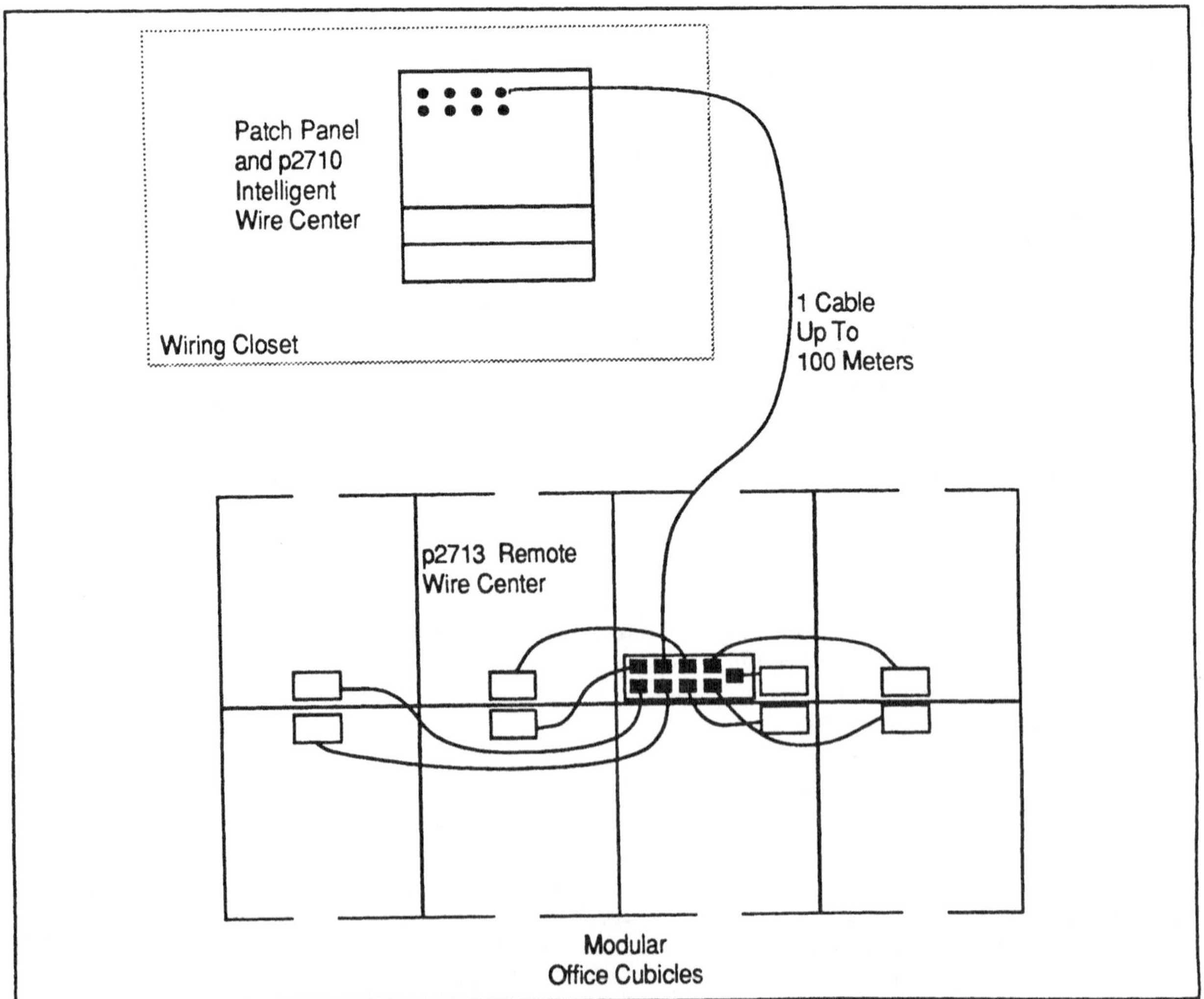


**Figure 17:** Proteon Multistation Wire Centers

previously wired or expected to be part of the network. The remote wire centers connect to an open port on an intelligent or non-intelligent ProNET-4 Wire Center to add another eight ports to an existing network. The remote wire center only joins the existing ring when there is an active device attached to it. The active device acts as a repeater, so that the eight additional ports can be added without violating the network distance design rules. The p2713 automatically removes itself from the existing ring when the devices attached to it are no longer active.

**4.5 Internetworking**

p4100 Router - Proteon's p4100 router interconnects Novell NetWare and TCP/IP networks in small workgroups, isolated departments, and remote offices. The p4100 allows users to develop medium-speed backbone networks, connect to wide area networks, and integrate Ethernet and token-ring LANs at a price/performance point that starts at $5,385. In addition to supporting the TCP/IP protocol frequently used in large internetworks, it introduces support for IPX--Novell's layer-three routing protocol. By supporting IPX, the p4100 provides a cost-effective entry into wide area networking or internetworking for LANs that run Novell's Advanced NetWare.

To maximize resources, network planners can use the p4100 Router to move file and print servers directly onto a ProNET-10 token-ring backbone. This arrangement distributes resources evenly across the network by transferring file service to the backbone to avoid performance bottlenecks.

In addition, "serverless" LANs, connected to a ProNET-10 backbone by the p4100 Routers, can obtain access to network services through the backbone itself, which acts like a server.

Proteon's p4100 Router, designed to serve locations requiring connectivity without the cost of dedicated T1 or CEPT facilities, operates at speeds of up to 64 Kbps. The p4100, when used in various configurations, extends the connectivity of several subnetworks or networks. For example, system managers can place the p4100 in a "hub-and-spoke" topology to provide WAN integration. In this scenario, p4100s, arranged like spokes around Proteon's high-performance p4200 hub, tie into a single, centrally placed p4200 Router that provides wide area connections to other buildings, office parks, campuses, cities, or states. Alternatively, p4100s can be grouped in a "leaf-node" format, interconnecting workstation clusters to the major "branches" that connect to the main "trunk" of a network.

Each p4100 Router interconnects as many as four local or remote networks into the larger internetwork. Proteon offers network interfaces for Ethernet Versions 1.0 and 2.0 (compatible with thin-wire and thick-wire Ethernet) and IEEE 802.3, as well as the IEEE 802.5 specifications implemented in IBM Token-Ring and ProNET-4 networks. When interfacing to Digital Data Service (DDS) and other serial lines, the p4100 handles up to three synchronous ports and is configurable for RS-232, RS-449, or V.35 use. Interfaces to Proteon's ProNET-10 LAN provide optional direct fiber plus standard twisted-pair connections.

The p4100 implements the Simple Network Management Protocol (SNMP), which allows the p4100 to work with Proteon's OverVIEW Network Management System (see below). Together, OverVIEW and the p4100 Router provide the capabilities necessary for checking the operational status of Proteon and non-Proteon networks that support SNMP.

p4200 Router Series - The p4200 Router Series design delivers twice the throughput of Proteon's first-generation design (which was introduced in 1986) and implements the Internet Standards Group's SNMP. It is said to be the first commercially available router to offer support of the SNMP, which allows users to use a common network management package to monitor and control all of the equipment on the network regardless of its type or make.

The new design includes Proteon's newly Version 8.0 router software, a new high-speed CPU, an Ethernet interface, and an optional, solid-state, integrated boot facility.

Used in conjunction with Proteon's high-speed ProNET-80 network, the p4200 Router allows users to create very large, high-speed, fiber-optic backbone networks. Ethernet networks, for example, can now be tied to token-ring networks over a high-speed medium, such as fiber-optic cable, to form a large organization-wide network. The p4200 also connects multiple backbone networks, providing virtually limitless network expansion. The system can easily migrate to the Fiber Distributed Data Interface (FDDI) standard when FDDI becomes a commercial reality. The p4200 also provides wide area network (WAN) access as well, linking to T1 and DDS facilities using a customer's existing voice and data facilities.

The Proteon p4200 handles all of the protocols used by today's most popular computing and communications systems, including TCP/IP, DECnet, and XNS. The system is constantly updated to accommodate emerging standards such as the ISO standard or ISDN. The p4200 Router Series is priced at $7,900.

ProNET CNX Family - The ProNET CNX Line--based on the AMD 29000 RISC processor--provides a platform for Proteon's Transportable Software Architecture (TSA).

The CNX Family is designed for industry-standard back-bone topologies. The CNX Family provides multiple access points that connect departmental LANs dispersed throughout a building or campus to a backbone.

The ProNET CNX 500, the first member of the CNX family, consolidates IBM SNA/multiple-protocol environments and remote sites into an enterprise-wide network. At 25,000 packets per second, the ProNET CNX 500 delivers Ethernet/token-ring performance and multi-protocol connectivity.

The CNX 500 is designed to provide comprehensive LAN/WAN integration, supporting many network protocols including TCP/IP, IPX, OSI, DECNet Phases IV and V, XNS, AppleTalk, and Apollo Domain. Internetworking for mixed-IBM/SNA environments includes simultaneous bridging support for 1:1 and 1:N Source Routing Encapsulation over TCP/IP, and Spanning Tree Bridging for non-routable protocols such as DEC LAT. The ProNET CNS 500 supports network interfaces including 4/16-Mbps token ring, Ethernet, and FDDI. Wide-area protocols supported include T1, X.25, Frame Relay, and PPP. All protocols are managed through the industry-standard Simple Network Management Protocol (SNMP), co-developed by Proteon. The ProNET CNX family is said to support all routing protocols, including Open Shortest Path First (OSPF).

Proteon and Texas Instruments (TI) are working together to develop new enhancements that will enable Proteon token-ring LANs to operate at the maximum throughput speed specified by the IEEE 802.5 standard (wire speed). Proteon expects enhancements to the MAC-layer software driving TI's 16-Mbps chip to accelerate data movement.

The ProNET CNX 500 will be offered in a range of local/remote configurations, priced from $10,995 to $19,495, and will be offered in two phases. Phase I will be available in limited quantity in first-quarter 1991, with full availability slated for second-quarter 1991, and it will support token-ring, Ethernet, T1, 640Kbps, Source Routing Bridging, Spanning Tree Bridging, NetWare/IPX, TCP/IP, OSI, DECNet Phase IV, and SNMP MIB II. Phase II, scheduled to be available in the second half of 1991, includes SNA support, multi-porting, FDDI, DECNet Phase V, X.25, Frame Relay, Point-to-Point Protocol (PPP), AppleTalk, Apollo Domain, and SRT.

OverVIEW - The OverVIEW network management system implements the Simple Network Management Protocol (SNMP), specified by the Internet Activities Board (IAB) as the immediate solution for the Internet community's network management needs. OverVIEW also implements the Simple Gateway Monitoring Protocol (SGMP), a precursor of SNMP, as well as the ability to integrate new protocol standards--e.g., ISO's Common Management Information Protocol (CMIP), when it becomes available.

A graphical, database-oriented system, OverVIEW provides centralized configuration and fault management for multi-vendor, multi-protocol internetworks, enabling network managers to increase system availability by detecting system faults and performance problems and minimizing downtime.

OverVIEW is a turnkey system that includes an IBM PC AT-compatible computer bundled with a high-resolution graphics card, mouse, and multi-tasking network management software.

OverVIEW permits the network manager to define the internetwork topology in a hierarchical fashion using "group", "network," and "node" icons on a Network Map. By providing graphic representations of the network topology, OverVIEW helps network managers quickly identify problem areas; icons and connections change color if their status changes; a "zoom" feature provides six levels of magnification so that the user can "explode" an area to determine the exact location of a malfunction; and editing capabilities permit insertion or deletion of elements from any configuration. Also, an Alert Log shows critical network-generated events which the system manager can use as a current "Things to Fix" list. In addition, an Event Log lists every status change.

OverVIEW supports Wide Area Networks with point-to-point serial, DDN, PDN X.25, and ARPANET DDN 1822 connections, as well as IEEE 802 and Proteon token-ring requirements.

### 4.6 Unshielded 16-Mbps Token-Ring

In a surprise move, Proteon, Inc., the first vendor to make available a new generation of ProNET-4/16 token-ring network adapters and intelligent wire centers that support unshielded twisted-pair (UTP) cabling over IEEE 802.5 4-Mbps and 16-Mbps token-ring networks. Proteon's new products feature unified media support and network management capabilities.

The key to Proteon's UTP support is a new multi-access unit (MAU) called the Series 70 Intelligent Wire Center. This modular hub presently supports 4-, 10-, and 16-Mbps networks on UTP and shielded twisted-pair (STP) cables, as well as fiber optics in the future. The Series 70's unified cabling approach is intended to offer long-term solutions to corporate users.

The Series 70 is compatible with the AT&T Premises Distribution System (PDS) and the IBM Cabling system. Proteon said PDS is often considered to be the best way to run networking cable when the wiring system is in place for telephone communications. The IBM Cabling system is also supported by the Series 70 for both UTP and STP wiring.

The Series 70 offers immediate support of both 4-Mbps and 16-Mbps UTP wiring. This allows users to build 4-Mbps networks now and 16-Mbps UTP networks in the fall--when Proteon will offer an entire family of 16-Mbps adapters using the same wire center. IBM cards will also work on 16-Mbps UTP networks using Proteon's Series 70 with a new Proteon media filter.

UTP is presently one of the most widely used network cabling options, because it is inexpensive and is readily available in most buildings. However, UTP has often been considered impractical for high-speed network transmissions because of its susceptibility to external electrical emissions.

Together with AT&T, Proteon has proposed to the IEEE 802.5 standards committee that they define the technical specifications for incorporating 16-Mbps UTP into the 802.5 standard.

Proteon recommends passive filtering as a simple and pragmatic way to address the technical challenge of 16-Mbps running over UTP: passive filtering at both ends of the UTP cable eliminates electro-magnetic interference (EMI) and facilitates reliable signal transmission, says Proteon. Proteon's filtering approach also limits radio frequency interference (RFI) within the acceptable frequency range.

Proteon's 16-Mbps UTP networks will support distances of at least 85 meters (about 279 feet) between the wiring closet and the workstation. According to AT&T surveys, this distance covers 99% of practical distances between network wire closets and workstations. Proteon supports at least 72 devices on 16-Mbps UTP networks. The Series 70 Intelligent Wire Center's modularity will provide future support for even larger 16-Mbps UTP networks.

Proteon's new Series 70 Intelligent Wire Centers simplify corporate networking through media independence, network modularity, and intelligent network management. These features provide a high level of network availability, which is a critical requirement of most corporate network managers.

The Series 70 uses an independent, out-of-band communications channel for management command and control. This channel enhances the network management capabilities already built into the IEEE 802.5 standard. Network managers using the Series 70 with Proteon's TokenVIEW-4 Network Management software can reconfigure the network to partition large portions of the LAN or individual PCs through the out-of-band channel. Faulty network components and broken cables can be diagnosed and isolated from the rest of the network in five minutes or less, even when the network is down.

Proteon, Inc., has introduced integrated fiber-optic connectivity for the Series 70 Intelligent Wire Center and 16-Mbps support for TokenVIEW Plus and TokenVIEW Manager Network Management Software. The company also introduced TokenVIEW site-licensing packages that lower the cost of operating and managing multiple rings in a building or campus.

The 4/16 new fiber connectivity complements the Series 70's existing support of unshielded-twisted-pair (UTP) and shielded-twisted-pair (STP) cabling. Because it combines all three media within a single multistation access unit (MAU), the Series 70 lets users manage the fiber backbone as an integrated aspect of the enterprise-wide network, rather than relying on external fiber modems.

TokenVIEW Plus and TokenVIEW Manager Network Management Software together provide a distributed, fault-tolerant means of managing dispersed 4/16-Mbps departmental LANs and the fiber backbone interconnecting them.

TokenVIEW Plus employs both in-band monitoring and an out-band communications channel that works independently of the physical layer for detection, isolation, and correction of network faults, even when the network is down. If the network or a portion of the network fails, TokenVIEW Plus allows network managers to troubleshoot the problem from remote location through the Series 70's out-band communications channel. According to Proteon, physical layer faults--which account for more than 75% of all network failures--are typically corrected with TokenVIEW in five minutes or less.

New site-licensing for the TokenVIEW family is said to reduce the ownership costs associated with providing distributed management for multi-ring networks.

The Series 70 Fiber Link Pair lists for $2,995; TokenVIEW Plus and TokenVIEW Manager Network Management Software for 4/16-Mbps token rings have site licenses ranging from $1,995 for three rings to $9,995 for 64-ring licenses.

For more information, contact Maureen McGregor, Proteon, Inc., Two Technology Drive, Westborough, MA 01581; (508) 898-2800.

### 4.7 Conclusion

Proteon has been successfully selling token-ring networks since 1981. With this experience, the company is well-placed to take advantage of the demand generated by IBM adopting a token-ring scheme as the basis for its strategic network offering.

Not only will Proteon sell <u>compatible</u> products and look-alikes to IBM-based networking environments, but its strategy is to offer them in versions that have significantly improved and enhanced features.

Proteon currently has more host interfaces and media choices for token-ring networks than any of its competitors. Its Intelligent Wire Centers are a must for any token-ring environment.

# 5. Racore Computer Products, Inc.

## 5.1 Introduction

Racore Computer Products, Inc., designs, manufactures, and markets local-area network (LAN) products for interconnecting PCs for the purpose of sharing data, software, and peripherals at the departmental level. The company is committed to producing quality products and advancing IEEE 802.5 token-ring and FDDI industry standards through participation in organizations such as the Open Token Foundation.

Racore has developed three main product lines and a group of related LAN products and accessories:

- LANpac II proprietary 16-Mbps network interface adapter cards for Novell NetWare
- Racore 802.5/802.2 IEEE standard token-ring network interface adapter cards
- LANstation diskless and administrative workstations
- Related products and accessories--includes Type 1 and Type 3 token-ring Multi-station Access Units (MAUs), media line filters, Remote Program Load (RPL) options, connectors, and repeaters

## 5.2 LANpac II Network Interface Cards

LANpac II adapters--Novell Labs-tested and -approved and summarized in Figure 1--are network interface cards for use with Novell NetWare, the defacto industry standard for network operating systems. Designed specifically for NetWare, LANpac II transfers data at 16 Mbps. Tested with Novell's "Perform2" benchmark software, LANpac II is said to operate nearly three times faster than 3Com's Etherlink Plus network adapter and more than four times faster than IBM's Token-Ring.

LANpac II can be configured in a linear bus and branching topology, with a base network end-to-end length of 1000 feet. Sixty-four nodes can be connected to the network cable without the use of repeaters. Up to 254 communicating nodes are possible with multiple cards in the file server, and overall network distances of 10,000 feet can be achieved with the use of multiple LANpac II Repeaters.

Racore says LANpac II's performance does not degrade significantly under heavy network load, due to its intelligent, high-speed, polling accessing scheme, which eliminates collisions and the retransmission of data packets caused by such collisions. With LANpac II, only one workstation can transmit data packets at a given time, thus avoiding collisions. LANpac II is intended for any office or business environment and is well-suited to intensive data entry and graphic applications such as CAD/CAM, desktop publishing, and accounting.

LANpac II cards use 7.5 watts of power, are full-length expansion boards, and are available in three versions:

- 8-bit (PC and XT) with 24K RAM buffer
- 16-bit (AT and server) with 32K RAM buffer
- PS/2 Micro Channel with 24K RAM buffer

A Remote Program Loading (RPL) option is available for all LANpac II cards, which enables a diskless workstation in which the card is installed to boot directly from the file server.

### 5.3 Racore 802.5 Token-Ring Network Interface Cards

Racore's Token-Ring adapter series--also Novell Labs-tested and -approved--offers three IEEE 802.5-compatible interface cards which operate at 4 Mbps.

Racore's 802.5 Token-Ring interface uses the Texas Instruments TMS380 chipset to provide an IBM-compatible adapter which can be used exclusively or intermixed in an existing LAN with IBM cards.

The 802.5 Token-Ring interface from Racore is compatible with Novell's NetWare. With the 802.2 plug-in feature option installed, the card is compatible with software packages such as the IBM PC Network Program and Advanced Program-to-Program Communications (APPC) using PC/MS-DOS 3.1 or higher.

Like the IBM version, Racore's 802.5 Token-Ring interface is designed to be configured in a star-wired ring topology and can support up to 260 nodes. Devices can be connected in the ring with Type 1 shielded twisted-pair or Type 3 unshielded twisted-pair telephone cables. Network end-to-end distances are 100 meters (330 feet) with Type 1 cable and, depending on the MAU, up to 1000 feet with Type 3 cable. Workstations are connected to Type 3 cable with a media filter which converts the DB-9 connection on the Token-Ring card to an RJ11 modular connector.

Racore 802.5 Token-Ring cards also use 7.5 watts of power, are full-length expansion boards, and come in three versions:

- 8-bit (PC and XT) with 18K RAM buffer
- 16-bit (AT and server) with 18K RAM buffer
- PS/2 Micro Channel with 18K RAM buffer

The 802.5 Token-Ring cards are also summarized in Figure 18.

| Product Name | Model # | Transfer Rate | Hardware | Software | Access Scheme | Topology | RAM Buffer | Power Usage | Max. LAN Distance | RPL * | Max. Nodes | Bus | Retail Price |
|---|---|---|---|---|---|---|---|---|---|---|---|---|---|
| LANpac II | M3102 | 16MB/sec | IBM PC, XT, AT | Novell NetWare | High-Speed Polling | Linear Bus | 24K | 7.5 Watts | 1000 feet;10,000 ft/repeater | Yes | 254 | 8-Bit | $325 |
| LANpac II | M3107 | 16MB/sec | IBM PC AT | Novell NetWare | High-Speed Polling | Linear Bus | 32K | 7.5 Watts | 1000 feet;10,000 ft/repeater | Yes | 254 | 16-Bit | $425 |
| LANpac II | M3106 | 16MB/sec | IMB PS/2 Series | Novell NetWare | High-Speed Polling | Linear Bus | 24K | 7.5 Watts | 1000 feet;10,000 ft/repeater | Yes | 254 | Micro Channel | $395 |
| Racore Token-Ring 802.5 | M3112 | 4MB/sec | IBM PC, XT, AT | Novell or IBM PC Network | Token Passing | Star-Wired Ring | 18K | 7.5 Watts | 100 meters from MAU | Yes | 260 Active Users | 8-Bit | $399 |
| Racore Token-Ring 802.5 | M3110 | 4MB/sec | IBM PC AT | Novell or IBM PC Network | Token Passing | Star-Wired Ring | 18K | 7.5 Watts | 100 meters from MAU | Yes | 260 Active Users | 16-Bit | $499 |
| Racore Token-Ring 802.5 | M3111 | 4MB/sec | IBM PS/2 Series | Novell or IBM PC Network | Token Passing | Star-Wired Ring | 18K | 7.5 Watts | 100 meters from MAU | Yes | 260 Active Users | Micro Channel | $499 |

* Remote Program Load

**Figure 18:** Racore Network Interface Cards

A Remote Program Loading (RPL) option is available for all Racore 802.5 Token-Ring cards, which enables a diskless workstation in which the card is installed to boot directory from the file server.

## 5.4 LAN-Related Products

### 5.4.1 Multi-Station Access Units (MAUs)

Multi-Station Access Units (MAUs) are the center or hub of a token-ring LAN. Racore offers six for maximum flexibility: two Type 1 and four Type 3 cable versions.

Both Type 1 MAUs (one rack-mountable, the other free-standing) are IEEE 802.5 token-passing standard 8-port models, with two additional ports for daisy-chaining to other MAUs. Completely compatible with IBM Token-Ring products, the Type 1 MAUs may be used separately or in combination with them, thereby expanding existing IBM Token-Ring LANs.

The Type 3 MAUs differ in both the number of available ports and the overall network distance possible. Two 8-port models, designed for use with centralized workstations and wiring closets, and two 4-port versions, for small clusters of devices, are offered. Network distances of 500 or 1000 feet can be achieved, depending on the model selected. All Racore Type 3 MAUs are compatible, allowing models to be mixed and matched. Two Type 3 MAUs--M8321 and M8322--support the use of mixed media, meaning Type 1, Type 2, and Type 6 data cable can be used in combination with standard telephone wire.

All Racore MAUs perform all standard token-ring functions, including automatically connecting and disconnecting terminal segments and providing both pass-through and looping capabilities on the ring. Diagnostic displays provide fault isolation. Each port on a Racore MAU is individually monitored with an LED to indicate active terminal connections to the token-ring.

### 5.4.2 Repeaters

LANpac II Repeaters extend the distance of a LANpac II network up to a maximum cable length of 10,000 feet, if using RG-6/U cable and placing a repeater at every 1000 feet. Each LANpac II Repeater is equipped with three I/O ports, which enables "branching": branching gives the ability to split a single incoming cable into two outgoing cables of up to 1000 feet in length each, for a total of 2000 feet per Repeater.

The LANpac II Repeater is available in either a stand-alone unit (AC power supply adapter included) or an internal card model which plugs into any 8- or 16-bit I/O slot.

Racore's 802.5 Token-Ring Type 3 Repeater allows flexibility in a token-ring network by extending the distance between two Type 3 MAUs up to 1200 feet (one Repeater required at each MAU).

## 5.5 Switchable Token-Ring Network Interface Card (Pending)

A preliminary Racore spec sheet indicates that Racore is about to introduce a series of 4x16 Mbit/second 802.5 Token-Ring Switchable Network Interface Cards for 8-bit, 16-bit, and Micro Channel buses.

The Racore 4x16 Mbit/sec (switchable) 802.5 Token-Ring series of network interface cards will plug into an IBM PC, XT, AT, PS/2, or compatible, offering "competitively price" Token-Ring compatibility.

The Racore 802.5 Token-Ring board is compatible with Novell's NetWare. Built around the TMS380 chipset--compatible with the IEEE 802.5 standard and IBM's extensions to the standard--Racore's 802.5 Token-Ring boards can be used exclusively or mixed with currently installed IBM Token-Ring cards. With the 802.2 plug-in feature option installed, the Racore 802.5 interface is compatible with software packages such as the IBM PC Network Program or Advanced Program-to-Program Communications (APPC) package.

The Racore series of 4x16 Mbit/sec 802.5 Token-Ring boards includes three models:

- **Model M8115** has an 8-bit PC I/O bus interface and is compatible with the IBM PC, XT, AT, PS/2 model 30, or compatibles with a PC-bus. This model is intended primarily for LAN workstations.

- **Model M8113** has a 16-bit PC AT I/O bus interface and is compatible with the IBM PC/AT model or compatibles with a PC AT-bus. This model is intended for either file servers or LAN workstations.

- **Model M8114** has a PS/2 Micro Channel interface and is compatible with any IBM PS/2 systems equipped with the Micro Channel bus. This model is intended for either file servers or LAN workstations.

### 5.6 Conclusion

One word that best describes Racore is "Aggressive!" The Racore strategy is simple: quality, low cost, and high performance. As the market matures, these words will define the Racore niche. Small size (under 100 employees) has given Racore the ability to reposition itself rapidly from a PCjr add-on manufacturer to a major token-ring product builder.

# 6. 3Com

## 6.1 Introduction

3Com's token-ring products represent a complete networking system, compatible with both the IBM Token Ring and the IEEE 802.5 standard. 3Com's token-ring products fall into two main categories: adapter boards and transmission systems. 3Com token-ring adapters are fully compatible with their IBM counterparts; 3Com transmission system products provide compatible alternatives to IBM cabling systems for token-ring networks, with added features that allow users to adapt existing wiring schemes to support local area networks.

3+ and 3+Open software can be used for networking with token-ring adapters from both 3Com and IBM, and can be used in both PS/2 Model 30 and PC compatibles as either a workstation or a server. 3Com's 3S/200 and 3S/400 multifunction servers provide network services for token-ring networks and provide integration between token-ring and either Ethernet or AppleTalk networks.

## 6.2 TokenLink Products

### 6.2.1 TokenLink Adapter

The TokenLink adapter is an IBM Token-Ring and IEEE 802.5/802.2-compatible adapter for use in a single expansion slot of an IBM PC, XT, AT, PS/2 Model 25, 30, or compatible personal computer. The TokenLink adapter uses the Texas Instruments TMS380 token-ring chipset and IEEE 802.2 logical-link control (LLC) protocols to ensure IBM compatibility at the media-access control (MAC) level. 3Com's implementation of the data-link control (DLC) interface (adapter handler) provides an IBM-compatible software interface. This interface enables the adapter to run most software written for the IBM Token-Ring PC and PS/2 adapters. This includes the IBM PC LAN Program, IBM LAN Support Program, IBM PC 3270 Emulation Program version 3.0, Banyan VINES, and Novell NetWare for workstations.

The TokenLink adapter's dual-edge connector fits into both 8- and 16-bit slots, and is self-sensing to implement 16-bit bus master mode in an AT-class machine, which takes full advantage of an AT's high-performance capabilities. The TokenLink adapter also has 16 Kbytes of usable RAM for frame buffering.

The TokenLink adapter's two media interfaces, a subminiature DB 9-pin connector and an RJ11 "phone jack" connector, allow users to choose between the IBM Cabling System (shielded twisted-pair in a star topology) or IBM-specified Type 3 cable ( unshielded twisted-pair in a star topology). Type 3 cable can be connected directly to the TokenLink adapter without adding additional components, because the media filter and the RJ11 connector are built into the TokenLink adapter.

The TokenLink adapter comes with adapter and network diagnostics. On startup of the computer, the adapter verifies proper operation of the adapter, the cable, and the network. Problems are reported, and, in addition, a set of diagnostic tests checks the status of the ring and notifies the station of users on the network. The board has on-board jumpers to select base I/O address and memory for a remote boot PROM. The optional Token Start ROM allows remote booting of the 3+ operating system.

### 6.2.2 TokenLink Plus Adapter

The TokenLink Plus adapter is an intelligent microprocessor-based adapter that lets IBM PCs, XTs, ATs, PS/2 Model 30s, and compatibles act as workstations and servers on token-ring networks. The TokenLink

Plus adapter uses the TMS380 token-ring network chipset supplied by Texas Instruments to ensure IBM compatibility at the media-access control (MAC) level. TokenLink Plus adapters can be intermixed with IBM Token Ring PC and PS/2 adapters using 3+ software. The TokenLink Plus adapter does not implement the LLC protocols or the DLC interface.

The TokenLink Plus adapter features a 10 MHz on-board 80186 microprocessor, 256 Kbytes of RAM, 16 Kbytes of ROM, and a FIFO (first-in/first-out) buffered 8- or 16-bit I/O path. These provide buffering of transmit and receive packets and 8- and 16-bit direct-memory access (DMA) transfers. The adapter's dual-edge connector fits into 8- and 16-bit slots, and its on-board intelligence automatically senses and configures for the appropriate DMA transfer. The 20-byte FIFO buffer between the TokenLink Plus adapter and the computer's bus ensures that the TokenLink Plus adapter has data ready and waiting in the buffer when the PC is ready to process network data.

Link Plus Optimizer software allows downloading of 3+XNS protocols and the NETBIOS interface onto the adapter, creating a "network computer on a card." The software is downloaded from the PC into the 256-Kbyte RAM on the TokenLink Plus adapter. The on-board 80186 processes the protocols. When used in a PC workstation running 3+, this frees up 60 to 90 Kbytes of host memory in the PC. This on-board network protocol processing proceeds on the adapter at the speed of a 10 MHz 80186, improving network performance for 808X and 80286 PCs/XTs/ATs.

The TokenLink Plus adapter is based on the same architecture as 3Com's EtherLink Plus adapter. They offer the same firmware interface, so that a software developer can take software written for one 3Com Plus board and easily port it to the other. The adapter also includes menu-driven diagnostic software for network and adapter troubleshooting.

### 6.2.3 Competitive Positioning of Adapters

IBM markets two token ring PC adapter boards that operate with 3+ software or IBM PC LAN software. A comparison of the PC adapter boards from 3Com and IBM are shown in Figure 19.

### 6.2.4 Type 3 Modular Access Unit (Transmission System)

The Type 3 Modular Access Unit (MAU) (see Figure 20) simplifies network connection in a token-ring network using IBM-specified Type 3 cable. It is a four-port multistation access unit that can be substituted for the IBM 8228 Multistation Access Unit for Types 1, 2, 6, and 9 cable using IBM data connectors. The Type 3 Modular Access Unit uses RJ11 connectors, allowing easy installation of Type 3 cable. Type 3 Modular Access Units can be daisy-chained through their ring-in/ring-out connectors to form networks of up to 72 nodes. One power supply is required for every five Type 3 Modular Access Units.

Network adapters must have a media filter to reduce noise on an unshielded twisted-pair token-ring network. The TokenLink adapter contains a built-in media filter and RJ11 connector, so that an additional external media filter is unnecessary. Other adapters require an external Type 3 media filter, which attaches to the DB9 connector, filters the signal, and provides the RJ11 connector for telephone twisted-pair wiring connection.

Token-ring networks operating on unshielded twisted-pair wire must use IBM-specified Type 3 cable. Commonly referred to as "telephone twisted-pair," this cable comprises four pairs of 24 AWG solid copper wire with at least two twists per foot in an insulated PVC jacket. It meets the specifications of Belden 1154-A or equivalent cable. This cable is installed by AT&T in its Premise Distribution System (PDS) and by most telephone cabling installers.

Computers connected with Type 3 wire can be plugged into a wall jack outlet specified for data connections. The data-carrying ring can use the same bundle of wires as used by the phone connections, but not

| | 3Com Token-Link | IBM Token-Ring PC Adapter I | IBM Token-Ring PC Adapter II | 3Com Token-Link Plus |
|---|---|---|---|---|
| **Standards** | | | | |
| IBM/IEEE 802.5-compatible | Yes | Yes | Yes | Yes |
| LLC Protocols/DLC interface | Yes | Yes | Yes | No |
| Licensed for us in all PC brands (according to patent holder 12/87) | Yes | No | No | Yes |
| **Software** | | | | |
| Runs 3+ | Yes | Yes | Yes | Yes |
| Runs 3+Open | Yes | Yes | Yes | Yes* |
| Runs IBM PC LAN Program | Yes | Yes | Yes | Yes* |
| Runs IBM LAN Support Program | Yes | Yes | Yes | No |
| Runs IBM Token Ring Bridge Program | No | No | Yes | No |
| Runs Link Plus Optimizer (XNS protocols/NETBIOS on-board) | No | No | No | Yes |
| **Features** | | | | |
| Built-in media filter for Type 3 cabling | Yes | No | No | No |
| Certified in high-speed PCs | Yes | NA | NA | Yes |
| Informative diagnostics | Yes | NA | NA | Yes |
| **Performance** | | | | |
| RAM | 16 KB | 8 KB | 16 KB | 256 KB |
| 16-bit interface | Yes | No | No | Yes |
| 8-bit interface | Yes | Yes | Yes | Yes |
| 8 MHz (1 wait state) AT-to-adapter data-transfer rate | 4 Mbps | 1.4 Mbkps | 1.3 Mbps | 2 Mbps |
| 80186 microprocessor | No | No | No | Yes |
| **Cabling** | | | | |
| Runs on IBM Cabling System | Yes | Yes | Yes | Yes |
| Runs on Type 3 cabling | Yes | Yes** | Yes** | Yes** |

(* Requires Link Plus Optimizer)
(** Requires a Type 3 media filter)
(NA = not available)

**Figure 19**: Comparison of PC Adapter Boards

the same pair that is carrying the telephone signal. It is important that the cable used be *twisted*-pair rather than the flat telephone extension cable often referred to as "silver satin."

### 6.2.5 Compatibility Summary

A Compatibility Summary is shown in Figure 21 and Supported Interfaces are shown in Figure 22.

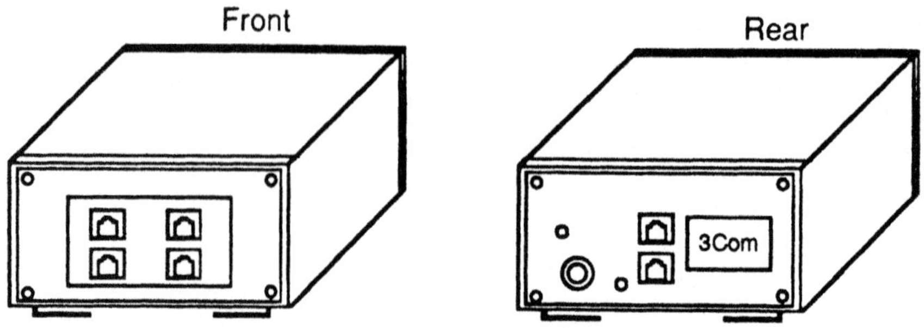


**Figure 20:** Front, Rear Views of Type 3 MAU

| **Adapters** | 3Com 3+ | 3Com 3+ Open | IBM LAN | IBM LAN Support | IBM 3270 | Banyan VINES Server | Banyan VINES Client | Novell NetWare Server | Novell NetWare Client |
|---|---|---|---|---|---|---|---|---|---|
| **TokenLink** | Yes | Yes | Yes | Yes | Yes | Yes | Yes | No | Yes |
| **TokenLink+** | Yes | Yes[1] | Yes[2] | No | Yes[3] | No | No | No | No |

1 TokenLink Plus is supported for DOS netstations running XNS protocols. TokenLink Plus with Link Plus Optimizer is supported for DOS and OS/2 netstations running XNS protocols.

2 Requires Link Plus Optimizer to download NETBIOS interface.

3 Requires Link Plus Optimizer to download NETBIOS interface. The TokenLink Plus adapter supports the synchronous gateway (NETBIOS-based) version of the 3270 Emulation Program but not the 3725 Token Interface Controller direct-channel attachment (DLC-based) option.

**Figure 21:** Compatibility Summary

## 6.3 Conclusion

In the PC LAN marketplace, 3Com strives to be compatible with the IBM PC LAN offerings, including the IBM OS/2 LAN Server, based on Microsoft's LAN Manager as its main goal.

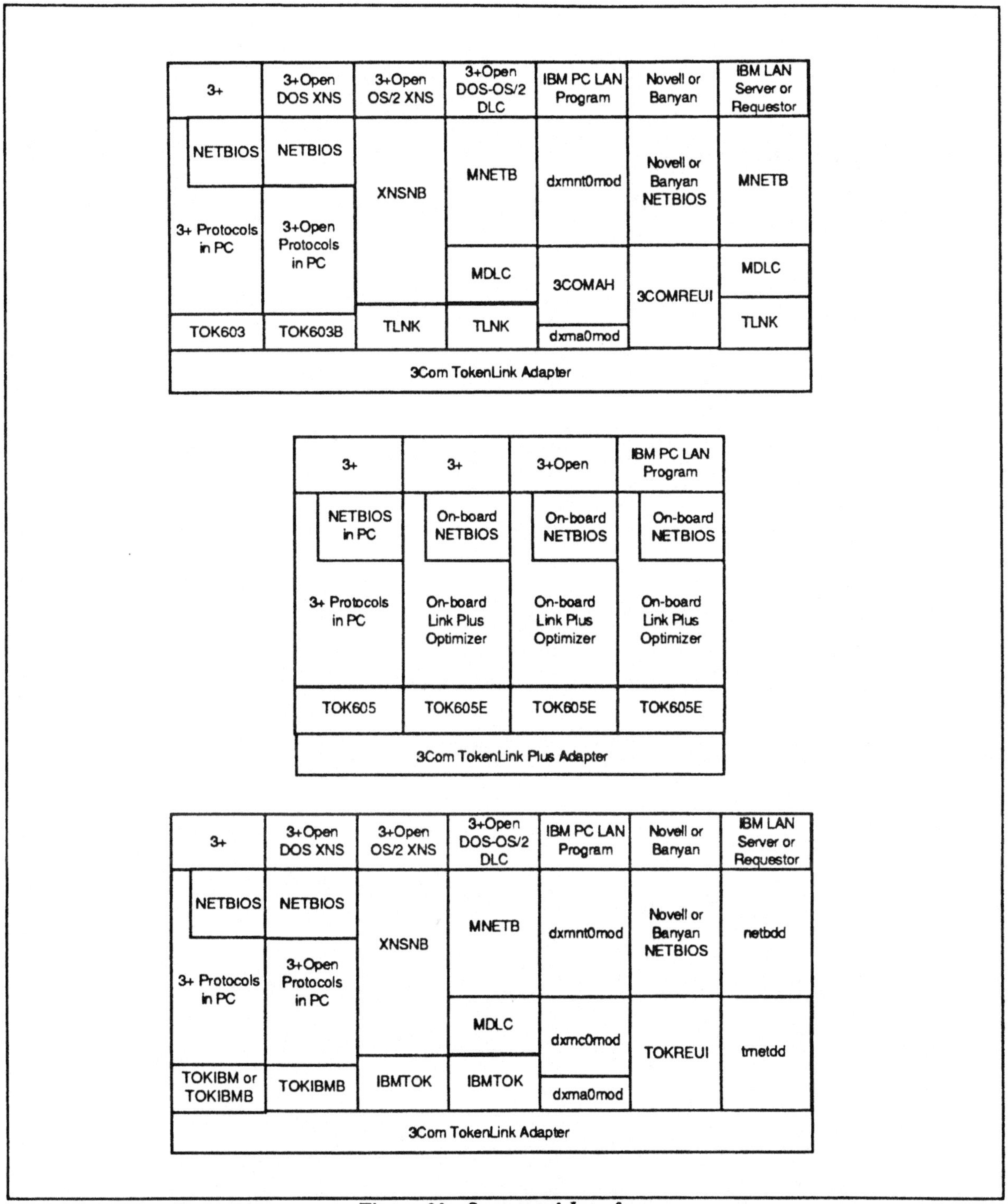


**Figure 22:** Supported Interfaces

# 7. Western Digital Token-Ring Products

## 7.1 Introduction

Western Digital Corporation, headquartered in Irvine, CA, with facilities worldwide, is a leading manufacturer of a range of storage management, intelligent disk drive, communications, imaging, core logic, and integrated systems products for both OEM and reseller markets.

Western Digital's involvement in the token-ring market includes participation in the IEEE 802.5 committee and development of token-ring products designed for both 4- and 16-Mbps data rates. Currently, Western Digital offers 4-Mbps token-ring products, as well as LAN product lines based on StarLAN, Ethernet, and Ethernet for twisted-pair media.

## 7.2 Token Card

The Western Digital Preference TokenCards are network adapters that connect PCs to a token-ring local-area network. The adapters support the Logical Link Control (LLC) IEEE 802.2 standard and use the IEEE 802.5 token-passing protocol. A Data Link Control (DLC) interface ensures IBM hardware and software compatibility.

A memory-mapped interface is used in PC XT-type environments and an optimized string I/O data transfer method is employed when the adapter is installed in PC AT-type systems. This method, combined with Western Digital's software drivers, is said to yield high performance.

The adapter is available in two versions: the TokenCard WS, with 2.8 Kbytes of RAM, is designed for use in network servers and in IBM applications environments. The server adapter uses its additional RAM as a data buffer and to offload network protocol processing and I/O functions from the host computer.

# Wiring Systems

## 8. STAR-TEK, Inc.

### 8.1 Introduction

With employees in the 60 range and revenues in the $10 to $20 million range, STAR-TEK, Inc., has its niche in providing products that enhance IBM wiring products for the 3270, System/3X, AS/400, and token-ring marketplaces. This section examines the products offered by STAR-TEK for token-ring, especially its 4- and 16-Mbps unshielded twisted-pair (UTP) products.

### 8.2 828AT MAU

The STAR-TEK 828AT Multi-Station Access Unit (MAU) provides users of token-ring local-area networks with an alternative to IBM's 8228 MAU. Used in conjunction with STAR-TEK token-ring media filters, the 828AT allows token-ring devices to be supported over unshielded Type 3 telephone twisted-pair cabling at full 4-Mbps data rates.

The 828AT Multi-Station Access Unit serves as the physical attachment point for the cable runs (lobes) associated with the devices to be connected to a token-ring LAN. The STAR-TEK 828AT functions as a 14-lobe wiring concentrator for token-ring environments. Each workstation connection is supported over an individual two-pair interface (RJ-11), with one pair serving as the transmit pair and the other as the receive pair. When an attached workstation requires access to the ring and a properly applied phantom current is detected on the corresponding device interface, the 828AT switches the transmit and receive pairs of the device interface into the ring. This process causes the corresponding workstation to be physically inserted into the ring.

The STAR-TEK 828AT is designed for fault-tolerant operation. A cable fault (i.e., a short or open circuit) on any lobe causes the immediate removal of that lobe from the ring, allowing the rest of the ring to continue operating.

The same fault-tolerance is available on main ring segment connections implemented via the front panel-mounted modular (RJ-11) ring in/ring out jacks. The 828AT can sense faults in the main ring segment connections and automatically isolate faulty segments, preventing such faults from leaving the entire ring open and inoperative. This process of automatically removing faulty portions of the ring protects the network from crashing as a result of a cable fault.

The STAR-TEK 820AT MAU provides diagnostic capabilities. A status LED for each workstation connection provides a real-time indication of insertion status. The 828AT indicates insertion status for any lobe by continuously lighting the corresponding LED as long as the workstation remains inserted into the ring. Ring In and Ring Out status LEDs display the condition of main ring segments. In addition, an internal self-test can be run at any time without disrupting activity on the ring.

Active lobe insertion modules provide active control of ring insertion/removal operations. This architecture allows fast ring insertion and removal (0.05 sec. insertion time vs. 2.5 sec for the IBM 8228, according to STAR-TEK) and facilitates a predictable start-up state for every device connection (i.e., isolated from the ring).

Two options are available for the 14-lobe versions of the STAR-TEK 828AT multi-station access unit:

- The 828AT model 1, which supports 14 device (lobe) connections and modular ring in and ring out connections

- The 828AT model 2, which supports 14 lobe connections, modular ring in and ring out connections, and ring in/ring out connections over the IBM cabling system via rear-mounted IBM 802.5 data connectors

**8.3 828AT Intelligent MAU**

The STAR-TEK 828AT-6 (also available as the 828AT-5 for shielded data cable) is an intelligent MAU for use in IEEE 802.5 token-ring LANs. An embedded microprocessor supports physical layer status monitoring, network control, fault tolerance, and communications with an optional network management PC or PS/2. Automatic fault-tolerance capability and network management tools support automatic recovery from and notification of physical layer network errors. All aspects of physical layer network configuration can be modified from the network management station. In addition, all network management functions are available remotely for off-site network control or troubleshooting.

The 828AT-6 MAU serves as the physical attachment point for the cable runs (lobes) associated with the devices connected to a token-ring LAN. Each workstation connection and main ring connection is supported over an individual modular interface (RJ-45). All connections are via unshielded telephone twisted-pair media which comply with IBM Type 3 cabling specifications. Attaching devices (nodes) are supported via STAR-TEK media filters. For networks running at 16 Mbps, STAR-TEK Dual Rate Media Filters (DRMFs) must be used. Networks operating at 4-Mbps may be implemented with either DRMF filters or standard (4-Mbps) STAR-TEK media filters.

The STAR-TEK 828AT-6 is designed for fault-tolerant operation. Unlike conventional MAUs, such as the IBM 8228, the STAR-TEK 828AT-6 is said to constantly monitor Ring In and Ring Out connections to maintain main ring integrity. On sensing a cable fault in a main ring segment, the 828AT-6 automatically isolates the faulty segment, preventing such faults from leaving the entire ring open and inoperative. This process of automatically removing failed portions of the main ring protects the network from crashing as a result of a cable fault.

A rear panel-mounted network management interface allows the STAR-TEK 828AT-6 to communicate with the serial port of a network management PC or PS/2. This capability allows physical layer network status monitoring and control. STAR-TEK Network Management--an application which runs under Microsoft Windows--provides a continuously updated diagram of the network and all of the attached devices: physically removing a lobe or powering-down the device associated with a lobe is immediately reflected in the on-screen network diagram. Bad cables and failed main ring segments are also displayed. A user at the network management station can remotely alter portions of the physical configuration of the network by manipulating the corresponding graphic element on the network management display. With this capability, physical layer troubleshooting can be performed without actually handling any cables. A person responsible for network management can trace through an entire network to isolate faults without leaving the network management console. This capability is particularly useful for large networks, where cabling may be widely distributed and not easily accessible. The serial network management can also support off-site monitoring and troubleshooting of remote networks, allowing a technician at a central facility to monitor and control the physical layer configuration of token-ring LANs installed in multiple remote branch offices.

Each 828AT-6 contains an internal ring path and switching modules which can insert any of the device connections (lobes) into this internal ring path. A single 828AT-6 can support up to eight lobes. To form larger rings, the internal ring paths of multiple 828AT-6s can be interconnected via the ring in and ring out (RI/RO) connections on each unit. These interconnections between MAUs are collectively referred to as the Main Ring Path. Up to nine 828AT-6s can be interconnected on any single ring. Larger networks can be constructed by linking multiple rings together through local bridges. Data cabling must conform to IBM Type 3 media specifications for unshielded twisted-pair (UTP).

The 828AT-6 provides eight IEEE 802.5 standard device attachments (lobe ports) and a Ring In and a Ring Out port. Each device in the network can, under normal operation, control the switching mechanism in the 828AT-6 which inserts or removes its lobe from the ring path. While not inserted into the 828AT-6 ring path, loves are self-looped, with transmit and receive pairs connected together.

### 8.3.1 Fault Tolerance on Lobe Connections

Like other MAUs, the 828AT-6 automatically protects against cable faults on lobes by operating in conjunction with the attaching LAN adapter cards. Any attached device which requires access to the ring must first apply a "phantom current" which is superimposed on the transmit and receive pairs of a lobe. If the phantom current is present, the 828AT-6 inserts the corresponding device into its internal ring path. If the phantom current is present, the 828AT-6 inserts the corresponding device into its internal ring path. If the phantom current is disrupted by a break in the cable or by a short circuit, for example, the 828AT-6 automatically isolates the lobe from the rest of the ring, and the remainder of the network continues to operate.

If used, an attached network management station is automatically informed of any changes in lobe insertion status.

### 8.3.2 Fault Tolerance on Main Ring Connections

The 828AT-6 automatically protects the main ring from cable failures. Fault tolerance on the main ring is implemented by sending a phantom current over RI/RO connections in much the same way that attaching devices send phantom current to the MAU over lobe connections. This capability protects the network from crashing when bad cables are installed on the main ring path, by automatically preventing these cables from being inserted into a live network. Main ring cables which fail in an operating network are automatically removed, allowing the remainder of the network to continue operating.

In order to provide backward compatibility with MAUs from IBM and other manufacturers which do not implement fault tolerance on the main ring path, 828AT-6 Ring In and Ring Out connections can be set to operate without fault tolerance.

### 8.3.3 Network Management

With conventional MAUs, if a cabling problem on the main ring path leads to a network crash, the person responsible for maintaining the network must physically visit the wiring closets through which the crashed ring is installed and methodically unplug cables until the problem has been located.

To speed the troubleshooting process, the 828AT-6 incorporates local intelligence and an out-of-band network management channel. A dedicated microprocessor in each 828AT-6 constantly monitors the status of all device (lobe) and main ring connections. Serial ports (RS-485) mounted on the rear panel of each 828AT-6 support an independent network management bus which connects all of the 828AT-6 MAUs to a network management console. Fault location and removal is said to be more efficient on rings implemented with 828AT-6 MAUs for two reasons:

- Fault tolerance on main ring connections automatically isolates cable faults on main ring segments, thus preventing many types of network crashes.

- If for some reason a ring still crashes, the status of all lobe and main ring connections can be inspected from a central network management console. In addition, all lobe and main ring connections can be controlled from the network management station, meaning that cables can be isolated or inserted into the network without sending a maintenance person to the wiring closets.

Figure 23 depicts network management bus connection details. Each 828AT-6 has two rear panel-mounted DB-9 connectors. The network management bus is configure by chaining 828AT-6s together with serial cables. One end of the chain is connected to the serial port of a PC or PS/2 through an RS-232 to RS-485 converter. Up to 33 828AT-6 MAUs can be connected to a single serial network management bus, and the bus can be up to 4000 feet long. The serial network management protocol is designed for reliability: even if multiple 828AT-6s power down, those remaining in operation can still communicate with the network manager over the serial bus.

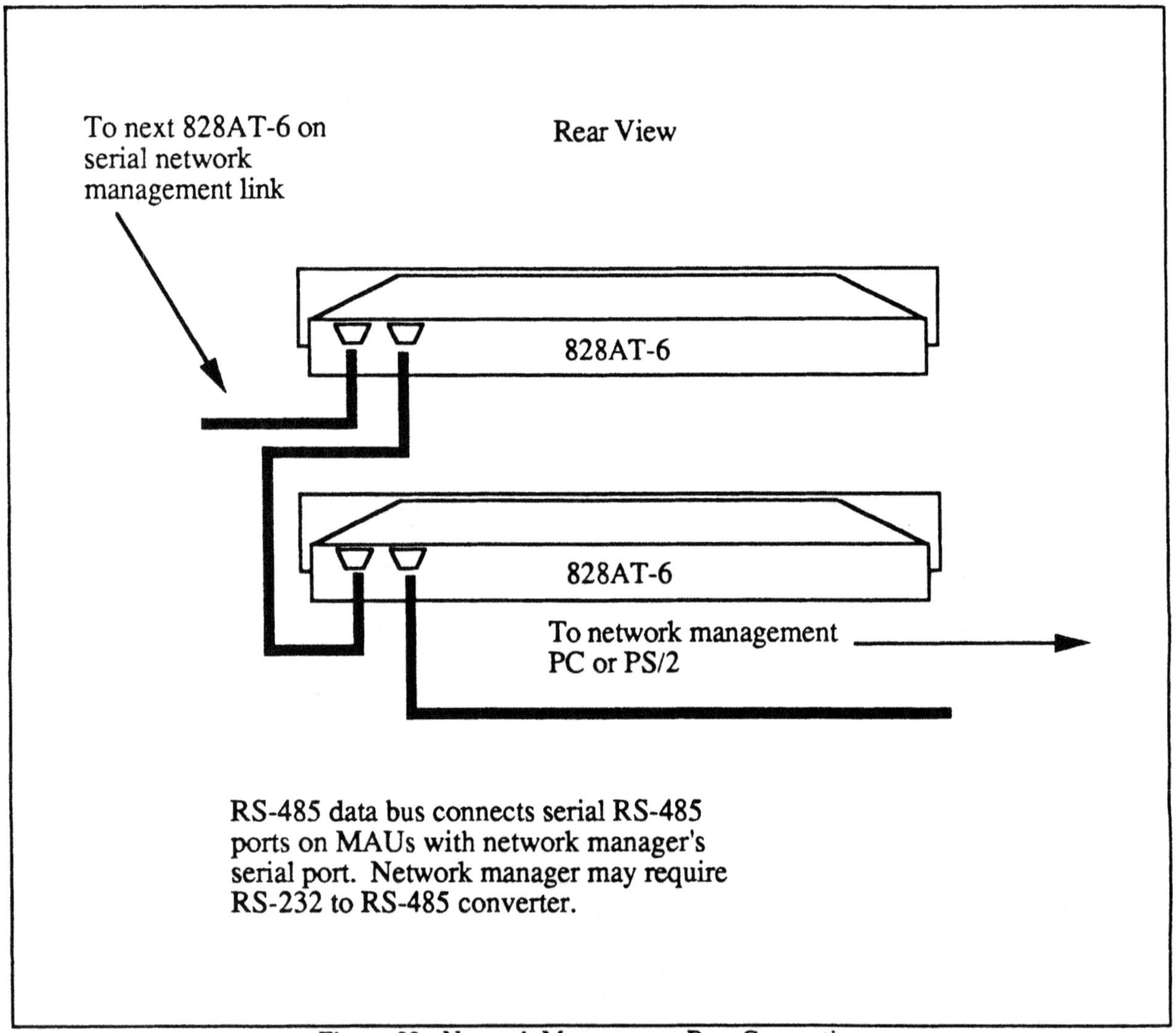


**Figure 23**: Network Management Bus, Connection Detail

STAR-TEK says the advantages of using a separate serial bus for network management are:

- The network manager can communicate with all MAUs even if the token-ring network is down; since network management capability is most needed when the network is down, this capability is advantageous.

- Remote sites can be managed from a central location via standard dial up modem links; this capability can provide savings in support and travel costs.
- The network management station does not require a token-ring adapter board.

### 8.3.4 Local Site Network Management

For installations where the network management station is within 4000 feet of all 828AT-6 MAUs, the serial port of the network management station can be connected to the network management bus through a STAR-TEK RS-232/RS-485 converter. The network management station does not need to be active on the token-ring network in order to run the serial network management bus. Figure 24 illustrates this configuration.

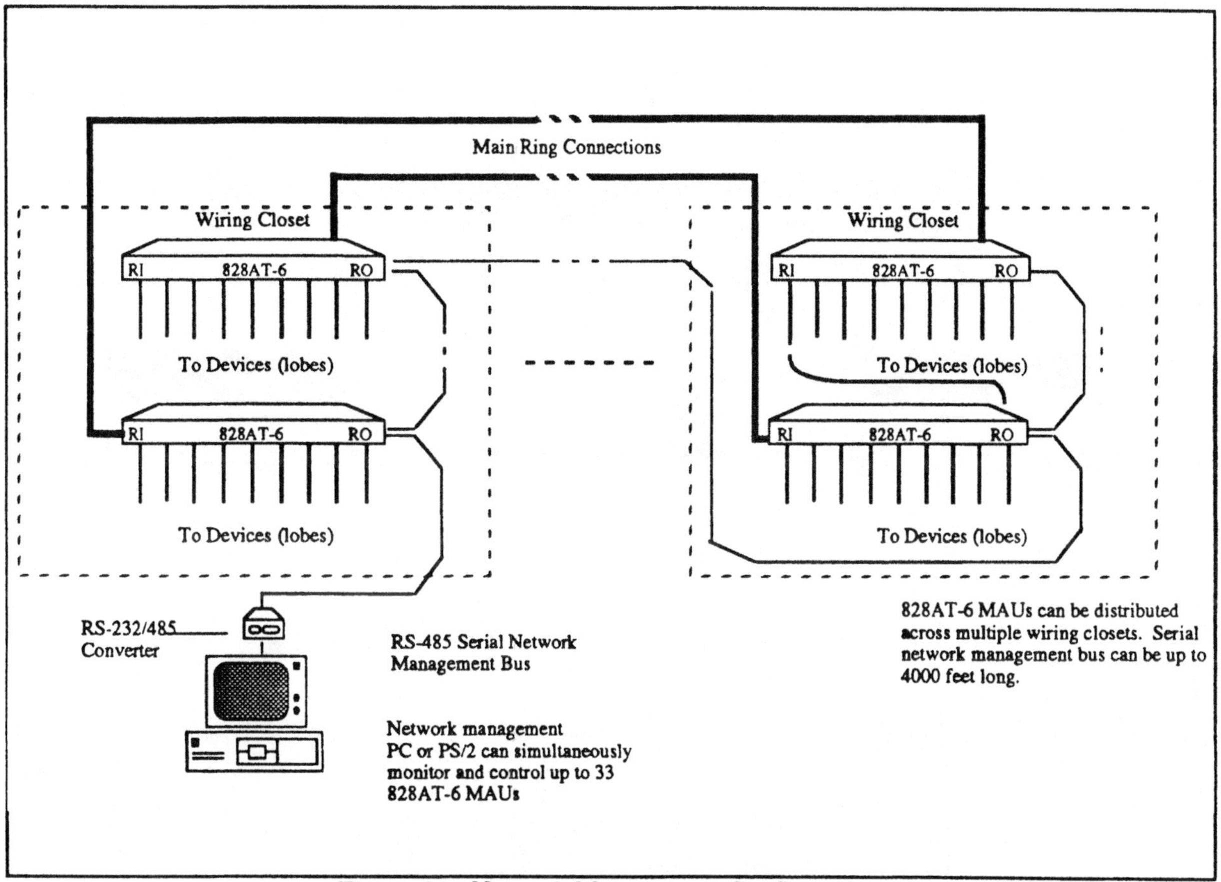


**Figure 24**: Network Management Configuration, Local Site

Each serial network management bus can support up to 33 828AT-6 MAUs. Additional serial management buses--up to a maximum of four--can be locally supported. Each requires a separate serial port on the network management station.

### 8.3.5 Remote Site Network Management

Token-ring networks at remote sites implemented with STAR-TEK 828AT-6 MAUs can be managed from a central site via standard 2400 baud dial-up modem links. At each remote site, an RS-485 serial bus interconnects the network management ports of up to 33 828AT-6 MAUs. A STAR-TEK RS-232/RS-485 converter links this management bus to the DTE port of a standard 2400 baud dial-up modem.

At the central management site, a serial port on the network management station is connected to another 2400 baud modem. By dialing into the modem at the remote site, the network manager can monitor and control the attached 828AT-6 MAUs. The number of remote sites which can be supported from a central site is limited only by the disk space available on the network management station.

The network management station (PC or PS/2 equipped with a serial port) provides central access to the monitoring and control functions embedded in the 828AT-6 MAU.

The STAR-TEK Network Management Application displays a graphic representation (refer to Figure 25) of the physical configuration of networks implemented with STAR-TEK 828AT-6 MAUs. Icons

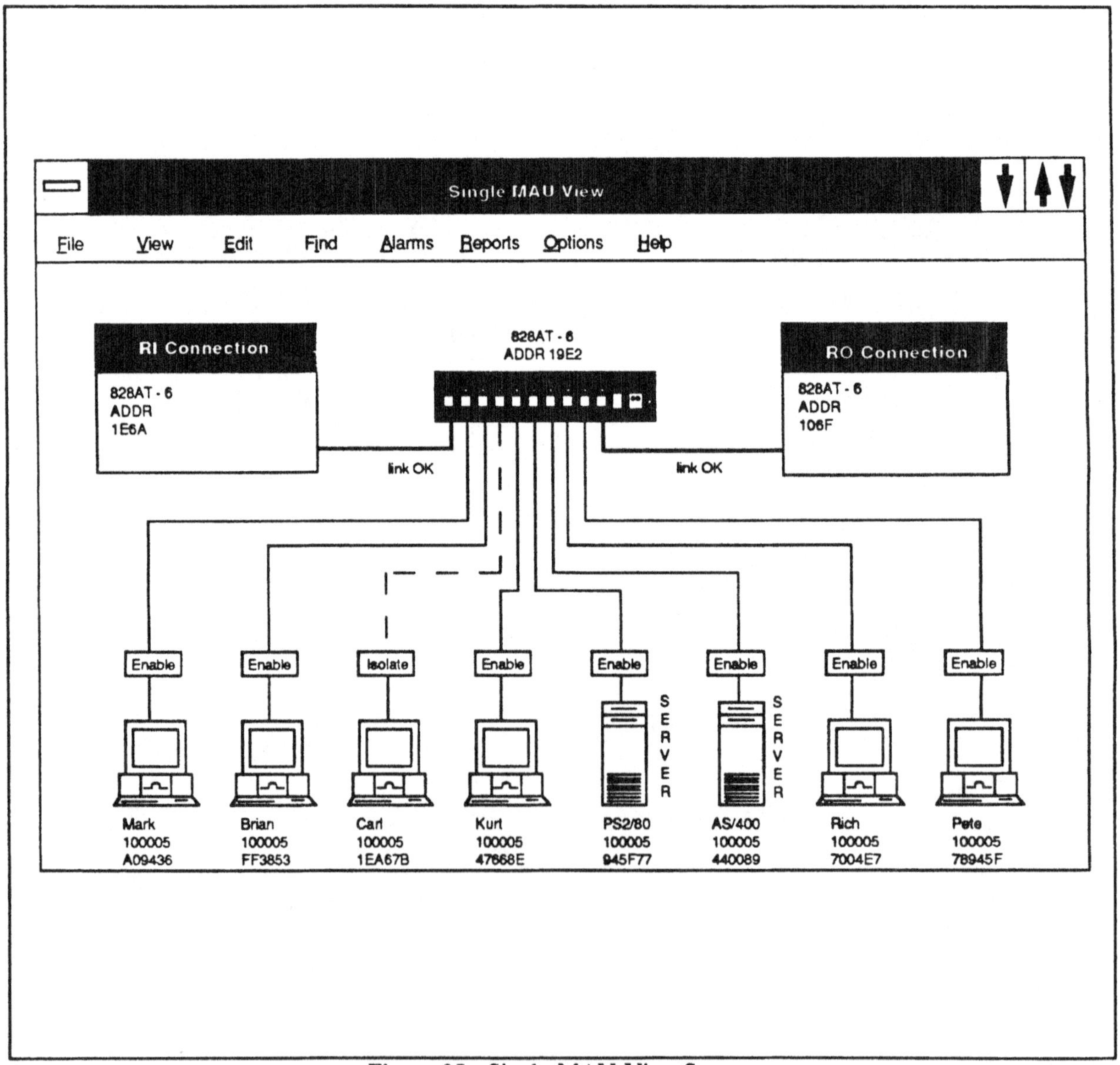


**Figure 25**: Single MAU View Screen

representing network components and the devices attached to the network are interconnected by lines attached to the appropriate MAU. Main ring links (interconnections between MAUs) are displayed which represent the network cabling. Devices operating on the network are shown with their cable graphically. Any problems detected by the fault-tolerance circuits in the 828AT-6s are displayed both graphically and as text adjacent to the failure. The screen display is updated in real time: any change in the network configuration or status is immediately reflected on-screen.

Networks can be viewed at five levels: Network Management Domain View; Ring View; Main Ring Sequence View; Single MAU View; and Expanded Cable View.

In addition to status monitoring and control capabilities, STAR-TEK Network Management provides configuration checking, which automatically calculates maximum ring size for the displayed configuration. This capability simplifies the network design and planning process. An integrated database for user-defined information associated with every element in the network helps to further organize network management information.

The program uses the Microsoft Windows graphic interface. Pull-down menus, mouse support, dialog boxes, on-screen control buttons, and on-line help screens are provided.

### 8.3.6 Configuration

The STAR-TEK 828AT-6 provides the data transport functions defined for MAUs under the IEEE 802.5 standard. Configuration rules are derived from two critical limitations:

Network Timing--Each device on a token-ring network acts as a repeater, receiving signals from an "upstream" neighbor and re-transmitting these signals to a "downstream" neighbor on the ring. As a consequence of this architecture, any timing errors introduced during this process can accumulate and interfere with proper data transfer around the ring. This effect (known as jitter) increases with the number of devices (workstations and repeaters) on the network. Because the accumulation of jitter can depend on site-specific factors, there is a variance in the maximum number of devices supportable on a single ring. A maximum of 72 devices per ring is recommended for most applications.

Larger user populations can be supported by interconnecting multiple rings with bridges. Bridges are devices which connect to two similar networks, passing traffic between the two. Because bridges do not pass timing errors, users can support a virtually unlimited number of network users by interconnecting multiple rings in this way.

Cabling Distances--Each device on the ring functions as a repeater, receiving a signal from its upstream neighbor and re-transmitting to its downstream neighbor. The signal received at each device must exceed a minimum threshold. This threshold defines the maximum attenuation permissible between any two neighboring devices on the ring. Many factors determine signal attenuation. The most significant of these are cable type, cable length, data rate, and the number of MAUs between a transmitting and a receiving device.

The following guidelines for maximum cable lengths ensure that signal attenuation is kept within acceptable limits throughout the network.

### 8.3.7 Definitions

Adjusted Main Ring Length (AMRL)--Main ring path distances must be taken into account when calculating maximum lobe lengths for networks containing multiple MAUs. The Adjusted Main Ring Length represents the worst-case distance around the main ring path that a signal must travel if the main ring is broken and forced to self-loop over the back-up pair. The AMRL is calculated as the sum of all main ring path connection distances for a fully-connected ring (i.e., all RI/RO connections complete) minus the length of the shortest main ring path connection. All main ring cables (including patch cables) must be counted when calculating AMRL. Figure 26 provides an example of AMRL calculation.

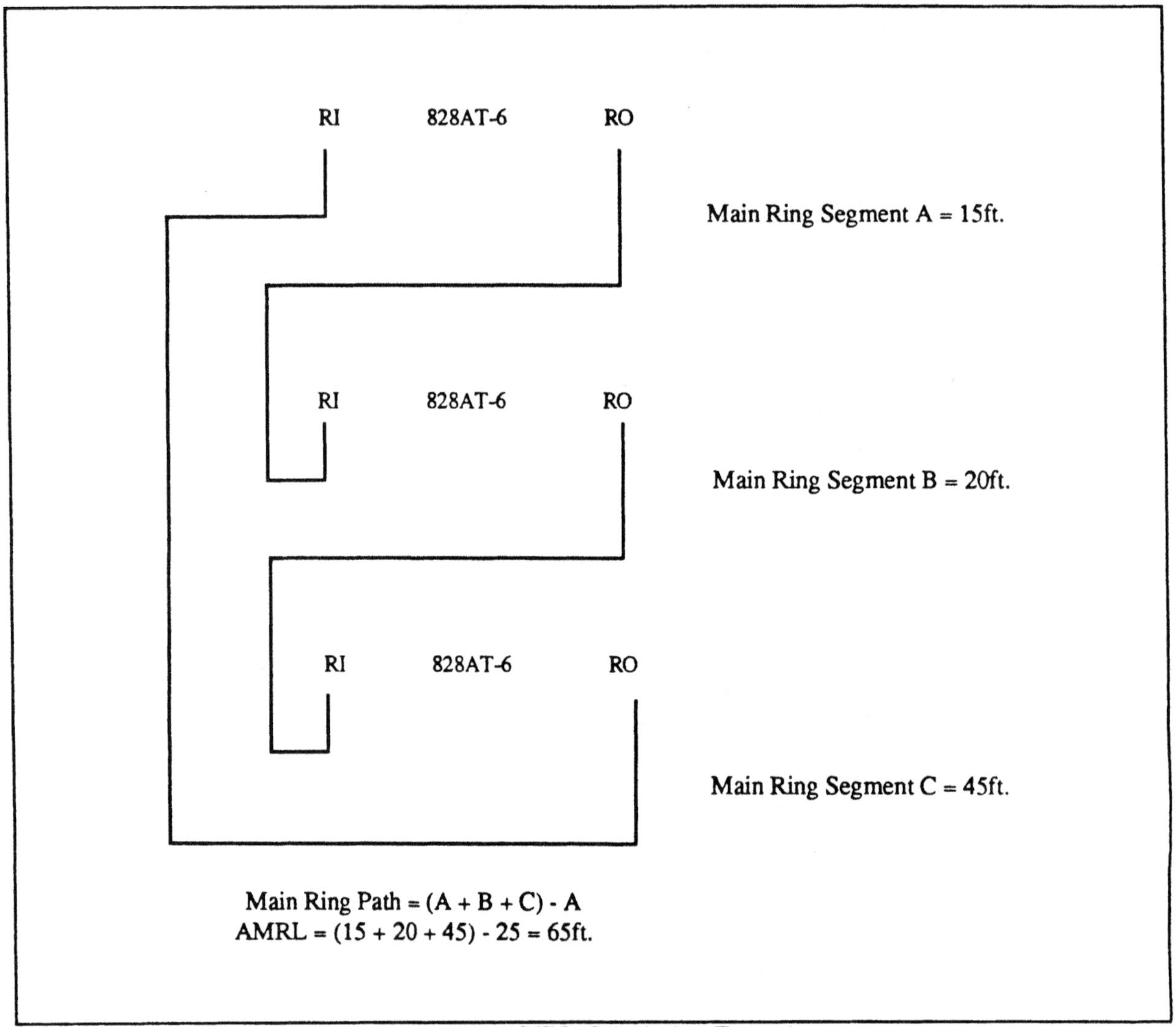


**Figure 26**: AMRL Calculation Example

Ring Drive Distance (RDD)--The sum of the AMRL and the longest permissible lobe length on a ring defines the longest total transmission path around the ring. This quantity is referred to as the Ring Drive Distance. Maximum ring drive distance (RDD) varies with data rate, cable type, the number of MAUs on a ring, and accumulated insertion losses.

Insertion Loss (IL)--Each time a cable path is spliced, punched down, connectorized, or otherwise altered, it become a slightly less ideal signal transmission path. Each of these alterations causes a slight loss in signal strength. This effect is known as insertion loss. For the purposes of the following relations, IL is expressed in terms of equivalent cable distance.

General Rule--The following rule must be satisfied for successful network operation:

Max. Lobe Length = RDD - (20N) - AMRL - IL

Notes: N = The number of MAUs in the ring

For 10-Mbps operation, STAR-TEK DRMF media filters must be used; for 4-Mbps operation, either STAR-TEK DRMF or TR-PD-8 media filters may be used.

Insertion Losses (IL) are calculated as per STAR-TEK publication TR-4 *Token Ring Planning Guide.*

For 16-Mbps operation over 2-pr 24AWG cable which complies with the Type 3 media specification, the following values for RDD are valid:

16 Mbps: RDD = 350 ft. 4 Mbps: RDD = 520 ft.

### 8.4 818AT-1 Regenerative Repeater

The STAR-TEK 818AT-1 (also available as the 818AT-2 for shielded data cable) Regenerative Repeater allows token-ring users to configure large networks over unshielded twisted-pair (UTP) cabling. Each 818AT-1 functions as two fully independent 4-Mbps repeaters, simplifying configuration and reducing by half the number of repeaters needed in the network. Active re-timing and embedded support for STAR-TEK fault tolerance allow the network to recover from errors transparently, preventing failures of the main ring.

The 818AT-1 supports two principal applications:

Main Ring Repeater--The STAR-TEK 818AT-1 extends the maximum length of the main ring path (the part of the ring between multi-station units). Wiring closets up 1,000 feet apart can be supported over Type 3 unshielded twisted-pair. Each STAR-TEK 818AT-1 receives and regenerates token-ring data on both primary and backup pairs of the main ring path, offering the same functionality as two IBM 8218s.

Lobe Repeater--The 818AT-1 can be configured as a single lobe repeater to support individual devices up to 1,000 feet from the Multi-Station Access Unit. Each 818AT-1 can extend one lobe in this configuration.

The 818AT-1 regenerates token-ring data in two ways:

Signal Strength--The 818AT-1 restores 4-Mbps token-ring data signals to original transmission levels, allowing for a maximum separation between repeaters of 1,000 feet for Type 3 cable.

Ring Timing--The 818AT-1 regenerates signal timing. An active synchronization circuit minimizes network timing error by reclocking outgoing data. This process compensates for the timing errors which otherwise accumulate on large networks.

The STAR-TEK 818AT-1 is designed for fault-tolerant operation. When used with STAR-TEK fault-tolerant MAUs, the 818AT-1 provides for automatic removal and bypassing of faulty main ring segments. This process ensures that only properly wired cable segments will actually be inserted into the main ring path. Once inserted, cable segments are constantly monitored for faults and are automatically removed from the ring as soon as a fault is detected. This capability allows the ring to recover transparently from cable faults on the main ring.

Each user connection, or lobe, is connected to the network through a MAU. Each MAU contains an internal ring which interconnects the lobes attached to it. This internal ring can be accessed via Ring In (RI) and Ring Out (RO) connections on each MAU. Large networks are configured by interconnecting MAUs via RI/RO ports. These RI/RO connections between MAUs constitute the main ring path.

For networks configured around a single wiring closet, maximum allowable lobe lengths are not significantly affected by the length of the main ring path. For networks in which the MAUs are distributed between two or more wiring closets, however, the length of the main ring path becomes significant in determining maximum allowable lobe lengths. Without repeaters, every additional unit length of the main ring path decreases the maximum possible lobe length of the network proportionately. Consequently, as networks extend beyond a certain main ring size, repeaters on the main ring path become necessary in order to allow for partial lobe lengths.

The most common application for STAR-TEK 818AT-1 is as a main ring repeater. Figure 27 depicts a typical configuration for a large network organized around three wiring closets. An interconnected "stack" of MAUs supports locally attached lobes in each wiring closet. The Ring In (RI) of the first MAU and the Ring Out (RO) of the last MAU in each closet provide connection points to the portions of the main ring path which run between the three closets.

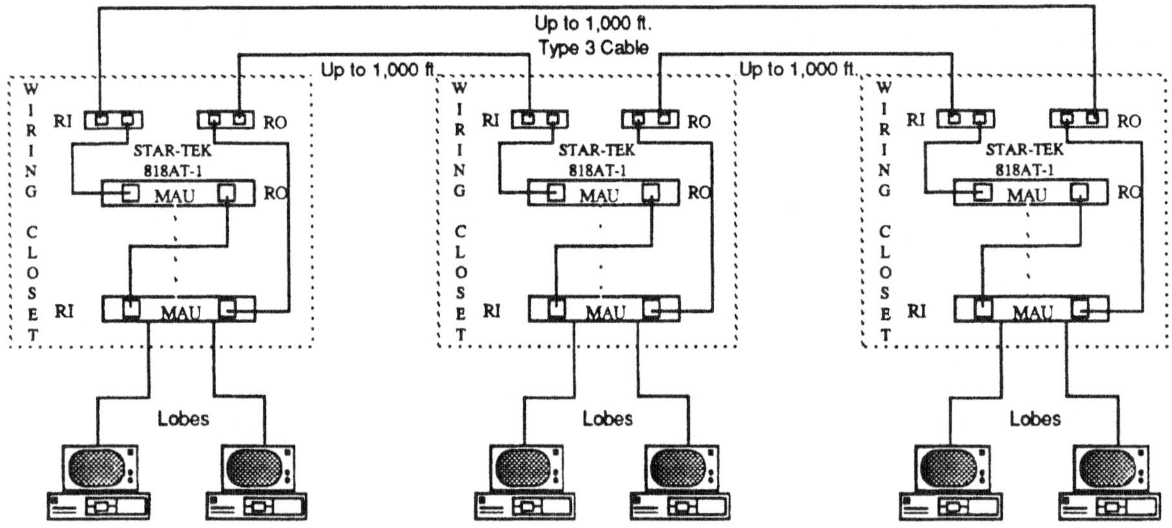


**Figure 27:** Redundant Main Ring Configuration

In this example, the main ring between wiring closets is implement over Type 3 twisted-pair. By placing an 818AT-1 repeater at each end, main ring segments between wiring closets can be up to 1,000 feet long. Longer spans can be supported with additional repeaters. This configuration essentially removes the trade-off between overall main ring length and maximum allowable lobe length.

An alternate application for the STAR-TEK 818AT-1 is as a lobe repeater. In this configuration, the 818AT-1 is installed in-line on a lobe, or device connection. This arrangement allows the lobe to be extended up to 1,000 feet for each repeater installed in-line. If the 818AT loses power while the attached lobe is inserted into the ring, the 818AT disrupts the phantom current path from the attaching device, allowing the MAU to automatically bypass the failed lobe. Figure 28 illustrates this configuration.

## 8.5 Conclusion

STAR-TEK is taking somewhat of a risk by offering products that go beyond the IBM standards. STAR-TEK is one of the few companies willing to take this risk in order to provide innovative products that differentiate it from other IBM token-ring cabling system product vendors.

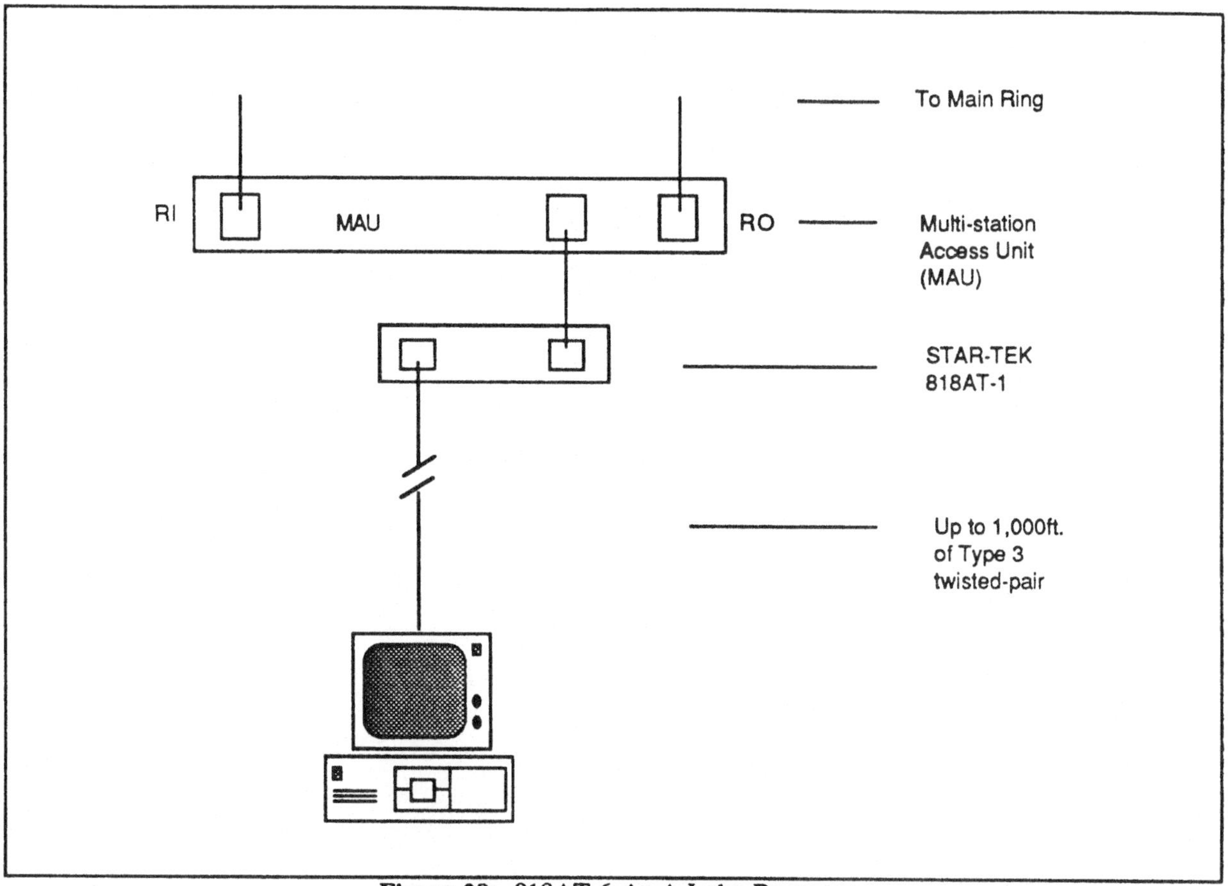


**Figure 28**: 818AT-6 As A Lobe Repeater

# 9. SynOptics Token-Ring Support Within Network Utility Architecture

### 9.1 Introduction

SynOptics Communications, Inc., developed its Network Utility Architecture (NUA) to address the concerns of MIS and network managers who are grappling with bringing large complex networks into line. The Network Utility Architecture defines networks as widespread communications utilities similar to the telephone system. It is composed of three basic components: connectivity, internetworking, and network management. The architecture strategy hold that these components are incorporated as networks grow larger and more complex, to provide capabilities required for a network to serve its users effectively and still maintain its utility functionality.

The Network Utility Architecture is delivered through a system strategy that provides customers with the function and capabilities required to transform their LANs into data communication utilities. Utility attributes applicable to the LAN include:

- Reliability
- Recovery from failure
- Adherence to standards
- Flexibility
- Advanced planning
- Growth potential

These attributes tend to be found at the lower layers of the ISO model--physical, data link, and network. These layers provide the connectivity required in a network so that information can be transmitted from one point to another. The goal of an effective network utility is to remain invisible while providing the lower-layer utility functions reliably, consistently, and automatically.

### 9.2 Mixed Token-Ring and Ethernet Support

A complex issue is that of bringing two disparate network access methods together into a manageable whole. The choice of access method is typically based on application needs, and the choice of cabling has been dependent on the access method. Now, because the Network Utility Architecture integrates all aspects of LAN wiring into a single unit in a centralized wiring closet, cabling and access decisions are independent of access method choice.

Using SynOptic's LattisNet System 3000 LAN hardware platform, token-ring and Ethernet connectivity can be implemented in the same wiring concentrator, eliminating the need for two separate cabling systems (see Figure 29). Further, as SynOptics unfolds token-ring internetworking and network management function, the entire spectrum of token-ring and Ethernet LAN planning and management is centralized.

The System 3000 platform is designed for growth. Initially, Ethernet connectivity, internetworking, and network management options were available, connecting to a single bus on the System 3000 backplane. Now, with the availability of LattisNet Token-Ring, a new backplane is available featuring multiple buses. One bus accommodates Ethernet connectivity, Ethernet network management, and power. The new Token-Ring bus supports two independent rings, each operating at either 2 Mbps or 16 Mbps.

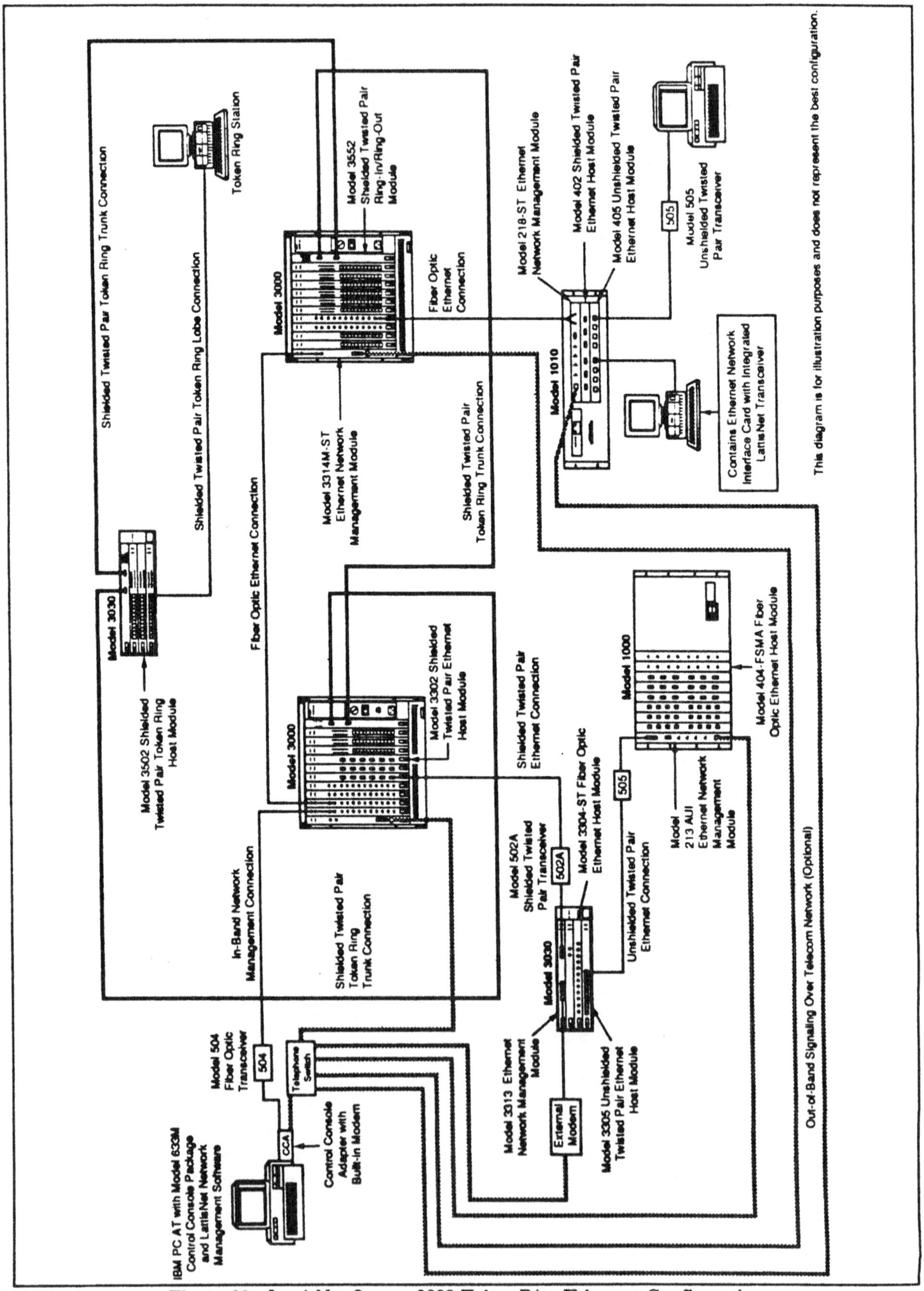


**Figure 29:** LattisNet System 3000 Token-Ring/Ethernet Configuration

**9.3 Lattis Token-Ring**

LattisNet Token-Ring provides token-ring connectivity at 4 Mbps and 16 Mbps over the IBM Cabling System's shielded data cables, including cable types 1, 2, 6, 8, and 9. A LattisNet Model 3000 Concentrator with token-ring host modules can support a maximum of 132 token-ring lobes while the Ring-In/Ring-Out Module is used to extend the ring beyond the concentrator.

LattisNet Token-Ring components include:

- The Model 3502 Shielded Twisted-Pair Host Module provides 12 shielded RJ-45 Token-Ring connections for enhanced connectivity options. Shielded RJ-45 modular receptacles are said to provide higher port densities than traditional token-ring installations using IBM multi-station access units.

- The Model 3552 Ring In/Ring Out Module connects concentrators in networks of up to 260 stations by linking concentrators via the DB-9 ring-in and ring-out connections. Non-LattisNET multistation access units, including those from IBM, can also be connected with the Model 3552.

- The Model 950-8 STP Patch Cable connects the concentrator to the IBM patch panel. This Shielded RJ-45-to-IBM Data Connector cable is specially designed by SynOptics to work with the Model 3502 Host Module.

- The Model 909-8 STP Wall Outlet/Trunk Patch Cable (DB-9 IBM Data Connector) connects a Model 3552 Ring In/Ring Out Module to an IBM patch panel or an adapter card to a wall outlet.

- The Model 951-8 STP Patch Cable, compatible with IBM's Model 8642551 Patch Cable, is used to extend the distance of the Model 950-08 or Model 909-8 cables.

The System 3000 concentrator backplane architecture is designed to accommodate three separate buses: the lower third of the backplane houses buses supporting Ethernet connectivity, Ethernet network management, and power. With the introduction of LattisNet Token-Ring, a new backplane which includes a token-ring bus is available. This design provides both Ethernet and token-ring connectivity from the same wiring concentrator. The LattisNet Token-Ring modules connect to the lower portion (for power) and the mid-section (for token-ring connectivity).

One of the most crucial utility attributes embodied in the Network Utility Architecture is room for growth. Next steps for the LattisNet Token-Ring system include integrated repeater functions, internetworking options, and integrated network management.

To address the use of ordinary telephone wire for data communications, SynOptics Communications, Inc., has announced its 4- and 16-Mbps token-ring module options for its System 3000 intelligent wiring hub. SynOptics says its new "active hub" approach allows use of ordinary unshielded-twisted-pair telephone wire for high-speed data transmission over longer lengths of cable than has previously been possible.

Also, additional new technology developed by SynOptics is said to increase the logistical number of stations that can be configured in a single token-ring network. Traditionally, the maximum ring count for unshielded twisted-pair token-ring has been limited to 72 nodes; raising the available station count reduces the number of bridges that would be required to build larger physical rings. Further, the addition of a new fiber-optic repeater module is said to extend trunk ring interconnections between concentrators of up to two kilometers.

SynOptics employs a dual strategy: a passive approach for use with shielded-twisted-pair and LAN cables such as those from AT&T and Northern Telecom, and an active hub approach which achieves standard building cabling distance requirements using ordinary telephone wire, commonly called D Inside Wire, or DIW.

The LattisNet Model 3502A STP/UTP Token Ring Hhost Module, an enhancement to the Model 3502 that was announced last March, uses the passive approach for 4-Mbps UTP installations of DIW, 4- or 16-Mbps installations using high-performance cable, and 4- or 16-Mbps installations using shielded-twisted-pair.

The LattisNet Model 3505 Token Ring UTP Host Module is intended for sites where ordinary DIW is installed and operation at 16 Mbps is required. This option uses SynOptic's active hub approach, employing both an equalizer and a filter on each channel of the host module to reduce cross-talk introduced at higher data rates. This approach allows distances of 330 feet (100 meters) over ordinary DIW. Even longer distances are achieved with the Model 3505 using high-performance cable: up to 600 feet (180 meters) at 16 Mbps and up to 1,000 feet (300 meters) at 4 Mbps.

Token-ring host modules can share the same concentrator with Ethernet host modules for unshielded-twisted-pair, shielded-twisted-pair, and fiber-optic cable, as well as the LattisNet local and remote bridge modules. The backplane design of the System 3000 concentrator chassis allows both Ethernet and Token Ring to operate together in the same wiring enclosure.

The Model 550 UTP Lobe Media Filter connects directly to the network interface card on a token-ring station to limit RF emissions on the unshielded-twisted-pair cable at both 4- and 16-Mbps data rates. The Model 551 Repeater Media Filter connects an external IBM Repeater (Model 8218 or 8220) to a LattisNet Model 3552 Ring-In/Ring-Out Module and concentrator populated with Model 3502A STP/UTP Host Modules supporting UTP lobes. A series of low cross-talk patch cables are also available to connect between the host module and the wiring closet patch panel or punch down block, and between the Token-Ring adapter card and the wall outlet.

To build enterprise-wide Token RingLANs, the LattisNet Model 3534-ST Token Ring Fiber Optic Repeater Module increases allowable trunk cable distances between concentrators by up to 2 km. Availability of the fiber-optic repeater module is dependent upon completion of successful field tests which are currently underway.

Using a sample configuration of 144 stations (lobes), LattisNet Token Ring is priced at about $235 per lobe using the passive approach (Model 3502A), and at about $300 per lobe using the active approach (Model 3505).

### 9.4 Pricing

Available now from SynOptics Communications and its authorized resellers worldwide, LattisNet Token-Ring is compatible with token-ring multistation access units, repeaters, bridges, and the LAN Manager from IBM. LattisNet Token-Ring products are designed to meet both the IEEE 802.5 standard and the de facto IBM Token-Ring standard. Existing token-ring equipment can be retained while networks are expanded with fully-compatible LattisNet Token-Ring products. In a typical configuration, LattisNet Token-Ring costs about $150 per connection.

### 9.5 Conclusion

Comprehensive twisted-pair networking wiring solutions for both Ethernet and token-ring are fast becoming a reality. As the trend toward mixed LAN environments gains momentum, the differences between deploying token-ring and Ethernet will diminish. SynOptics believes that in a typical Fortune 1000 organization--many of which already use LattisNet--LattisNet Token-Ring will gain significant penetration. To date, more than 450,000 nodes of its LattisNet product have been installed worldwide.

Competition for wiring 16-Mbps token-rings with LattisNet comes from other vendors with support for 16 Mbps on unshielded twisted-pair, including Proteon, Cabletron, STAR-TEK, and Ungermann-Bass. For more information, contact SynOptics Communications, Inc., at 501 E. Middlefield Road, Mountain View, CA 94043; (415) 960-1100.

# Testing

## 10. Bytex Systems ATS 1000 Token-Ring LAN Analysis System

### 10.1 Introduction

The ATS 1000 from Bytex Systems is a family of analysis systems for LANs based on the IEEE 802 standard. THe ATS 1000 is available in models that support Ethernet (802.3), token-ring (802.5--the subject of this section), and token-bus (802.4) topologies, used by the Manufacturing Automation Protocol (MAP) 2.1 and 3.0 protocols.

### 10.2 ATS 1000 Token-Ring LAN Analysis System Architecture

Bytex designed the ATS 1000 Token-Ring LAN Analysis System to give LAN managers comprehensive LAN management, analysis, and testing capabilities on token-ring networks. The system's platform provides high-speed, unrestricted access and logging of all network events. This platform also offers analysis facilities for use during and after event collection. The ATS 1000 also allows a LAN manager to de-insert malfunctioning workstations from a remote location, rather than visiting the site.

The ATS 1000 attaches to the token-ring LAN via a LAN I/O Module (LIOM, patent pending). A dedicated high-speed "front end" Data Control Module (DCM) processes the network events captured by the LIOM. These events are them made available via a VMEbus for storage, display, and post processing in the PC environment.

The LIOM was designed to allow easy access to the token-ring LAN. Physical connection of the ATS 1000 can be made between a workstation and the LAN (daisy chain), eliminating the need to use an MAU port. Optionally, the MAU may be used as the point of connection. Once the LIOM is attached, the Data Control Module has total simultaneous transmit and receive access to the network.

The DCM acts as a "front-end," responsible for preprocessing the network events. A network preprocessor configured with multiported memory is used to perform this function. The DCM acts upon network events based on a Filter/Trigger mechanism available via a menu-based used interface. Most of the more common Filter/Trigger combinations for performing specific analyses have been predefined and stored in a System Library.

The ATS 1000 operation is transparent to the network. It places no additional overhead on the LAN, sees all error conditions, causes no loss of operation, and allows the user to gain on-demand access to the ring. This is especially useful when troubleshooting "beaconing" rings, because inserting stations other than the ATS 1000 is impossible at the time.

DCM technology allows the ATS 1000 to see all events on the network, as well as events occurring at selected higher-layer protocols. Errors normally masked from a workstation (frame fragments, truncated frames, invalid MAC frames, network silence, and tokens themselves) are collected and available for problem analysis.

Loss of data caused by a sudden and/or long burst of network events is not a concern with the ATS 1000, due to the throughput achieved by the DCM.

Network events processed by the DCM are time-stamped and written to the ATS 1000 hard disk as they are collected. Time-stamps are at a one-microsecond granularity.

The ATS 1000 operates as an MS-DOS PC AT in post-processing mode and is MS-DOS-compatible for user processing via standard spreadsheet and word processors. The system includes: PC AT-class processor with 1 Mbyte of RAM; detachable keyboard/electroluminescent display; hard disk with floppy drive for offline storage; and ports for optional keyboard, monitor, printer, and serial communications for remote or local access.

The ATS 1000 architecture is depicted in Figure 30.

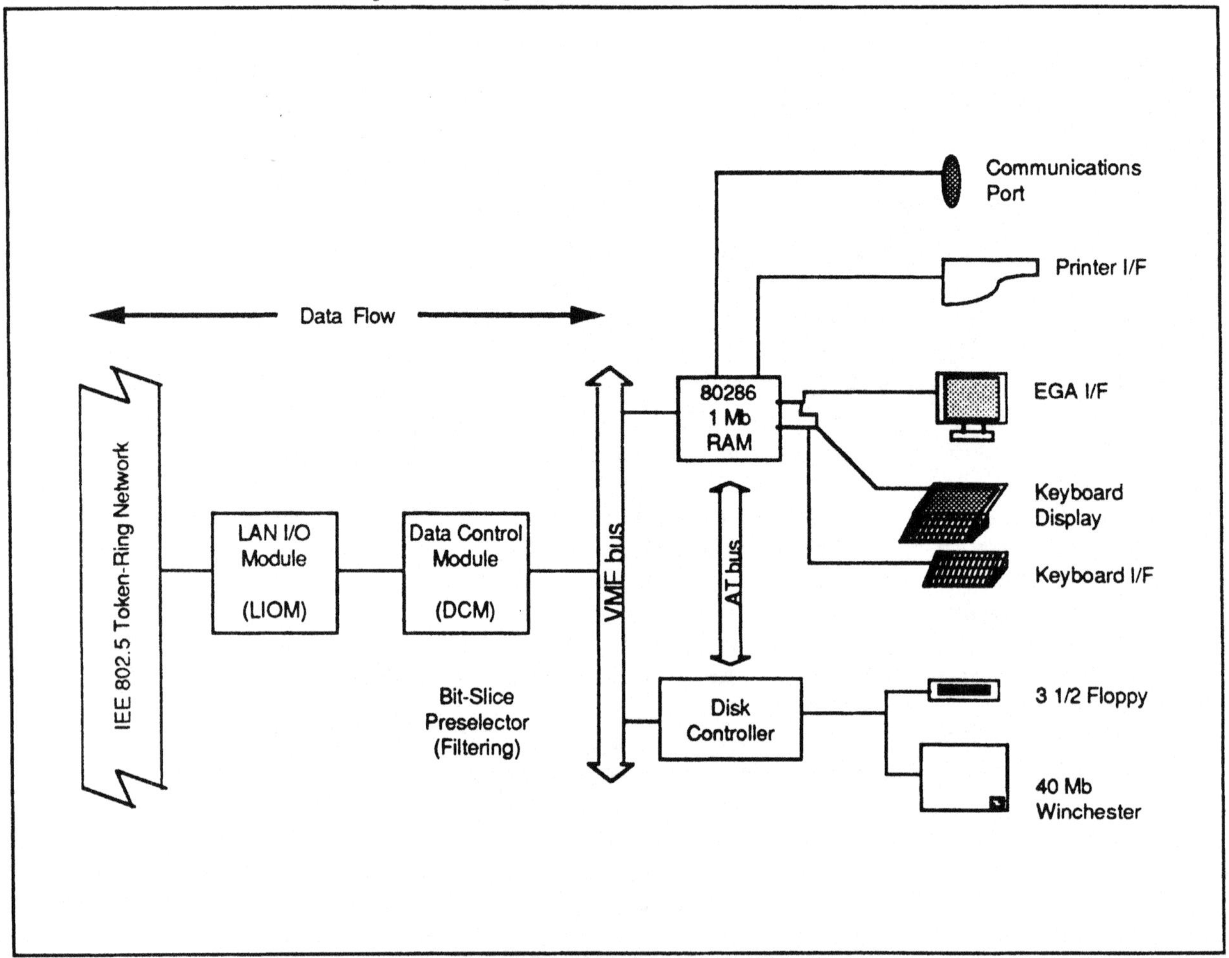


**Figure 30:** ATS 1000 System Architecture

### 10.3 ATS 1000 Data Collection And Display

#### 10.3.1 Event Trace

The most basic form of displaying information collected by the ATS 1000 is the Event Trace. This is a time-sequenced summary (trace) of all selected LAN events. Every event which occurred at the Physical, Media Access Control (MAC), Logical Link Control (LLC), and "upper" layers is displayed in the order it took place. The system displays typical LAN traffic and Token frames, as well as such anomalies as invalid MAC frames and network "silence."

Timing of events occurs at a resolution of one microsecond. Time-stamp reporting format is selected dynamically as either actual time-of-day, delta (the time between events), or relative (to the first event). Frames associated with the so-called upper-layer protocols supported by the ATS 1000 are automatically recognized and translated.

Input for this display can be either the live events coming from the network, or previously collected data stored on disk. The event's time, type, size, destination, and source are provided on the summary display. The ATS 1000's Station Address Database automatically translates the source and destination addresses to labels or functional addresses. The codes for known Link Service Address Points (LSAPs) are also translated.

The ATS 1000's function keys explode the events down to a finer level of detail via the Event Analysis Display. Complete decoding of the frame in Physical, MAC, LLC, and higher layers, coupled with a Help facility, provide the LAN manager/administrator with access to the value and description of major and minor data fields. (This is particularly helpful to the less experienced analyst.)

Additionally, the Frame Information field is provided in hexadecimal and displayed in either EBCDIC or ASCII. Source Routing fields are decoded to show direction (into or out of the ring) and path.

The ATS 1000 has access to fragmented or truncated frames. These occurrences can be viewed and isolated to help determine their source. Tokens can be recorded for use in calculating rotation timing statistics.

### 10.3.2 Filters And Triggers

During troubleshooting or focused analysis, neither capture nor display of all LAN events is required or desirable--manually sifting through thousands of entries is time-consuming and unproductive. The ATS 1000's platform provides Filters that can be applied to the LAN traffic in realtime by the high-speed DCM "front-end" and/or applied to previously collected data stored on disk. Filters can display certain frame types or isolate traffic to/from a particular destination/source, or all events to a particular functional manager such as the Configuration Ring Server.

Triggers also assist in the data collection process by determining when collection and display should begin. The Trigger can act as a trap that, when "sprung," captures all LAN events, or those specified by the user-defined Filters. The Trigger mechanism is sensitive to the occurrence of specific LAN events, as well as time-of-day and duration.

### 10.3.3 Experiments

Emulation--or the ability to place a traffic scenario onto the LAN--is provided as part of the Experiment facility. Because the ATS 1000's DCM provides simultaneous send/receive functionality, the effect of Emulation frames can be observed as it happens. Error conditions resulting from an overloaded bridge or response time sensitivity to traffic loads can be evaluated using the Event Trace Summary and Analysis displays. The Emulation facility is implemented as a scenario of sequenced user-defined frames.

Any unique group of Trigger, Filter, and Emulation parameter specifications is referred to as an Experiment. A number of Experiments that perform particular functions are included with the ATS 1000 and are kept in the System Library. These are available for direct use and also as a starting point or prototype for LAN manager/administrator-tailored Experiments.

### 10.3.4 Protocol Decodes

Standard features of the ATS 1000 include decoding of the Physical, MAC, and LLC layers of the OSI Reference Model. Protocol decodes are optionally supported for various upper-layer protocol suites. To allow users to develop tailored support, deeper decoding (i.e., control data within the information field), or to provide decoding capability for a proprietary or unsupported protocol, the system optionally includes a User Programmable Decode facility.

### 10.3.5 Station Address Database

Up to 1800 entries can be stored in this database to translate the station's hexadecimal address to a more meaningful name. Once supplied, the new names can be used in the various ATS 1000 displays. Functional addresses are also translated to provide recognition of the stations designated as the error, network, or configuration manager.

### 10.3.6 Realtime Displays

As events are captured from the network, they are displayed in realtime as entries on the Event Trace Summary. This allows the network manager/administrator to see the results of a troubleshooting experiment instantly. For example, an end-user of the LAN is unable to gain access to the network and calls for assistance; through collection/display of MAC control frames, the cause can be quickly isolated by looking for such events as the "Duplicate Address Test" or line errors.

### 10.3.7 Data Integrity

The ATS 1000 was designed to provide complete and comprehensive data traces for LAN analysis. The system's I/O buffers are large and circular, and its VMEbus internal architecture supports high-speed data movement within the unit. Combined with direct writing of LAN events to disk and protocol layer Filters, this eliminates concerns associated with buffer overflow. Compromises such as partial frame truncation (slicing) are not required. In some situations, such as when collecting tokens (where buffer saturation is expected), the Experiment will stop. All data collected up to this point is complete and valid.

## 10.4 ATS 1000 Token-Ring Monitors And Applications

The realtime monitoring features of the ATS 1000 provide the network manager or LAN administrator with an on-line snapshot of LAN performance for system-wide utilization, error identification, and point-to-point activity. Each of the monitor functions allows users to define their own thresholds for operator warning and/or alarm levels.

### 10.4.1 System Monitor

The System Monitor provides an on-line snapshot of LAN utilization for performance and load-level analysis. It provides information pertaining to network throughput, average frame size, total frames transmitted, Kbytes of data observed, and relevant time information. If user-defined thresholds for bandwidth utilization are exceeded, special markings or optional color coding appears on the monitor screen.

This function provides status information on system-wide LAN performance to administrators and management personnel to help ensure that the network is operating efficiently.

### 10.4.2 Error Monitor (Optional)

The Error Monitor provides statistics on token-ring errors in the form of hard (including beacon conditions) versus soft errors within isolating or non-isolating conditions. Because errors are displayed as they occur, the LAN administrator/manager can immediately respond and troubleshoot the problem.

The Error Monitor presents the following statistics in a Token Ring Environment:

**Isolating Errors**

| Hard | Soft |
|---|---|
| Set Recovery | Line |
| Signal Loss | Burst |
| Bit Streaming | ARI/FCI |
| CL-TK Streaming | Internal |
| | Abort |

**Non-Isolating Errors**

| Hard | Soft |
|---|---|
| Lost Frame | Active Monitor |
| Rx Congestion | Duplicate Address |
| Frequency | Duplicate Monitor |
| Frame Copied | Ring Poll Failure |
| Token | |

In addition, to facilitate troubleshooting and problem resolution, the system provides a distribution of isolating errors by location (fault domain).

### 10.4.3 Channel Monitor (Optional)

The Channel Monitor is a more in-depth analysis of information presented by the System Monitor and provides a monitoring capability that helps ensure that the network and its component stations are operating efficiently.

A "Channel" to the ATS 1000 is described as any specific source/destination address pair on the LAN. The Channel Monitor provides performance information on individual channels--as defined by the operator--on the token-ring. Each of the channels can be given a label for identification. Channels may also be defined for all traffic to/from an individual station. The system presents multiple performance perspectives via function key-driven screens displaying:

- SUMMARY (Single-Screen) Information
  - Throughput DETAIL summary for the system and each channel
  - Bandwidth UTILIZATION graph for the system and each channel
- CHANNEL Information (one screen per channel including the system)
  - Throughput DETAIL-complete statistic set
  - Frame size distribution graph

Current and cumulative time "windows" are provided and statistics are available as either actuals, or normalized as a presentation aid.

## 10.5 ATS 1000 Token-Ring LAN Analysis System Applications

### 10.5.1 Who's There Application

The "Who's There" application monitors the LAN to determine who is active on the network. The list presents active stations in the order of their logical configuration on the ring. The information captured for active stations on the network is presented using names via conversion from a physical to logical station address using the Station Address Database.

The Who's There application also facilitates the process of adding and maintaining station names corresponding to the station addresses resident in the ATS 1000 Station Address Database.

### 10.5.2 Station Control (Optional)

"Station Control" is an optional application program that provides the network management and configuration tools needed to control the operating parameters of all stations on the LAN. Through the use of the Station Control application, the LAN manager/administrator can query a station to obtain current functional parameter settings, including Upstream Neighbor identification. If applicable, for effective LAN configuration control the ATS 1000 operator can change any of the following parameters, station-by-station:

- Station Report Timer--for defining the no-response threshold
- Station Local Ring Number--for configuration control
- Station Physical Drop Number--for configuration control
- Station Authorized Priority--for ring security
- Station Function Classes--for network management to identify the station as:
    - Ring Error Monitor
    - Ring Parameter Server
    - Configuration Report Server
    - LLC Manager
    - Ring Station Only

### 10.5.3 Station Diagnose Application (Optional)

The "Station Diagnose" application enables a user to check workstation conformity to various elements of the IEEE 802.5 token-ring protocol standard. Any workstation destined to become an active station on a token-ring LAN can be checked "off-line" by a direct cable attachment to an ATS 1000. The ATS 1000 initiates the application, and the workstation to be checked is tested to determine if the initialization/sign-on procedure is performed according to the IEEE 802.5 standard. Workstations failing any of the five Station Diagnose tests are identified for resolution.

### 10.5.4 Token Rotation Time Application (Optional)

Token Rotation Time is the elapsed time for a token to rotate around the ring network. The "Token Rotation Time" application monitors token activity over a specified period and presents statistics, distributions, and graphs of the various elapsed times. By analyzing the distribution of various token times, LAN managers/administrators can pinpoint more detailed levels of activity, including sustained file transfer, operation of a fiber-optic link, or no activity at all.

### 10.5.5 Remote Operation (Optional)

As an option, the ATS 1000 can remotely run any installed Application Program. Through a combination of hardware, software, and ATS 1000 interfaces, this option enables Application Program results on one ATS 1000 to be displayed on any other remotely located ATS 1000 or PC AT MS-DOS-compatible workstation with a serial port.

## 10.6 SNA, 16-Mbps Capability

On October 25, 1989, at LocalNet '89 in Atlanta, Bytex Systems announced two major enhancements to the ATS 1000 Token-Ring Analysis System: 16-Mbps data capture and analysis, and IBM SNA protocol support.

Bytex's 16-Mbps capability for token-ring analyzers is embodied in its ATS 1000, which uses a bit-slice microprocessor--a proprietary Bytex design--to enable observation, filtering, and recording of all data on the network. This front-end technology, says Bytex, is the essential ingredient in providing the first deliverable 16-Mbps capability among Token-Ring LAN analyzers.

Priced at $17,995, the baseline 16-Mbps ATS 1000 includes an 802.5 network interface; a portable MS-DOS-based microprocessor with 1 Mbyte of memory, 40 Mbytes of fixed disk, and 2 Mbytes of floppy disk storage; turn-key system software for OSI lower-layer protocol decodes, experiment data collection, and control; a realtime system monitor and an active node Application Program; and a multi-frame emulation capability for simultaneous traffic generation and data capture. Additional statistical monitors, application programs, and protocol decodes are available as separately priced options. Customer shipments of the 16-Mbps Token-Ring ATS 1000 will begin 1st Quarter 1990. Upgrade pricing for a 4-Mbps ATS 1000 to include 16-Mbps token-ring capability is $4,000.

At LocalNet, Bytex Systems also demonstrated the immediate availability of SNA protocol support for its ATS 1000 Token-Ring system. The SNA protocol decode option enables the ATS 1000 to decode the SNA transmission header, the request/response header, and the request/response unit content (layers 3 through 7 of the ISO/OSI Reference Model, including LU2.0 and LU6.2 commands). As with all other protocol decode options, all decoded fields include context-sensitive help.

## 10.7 Conclusion

As the number of LANs and the number of vendors represented on them grows, questions regarding interoperability and network management are no longer just for system integrators and OEMs. Today, the vast majority of Fortune 2000 companies and other large organizations face connectivity as an issue that affects not only the day-to-day operations of individual departments, but the ability of entire companies to execute critical strategic plans.

With interoperability becoming important to a broader array of users, the nature of LAN testing/analysis and management changes as well. LAN analysis should--in fact, must--provide users with answers to critical questions regarding LAN design, performance, and suitability to job requirements.

It was user demand for interoperability of incompatible devices that led the industry to begin developing standardized LAN protocols. By adhering to these standardized protocols, products from different vendors are abe to communicate. The leading standard for LANs, developed by the International Organization for Standardization, is the Open Systems Interconnect (OSI) reference model. OSI represents a standardization approach to the way information is exchanged through a network so that independently developed devices can interoperate.

Going "up the stack" to analyze interoperability at higher levels often means simply looking at a different set of symptoms rather than the underlying problem itself. Properly functioning higher-level protocols may, in fact, conceal problems that exist at the physical and MAC layers until they become severe, disrupting communications and possibly causing loss of data. The reason other vendors focus on higher layers is that these do not demand the same specialization hardware required at the lower levels.

Bytex's strategy, however, is different: because all network traffic must go through the lower layers, Bytex feels management can most effectively be done at the lowest three levels of the ISO seven-layer stack. Bytex takes data predominantly from these levels and converts it into the information network managers need.

Providing that kind of information requires a LAN analyzer--such as the ATS 1000--that can see 100% of the data on the network--both good and bad--even during times of peak traffic. The ATS 1000 has significantly more power than a typical station on the network, because by using the same architecture as many high-performance engineering workstations, the ATS 1000 has off-loaded many of the functions of an analyzer (such as triggers, filters, statistics, and error data collection) into proprietary hardware specifically designed for those functions.

Based on a multi-processor architecture, utilizing an 80286 microprocessor and bit-slice technology, the ATS 1000 has three modes of operation: Monitor, data collection, and emulation. The Monitor Function provides network managers with an on-line real-time summary of LAN and individual station utilization statistics for performance and trend analysis, along with a compilation of error statistics. The Monitor Function allows users to set threshold levels that will generate warnings and alarms.

The Data Collection and Emulation functions make use of the high-performance bit-slice front end and can operate independently or concurrently, so the user can see all the traffic on the network while emulating various traffic patterns. This Bytex technology observes and records every bit of data transmitted over the network without actually becoming part of the network and thereby affecting its operations.

From a planning and management perspective, however, the more significant analysis is done by the ATS 1000's application programs. These programs use data collected by the bit slice processor and summary statistics stored on the hard disk to answer questions regarding network performance, utilization, management, design, expansion, and planning under an almost unlimited number of scenarios.

Bytex Corporation is now marketing a new product designed specifically for testing and monitoring token-ring networks. A hand-held, battery-operated device, RingOut identifies faulty cables and failed MSAU (multi-station access unit) ports on 4- and 16-Mbps IEEE 802.5 token-ring networks. RingOut is designed to work on both shielded- and unshielded-twisted-pair wiring.

Bytex boasts that it has packed the power and functionality of a portable PC, two 4/16-Mbps token-ring adapter cards, IBM Trace and Performance Program software, IBM Cabling System Tester, and additional custom software into a hand-held device.

As a cable tester, RingOut provides token-ring cable and MSAU port relay switch fault identification and isolation, DC continuity testing of cable conductors, and AC signal degradation identification and isolation.

As a monitoring device for active networks, RingOut enters the ring to monitor activity and determines if the netwokr is active or inactive. In addition, it can detect a ceaconing state and can be used to isolate the beaconing node.

RingOut carries a price-tag of $1,495.

For more information on ATS1000 or RingOut, contact Joe Skorupa, Bytex Corporation, 120 Turnpike road, Southborough, MA 01772-1886; (508) 480-0840, ext 236.

# 11. Time Domain Reflectometry Applications For Token-Ring Networks

## 11.1 Introduction

Time Domain Reflectometry has become a widely accepted and effective method for testing network cabling to locate and identify faults, as well as to verify that the cabling is working properly. Time Domain Reflectometry involves sending electronic pulses down the network cable being tested. Faults or changes in impedance in the cable cause some of the energy to be reflected back to the Time Domain Reflectometer (TDR). Because different anomalies and faults produce different types of reflections, the TDR is able to process the reflections and display the results. Knowing the speed at which the pulses travel down the cable allows the TDR to determine where the faults are located. The speed of the pulses down the cable is determined by the velocity of propagation (Vp) of the cable. The Vp of the cable is specified by the manufacturer or may be determined using the TDR.

This section addresses token-ring applications involving metallic cabling. Time Domain Reflectometry are also available for optical fiber applications. The basic concept is similar, with the exception that light pulses are used rather than electronic pulses.

### 11.1.1 Token-Ring History

Token ring was conceived in 1967, and Olaf Soderblom, who obtained the patent, is credited for its invention. At that time, data processing was evolving from a strictly centralized function to a decentralized function.

During the 1970s, extensive research was done on the nature of token rings, but it was not until the 1980s that the new token-ring products were introduced. IBM developed the "Zurich Ring," which is named for its geographical point of origin. The "Zurich Ring" is the basis for the European Computer Manufacturers Association 89 and the Institute of Electrical and Electronic Engineers (IEEE) 802.5 standards.

IBM introduced its Token-Ring Network in 1985. The initial excitement of the LAN community did not translate into instant acceptance. Not until early 1987 did the market for token-ring networks really materialize.

Most networks with centralized operation of the protocol entailed a high overhead for access arbitration. Token ring provided a protocol which was decentralized and efficient. Token ring also provided a high degree of adaptability and a high level of availability with its deterministic token-passing access protocol. Token-ring connections are expected to exceed those of the other LAN alternatives by 1991. The main reason is that PC connections are growing faster than any other segment in the networking marketplace, and IBM has been estimated to account for around 35% of all PC shipments.

### 11.1.2 The Network

Token ring is a baseband network that uses a logical ring configuration. Signals on the network are received and retransmitted by each active station, resulting in a unidirectional communications link. Access or permission to put data on the network is regulated by use of an electronic token which circulates on the ring. It is only when a station has the token that it may initiate data onto the network. Sequentially, the token is passed to the next station.

One of the strengths of the token-ring network is its ability to handle diverse levels of data priority. If prioritization is not desired, the network uses fixed times for which each station may hold the token. This results in equal access for all stations. The amount of data that can be transmitted by each station is determined by the size of the data field and the amount of time a station may hold the token.

When prioritization is desired, there are eight levels available. Using these priority levels determines which stations get access to the token. This can be essential for applications where certain stations must be assured of periodic access.

Although a Token-ring network is a logical ring, the most common implementation is a physical star topology with the transmission line from each station coming to a central wiring closet, or Multistation Access Unit (MAU). Up to 260 devices or stations may be attached to a ring. Rings can also be bridged to extend this limit.

An inherent vulnerability of ring networks is that if the ring is broken, the entire network comes down. As a result, a great deal of effort has been applied to safeguard against this total failure mode. The results have been alternate transmission path and bypass methods that maintain the integrity of the ring in the event of a failure.

MAUs provide this capability. Each MAU has the capability to provide access for up to eight stations to the ring. To obtain access, each station must provide a phantom signal to the MAU which causes the MAU to insert the station into the ring. Should the phantom signal cease to be present due to cable failure or a downed station, the MAU will bypass that station and maintain the integrity of the ring. Figure 31 is an example of a token-ring network with MAUs.

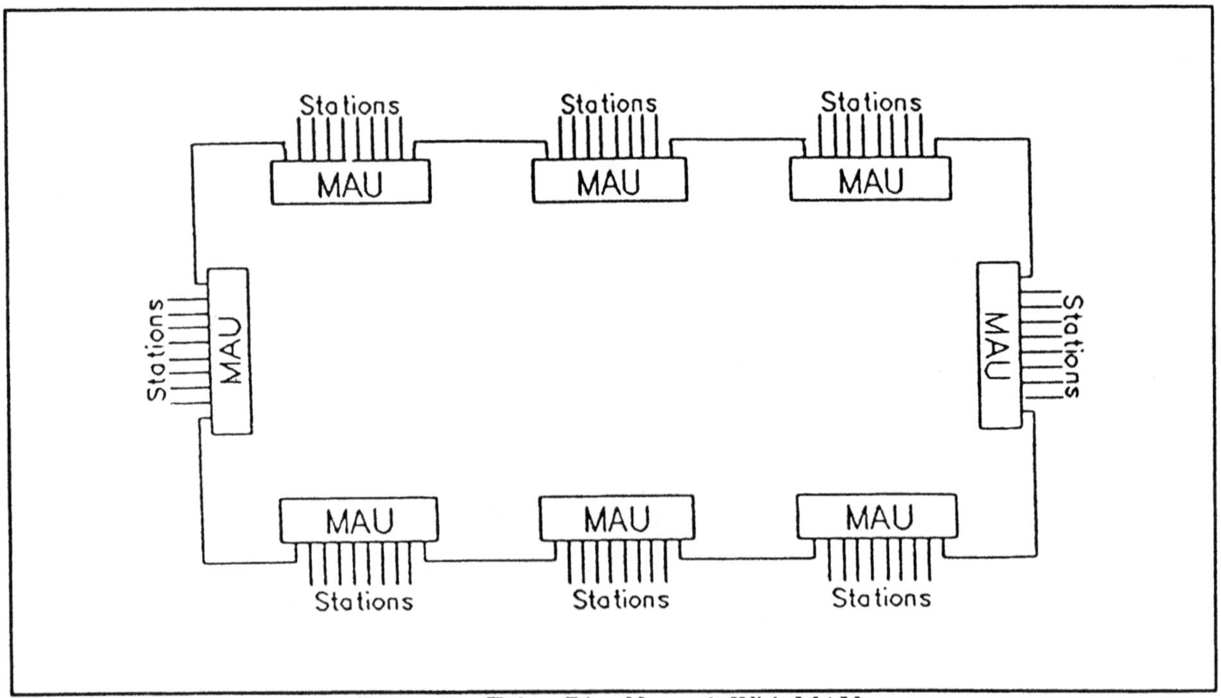


**Figure 31**: Token-Ring Network With MAUs

To maintain this level of reliability and restore the downed part of the network requires prompt identification, location, and repair of the affected segment.

Cabling used for token-ring networks includes IBM Types 1, 2, 3, 9 (metallic), and Type 5 (optical fiber), as well as others. Type 6 (metallic) is recommended for use as distribution panel patch cables only.

The new 16-Mbps token ring offers an Early Token Release option. Early Token Release allows the transmitting station to release a new token as soon as it has completed its frame transmission, without having to wait for its frame header to return from its trip around the ring. This optimizes the use of available bandpass when the average frame size is less than the ring length. It also decreases the time subsequent stations must wait for the token.

The use of shielded data-grade media is recommended for 16-Mbps token-ring networks. In many cases, the links between wiring closets--which were metallic in the 4-MHz networks--will need to be optical fiber to span the distance at the higher transmission rate.

## 11.2 TDR Applications

### 11.2.1 Cable Inspection

The first service a TDR provides in the life of a LAN is the verification of the basic cable. Manufacturers use the TDR for quality control. Installers use the TDR for incoming inspection to ensure that the cables are functional upon receipt. Also, the cable lengths can be verified against the purchase order.

The results of a TDR test can be reported in two ways. One is with an alphanumeric display, such as, for example, with the Tektronix TMA802 Media Analyzers, that tells users the status of the cable. Faults are reported with the nature of the problem such as OPEN, SHORT, or ERROR for complex faults (those other than pure opens or shorts) and the distance to the fault. The other is a graphic display or signature of the cable, such as with the Tektronix 1503B Time Domain Reflectometer.
The following displays are of a 50-foot length of fault-free IBM Type 1 cable.

Tektronix
TMA802

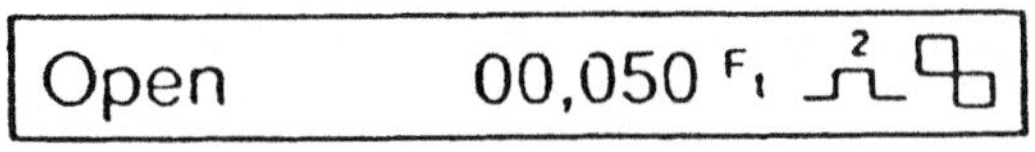


Tektronix
1503B

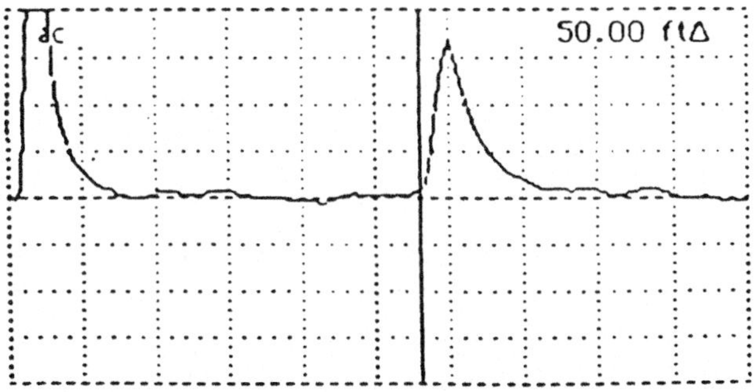


If Medium Interface Connectors (MIC) are installed, the connector at the far end loops the cable pairs, resulting in an actual conductor length of twice the physical length of the cable. This type of connector is also referred to as IBM Cabling System (ICS), Data, or Environmental Communications Link (ECL) connectors, depending on where they are used. When testing the cable in this situation, users are seeing both the send and receive pairs. By selecting the transmit pair or send pair on the Token Ring Interface, users are selecting which pair the TDR pulse is transmitted on.

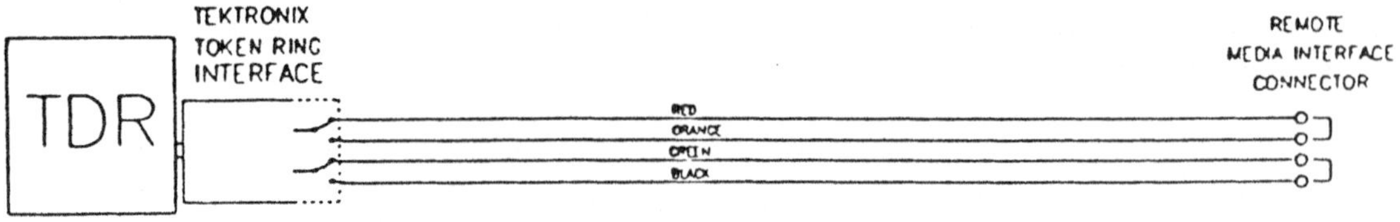


Tektronix
TMA802

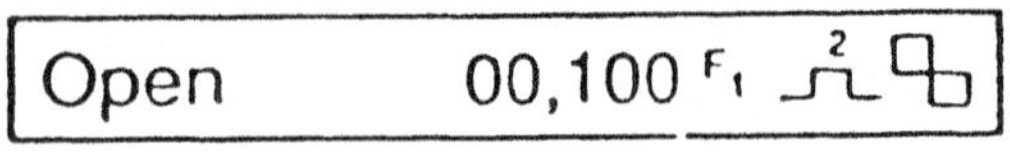


Tektronix
1503B

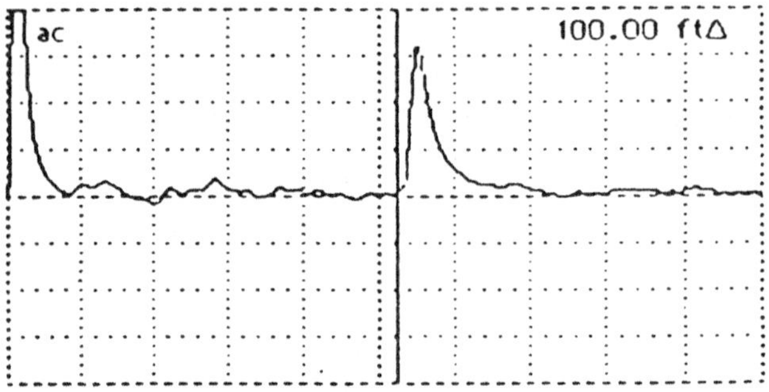


If a user wants to see just one of the pairs, the loopback feature of the MIC type connector can be defeated by inserting a matching connector with open leads. With the Token Ring Interface set to receive pair, the red and green pair is connected. When the transmit pair is selected, the orange and black pair is connected.

### 11.2.2 Installation

Verification of the network cabling after installation ensures that the cabling has not been damaged during the installation process. The TDR also tests the connectors prior to the network equipment being attached to the network.

Network mapping is also part of the installation verification process. Mapping involves verifying final cable lengths to produce accurate network documentation. Network maps provide documentation of successful installation of the network cabling. Prior to an installation, cable lengths are estimated using a floor plan, so that the proper amount of cable can be ordered. The network map is used to track and adjust the estimating process to minimize cable waste while maintaining an effective safety margin.

A Network map should be a living document that is updated whenever a change to the network is made. Such a map is invaluable when maintenance is required.

### 11.2.3 Restoration

Restoration may involve any part of the network. If the network is working normally but a particular station cannot get inserted into the ring, there are several issues to check. First are the basics, such as checking the power and data cable connection: the actual network cable or associated connectors that tie the station to its MAU could be the problem. The cable path between these two points can be easily checked using a TDR. The cable should be disconnected from the MAU and the station. If extension cables are used from wall sockets to connect devices, they should also be included in the tests.

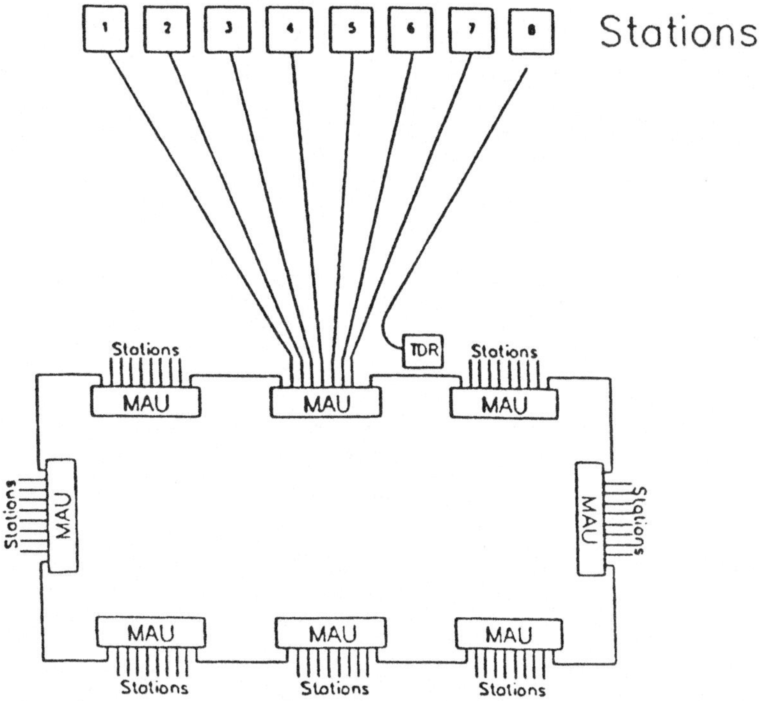


A short in the cabling will result in a reflected pulse of the opposite polarity to that of the launch pulse. The following displays are of a network cable with a staple in it. Crushed cables are also subject to shorts.

Tektronix
TMA802

Tektronix
1503B

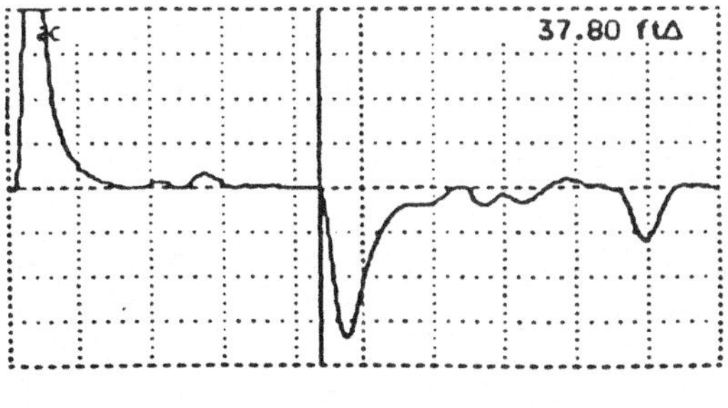


An open results in a reflected pulse of the same polarity as the launch pulse, as shown below.

Tektronix
TMA802

Tektronix
1503B

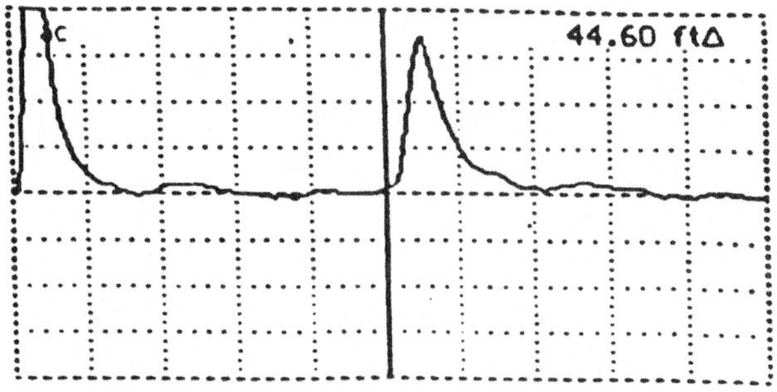

If the network goes down or a message such as "transmission fail" is displayed that indicates a possible cable problem, the backbone of the ring is a candidate for testing. To test the backbone of the ring, all the stations need to be off line.

Using the Tektronix Token Ring Interface (which provides the Phantom Signal) with the TDR allows the ring backbone to be tested through one of the station ports without disturbing the backbone.

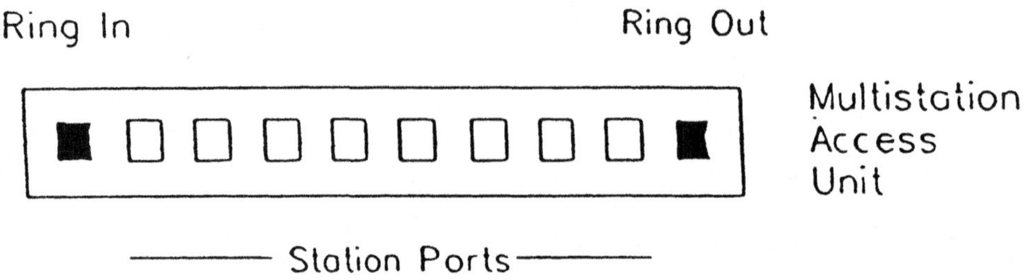


Using this method, the entire backbone can be tested at one time, and the loopback function discussed above in "Cable Inspection" does not come into play. The TDR pulse transverses the ring on the pair selected and returns to the interface, where the pulse is terminated into a user-selectable load. By changing the load selected, the return point on the ring can easily be distinguished from any faults on the ring.

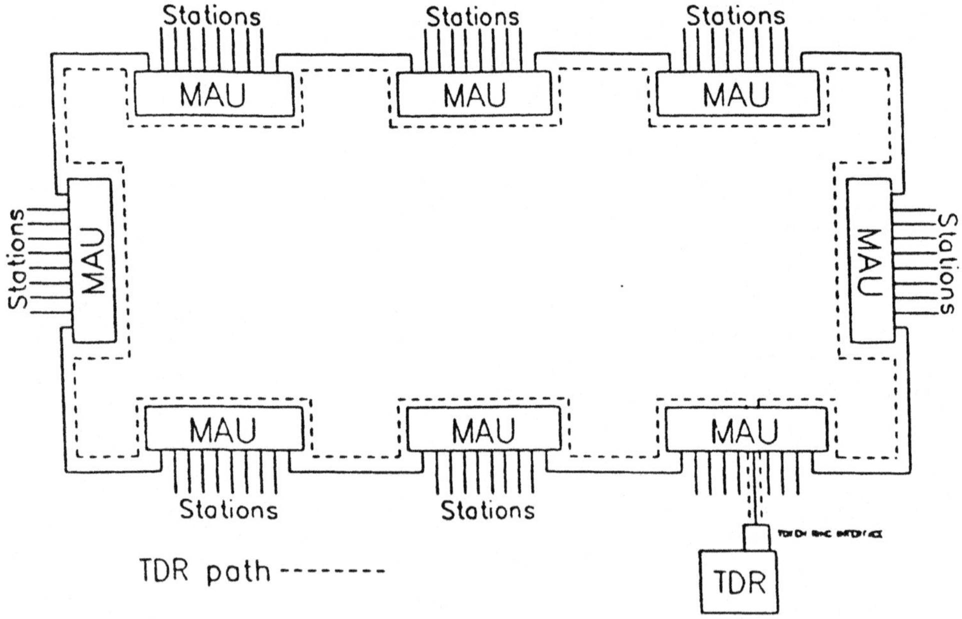


The distance measurement of the network reflects a combination of cabling and MAUs. The MAUs are electronically 5.5 feet long from the Ring-In port to the Ring-Out port. The cable measurement is the same as the physical length. The station ports are electrically six feet for each time they are included in the test configuration. For example, in the network shown above, the measurements would include:

| | |
|---|---|
| Station Port Entry | 6 feet |
| 8 MAUs | 44 feet |
| Eight 50-foot cables | 400 feet |
| Station Port Exit | 6 feet |
| | --------- |
| | 456 feet |

The cable used to connect the TDR to the MAU can be zeroed out and eliminated from the measurement.

### 11.3 Conclusion

As has been shown, a Time Domain Reflectometer is a valuable tool for network installation, verification, maintenance, and restoration. Because of the dynamic way the TDR works, it finds faults that other methods cannot. A cable that tests good on a continuity tester can, for instance, still fail to pass data: this is because the continuity tester only detects resistance. A TDR detects capacitance and inductance as well, which are also factors of impedance which attenuates, corrupts, or stops data. Not finding these faults compounds the problem when the cabling is incorrectly removed from the suspect list.

A TDR also tell users where the fault is. This simplifies network support and contributes to increased network uptime and productivity.

TDRs also have applications for networks such as Ethernet, Cheapernet, StarLAN, broadband, USOC (based), and others. Optical Time Domain Reflectometers are available for testing the fiber portions of networks.

# 12. Toshiba 16/4-Mbps Token-Ring Chipset

## 12.1 Introduction

Toshiba's TC35802G TRC (Token-Ring Controller) is an IEEE 802.5-based LAN controller which utilizes the token-ring protocol. The TC35802G has been designed to easily interface to the iAPX series of microprocessors. The TRC's built-in DMA controller and linked list buffer management scheme allows a system to be configured for high performance in node processor applications. For systems without a dedicated node processor, the system designer can choose between shared memory interfaces and bus master applications.

All MAC-level functions are supported. The Logical Link Control, Configuration Report Server, Ring Error Monitor, and Ring Parameter Server are implemented in software. The TB32042F MDR (Media Driver/Receiver) allows for easy connection between the ring network and the TRC. The MDR has built-in phantom drive control, loop-back, watchdog timer, and wire-error detection, and it is software switchable between 4-Mbps and 16-Mbps speeds.

The chipset has the following characteristics:

- 1.2 um CMOS Integrated Token-Ring Controller (TC35802G) and Bi-CMOS Media Driver/Receiver (TB32042F)
- Compatible with IEEE 802.5 specifications
- MAC-level function support
- Software-switchable 16-or 4-Mbps data rates
- Intelligent DMA utilizing linked list data structures
- Automatic execution of token-passing protocol
- Direct interface between the TC35802G Token-Ring Controller and the TB32042F Media Driver/Receiver
- Built-in self-diagnostic functions
- 16-bit bus interface allows for integration with iAPX86, 186, 286 microprocessors
- Built-in phantom drive control, loop-back, watchdog timer, and error detection in the TB32042F
- 144-pin flat package (TC35802G), 60-pin flat package (TB32042F)

## 12.2 Token-Ring Controller--An Overview

(This section is based on preliminary information. Please note that the specifications are subject to change without notice due to continuing standardization of JEDEC standards and improvements of characteristics.)

TRC (Token-Ring Controller) is an IEEE 802.5-based LAN controller LSI circuit which utilizes the token-ring protocol. All MAC functions can be executed, except for Network Manager, Configuration Report Server, Ring Error Monitor, and Ring Parameter Server, which are implemented in software.

Bridge station functions are also supported, so that the TRC can be used to design bridge stations.

TRC functions and features include:

- Automatic execution of token-passing protocol
- Active and standby monitor functions
- Ring error recovery functions
- Built-in error counters
- Built-in self-diagnosis function (lobe media test, internal return mode test)
- Network manager reporting
- Intelligent DMA functions which handle list data
- Routing information field detection and copy functions for bridge stations plus relay frame strip functionality
- Data signaling rate selective with software (16/4-Mbps)
- Direct interfacing with media driver TB32042
- Interfacing with iAPX86, 186, and 286 buses
- 1.2um CMOS Silicon Gate Technology
- Low power consumption (180mA Max. at 8MHz)

### 12.2.1 Token-Ring Adapter Configuration

Figure 18 shows an intelligent-type Token-Ring Adapter used to connect PC AT buses. In this example, the adapter is configured with the TRC (T5B79), media driver (TB32042), and iAPX186 network processor, a ROM containing software for the TRC controller, a buffer and work area SRAM, and an interface circuit for connecting PC AT buses.

Hereafter, the memory used for transmitting and receiving frames is referred to as FBM (Frame Buffer Memory).

Note: A processor for execution of communication software is called a network processor in this section.

### 12.2.2 MAC Protocol Execution

The TRC includes hardware capable of executing the IEEE 802.5 MAC (Medium Access Control) protocol.

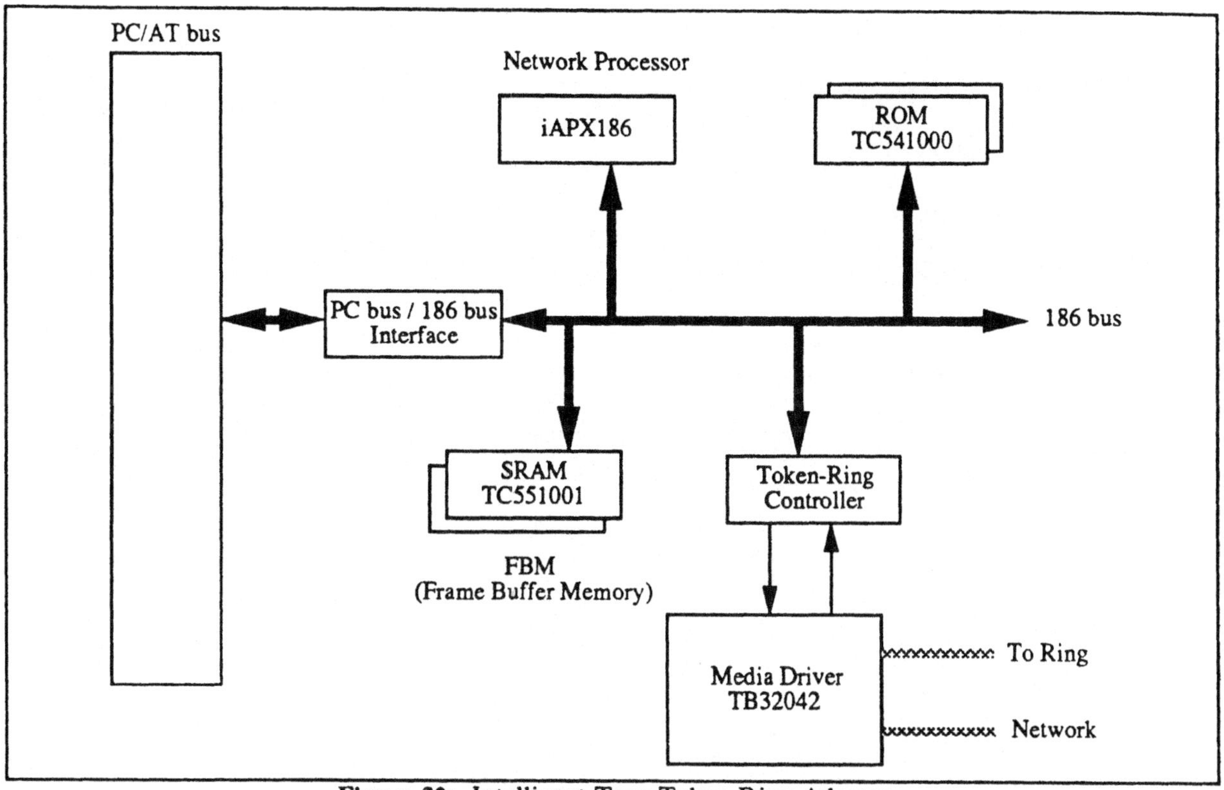


**Figure 32:** Intelligent-Type Token-Ring Adapter

This MAC protocol includes frame transmitting and receiving functions using the token-passing access method, a self-diagnostic function using the station attach process, active monitor/standby monitor functions required to support rings, and a ring error recovery function.

The TRC hardware automatically transmits the MAC frames required for ring control and also makes the required responses to MAC frames received. TRC can execute protocols requested by stations forming the TRC ring. In addition, TRC also has MAC protocol self-diagnosis functions.

A lobe media test is performed when TRC participates in a ring, or when a beacon frame is received at this station. This is for testing the continuity and bit error rate of the wire in a loop-back path.

### 12.2.3 Error Counter Types

The TRC contains ten different 8-bit counters for reporting errors to the ring error monitor. The counter values are obtained by executing the READ ERROR STATUS command in relation to the TRC.

The following is a list of error-counter types:

- Line Error Counter
- Internal Error Counter
- Burst Error Counter
- A/C Error Counter
- Abort Delimiter Transmitted Counter

- Lost Frame Error Counter
- Receive Congestion Counter
- Frame Copied Error Counter
- Frequency Error Counter
- Token Error Counter

### 12.2.4 MAC Frame Handling by TRC

The following MAC frames can be transmitted and received automatically by the TRC hardware:

- Beacon
- Claim Token
- Purge
- Active Monitor Present
- Standby Monitor Present
- Duplicate Address Test
- Lobe Media Test

When the following MAC frames are received, the TRC automatically performs the appropriate operation and transmits a Report MAC frame in response to a Request MAC frame. If the source class of a MAC frame is authorized as a function class for the station, the TRC can transmit the frame if the TRANSMIT FD command is executed; if the class is not authorized, the TRC refuses to transmit.

- Remove Ring Station
- Change Parameters
- Initialize Ring Station
- Request Ring Station Addresses
- Request Ring Station State
- Request Ring Station Attachments

The following MAC frames are transmitted automatically by the TRC. If the destination class of the MAC frame is authorized as a function class for the station, the MAC frame received by the TRC is copied to the FBM. If the destination class of the MAC frame is not authorized as a function class for the station and the source class of the MAC frame is not ring class, the TRC transmits Negative Response MAC frame.

- Request Initialization
- Report Station Address

- Report Station State
- Report Station Attachments
- Report New Active Monitor
- Report SUA Change
- Report Neighbor Notification Incomplete
- Report Active Monitor Error
- Report Error

The Response MAC frame is transmitted automatically by the TRC; also, MAC frames received by the TRC are copied to the FBM if the destination class is a function class authorized for the station. If the class is not authorized, the frame is ignored. No processing is performed if the destination class is a ring station.

The Hello MAC frame is for bridge stations. This MAC frame received by the TRC is copied to the FBM if the bridge function is authorized for the station. Also, the TRC can transmit this MAC frame by TRANSMIT FD command if the bridge function is authorized.

### 12.2.5 Network Manager Report Function

The Network Manager software configures and maintains a token-ring LAN system using Configuration Report Server, Ring Error Monitor, and Ring Parameter Server.

Network Manager uses special MAC frames to communicate with the stations forming a ring, and the TRC supports the transmitting and receiving of these special MAC frames. Consequently, TRC users can utilize these special MAC frames when implementing Network Manager in stations for network control.

The server functions are implemented in software, as called out below. Figure 19 shows their relationship to TRC.

- Configuration Report Server (CRS)--this function controls ring configuration:

  (1) Receives and compiles configuration information from the stations of a ring, creates reports on the overall configuration, and transmits these to the Network Manager.

  (2) The configuration information is used to maintain the ring configuration.

  (3) Monitors the status of ring stations, alters the operating environment, and removes stations from the ring in accordance with instructions from Network Manager.

- Ring Error Monitor (REM)--this function strips ring error data from ring stations: it reads and analyzes received errors and compiles error statistics.

- Ring Parameter Server (RPS)--this function makes the initial settings for the operating environment of stations on a particular ring.

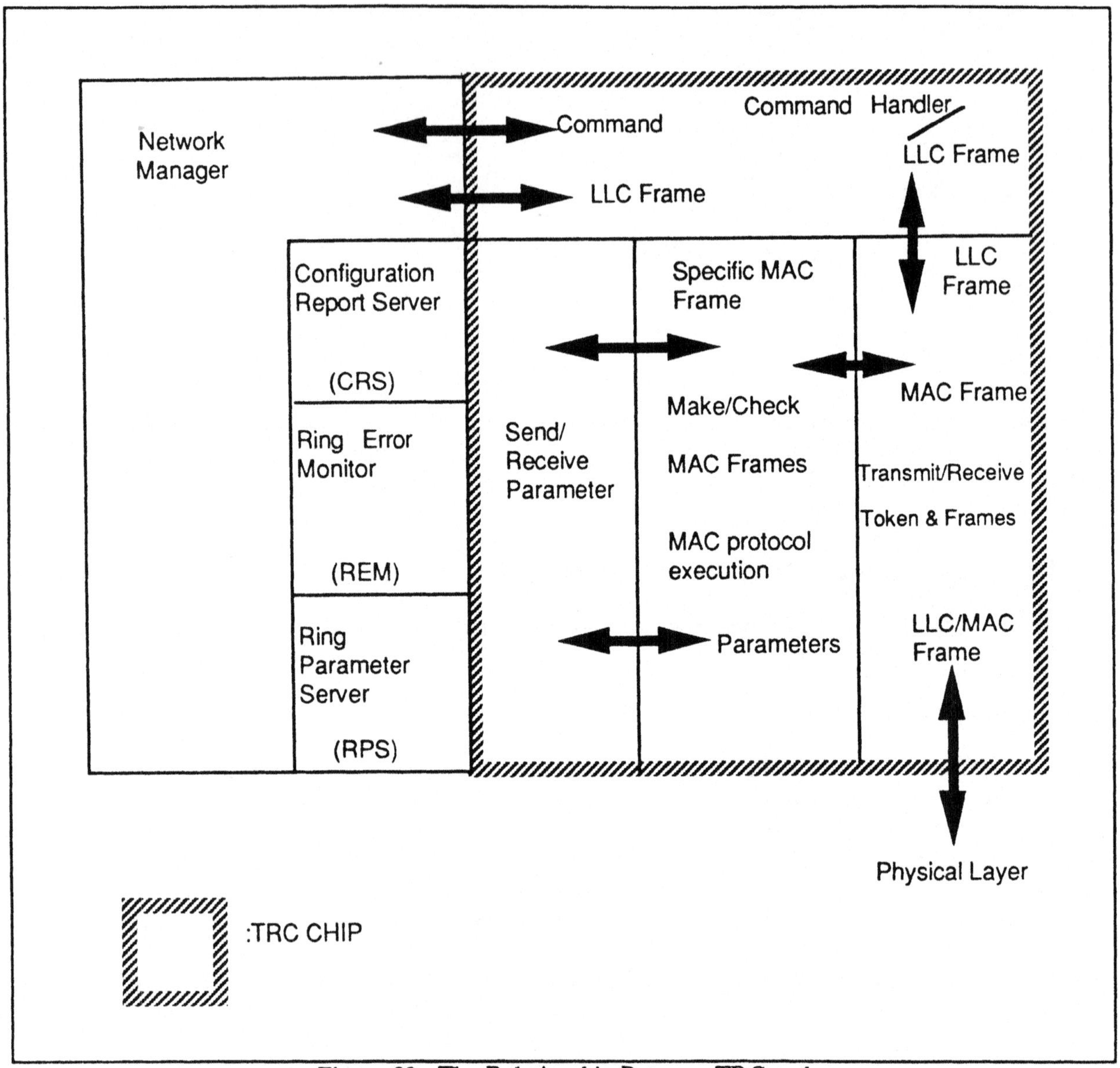


**Figure 33:** The Relationship Between TRC and Network Manager

### 12.2.6 Special Functions for Bridge Stations

In addition to its ring station functions, the TRC also has bridge station functions for connecting to other rings. The TRC can be used either as a bridge station or a ring station, by executing the RESET command.

When used as a bridge station, the TRC has the following special functions:

- If a frame is received with RII set to 1, an RI length field => 2, and any of the following conditions hold:

  (a) the explorer indicators set to 10X (10 hex), indicating an all-routes explorer frame where the ring-out number is not already contained in the routing information field

  (b) the explorer indicators set to 11X, indicating a spanning-tree explorer frame, the port the frame is receive on is enabled to forward spanning-tree explorer frame, and the ring-out number is not already contained in the routing information field

(c) the explorer indicators are set to 00X, indicating a non-explorer frame, the direction bit (D) is set to 0, with a ring-in number, bridge number, and ring-out combination match, in that order, in the routing information field

(d) the explorer indicators are set to 00X, indicating a non-explorer frame, the direction bit (D) is set to 1, with a ring-out, bridge number, and a ring-in combination match that order in the routing information field

then the TRC sets the address recognized bits to 1 in the repeated frame and copies it to FBM.

- Frames with source addresses different from the station address and including Routing Information Fields can be transmitted

The TRC has a DMA (Direct Memory Access) function for the direct transfer of lists from the FBM.

The TRC can operate over iAPX86, 186, and 286 buses.

Also, the TRC has an interface to Media Driver TB32042. The TRC can be physically coupled to a ring through this media driver, which is connected with a ring through phantom drive circuits.

### 12.2.7 Station Addresses Setting

Before starting communication by using the TRC, it is necessary to set the following addresses (there are three kind of addresses):

- Station Address (uniquely identifies the station)
- Group Address (identifies that the group consists of multiple stations)
- Functional Address (identifies the station which has a special function)

The network processor must give these addresses to the TRC by using the ATTACH command parameter.

With regard to setting the station address, there is also another way: the TRC can automatically read it from the special ROM in which Station Address is written. If the network processor cannot give the Station Address to the TRC by software, this method is useful for managing Station Addresses. This type of address setting is called FXSA (Fixed Station Address) setting.

When the TRC finds that the destination address of a frame is equal to one of these three station addresses, TRC copies the frame. When TRC transmits a frame, TRC inserts the Station Address into the SA (Source Address) field of the frame.

## 12.3 Conclusion

Toshiba appears to be the first semiconductor company to capitalize on TI's 16/4-Mbps chipset delay. Expect other semiconductor companies, such as Western Digital, to soon provide token-ring chipsets. LAN vendor Ungermann-Bass has been using its own token ring chips but operating at only 4 Mbps.

With multiple vendors entering the token-ring chipset fray, expect things to get more interesting in the token-ring marketplace in general--commodity pricing leading to low-cost, 16-Mbps adapters, performance and architecture comparisons, ease of design, compatibility with existing IBM and third-party token-ring software, adapter interoperability, etc.

Toshiba has been quietly working on these chips for the past year (preliminary information was available as early as April of 1989) and not making noise or preannouncing products. Toshiba has a reputation for delivering working parts when volume production is promised. The 16/4-Mbps parts (4-Mbps parts are now sampling) will be sampling in February, with volume production slated for April. If so, expect Toshiba to win new third-party token-ring adapter and bridge designs, possibly even upsetting TI in previous designs.

The two-chip set is expected to sell for near $100 in volume.

Printed in Dunstable, United Kingdom

91221445R00085